Buy-outs and Buy-ins

The Elimination of Defined Benefit Pension Scheme Liabilities

Consulting Editor **Steven Hull**

Consulting Editor
Steven Hull

Publisher
Sian O'Neill

Marketing manager
Alan Mowat

Production
John Meikle, Russell Anderson

Publishing directors
Guy Davis, Tony Harriss, Mark Lamb

Buy-outs and Buy-ins: The Elimination of Defined Benefit Pension Scheme Liabilities
is published by
Globe Law and Business
Globe Business Publishing Ltd
New Hibernia House
Winchester Walk
London Bridge
London SE1 9AG
United Kingdom
Tel +44 20 7234 0606
Fax +44 20 7234 0808
Web www.gbplawbooks.com

Printed by CPI Antony Rowe

ISBN 978-1-905783-26-7

Table of contents

Preface

Steven Hull
Ashurst LLP

With successive surveys indicating dramatic increases in the number of employers intending to cease future service accrual in their defined benefit schemes, those involved with operating such schemes will be aware of the change in trustee mindset this can generate. When faced with an employer that is seeking to limit the days it spends carrying the burden of a defined benefit scheme, the trustee response is often, "We are now on a one-way street to buy-out. The only question now is how fast can we get there."

Indeed, it now appears that many sponsoring employers may also be thinking the same.

According to Aon Consulting's Q1 buy-out survey released in May 2009, the number of buy-out providers actively seeking to underwrite business has reduced in recent months, mainly due to pricing which has inevitably been affected by the credit crunch (notably the increased risk of default on corporate bonds). Nevertheless, there is still a competitive market for buy-outs and, given the clear corporate intent shown in the surveys above, this competition is likely to be fed with significant amounts of potential new business in the years to come.

This book is designed to provide an overview of the various and complex types of buy-out and buy-in, focusing on how the market has changed in the past four years. It takes the reader through the historical development of today's expanding and evolving buy-out market, the attractions of the current buy-out market as well as its alternatives, the insured and non-insured buy-out options, buy-ins, the use of buy-out in various jurisdictions overseas and the future of the buy-out market.

Contributors have attempted to avoid great complexity in an effort to make the book readable and more readily understandable. The book is intended to appeal to a wide audience: from pension managers to finance directors; from prospective pension fund members to pensioners; from pension advisers to insurers. We hope that all those with an interest in the pensions world will find it useful.

We are fortunate to have had so many high-profile contributors willing to dedicate their time and expertise in contributing to this book, and special thanks go to them for their efforts. I would also like to give special thanks to my assistant, Maud Couget, without whose tireless efforts the project could not have been completed.

Steven Hull
Partner
Ashurst LLP

Steven Hull is a partner at international law firm Ashurst LLP. He has over 20 years' legal experience of a wide range of pension-related maters in acting for employers and trustees. He has particular expertise in pension scheme reorganisations and mergers, deficit recovery and funding issues, changing benefit structures, the pension aspects of corporate transactions, and dealing with the legislative regime introduced by the Pensions Acts 1995 and 2004 and Finance Acts 2004 and 2009.

Prior to joining Ashurst LLP in 2005, Mr Hull established and led the pensions team for over five years in the London office of a large US law firm. Prior to that, he spent over 12 years training, qualifying and becoming a partner in the pensions team at a well-known London law firm. His time there included a two-year secondment to the employee benefits department of a large New York law firm.

Background and evolution of today's growing and developing buy-out market

Jonathan Bloomer
Lucida plc

1. Introduction

Although now seen as one of the largest and most important new opportunities in the financial services arena, the UK pension buy-out market had a relatively quiet birth more than 20 years ago.

Back in the days when Margaret Thatcher first came to power, a small number of mandatory closures of solvent defined benefit pension schemes were handled through bulk annuity buy-outs by just two life companies – the Prudential and Legal & General. This is a far cry from the dynamic, highly competitive and rapidly evolving market that has taken root over the last five years.

So what has brought about this change?

For a start, there has been a relentless increase in the costs of running a defined benefit scheme. Significant and ongoing increases in longevity, changing government regulations increasing the benefits required from schemes, changes to tax treatment and volatile investment conditions have all served to increase costs.

To compound matters, changes to accounting disclosure requirements have made the impact of these costs all the more visible and increased their impact on the sponsoring employer's business by putting them directly onto the balance sheet.

These pressures have led to widespread closure of defined benefit pensions in the private sector, reducing the number of people in schemes open to new members from 8 million to just 3.6 million.

However, closing a scheme does not eliminate the existing costs and ongoing risks. It still leaves the significant problem of providing the benefits already accrued.

Another important factor has been the increasingly significant role of trustees. They have been given both increased responsibilities and greater power by changes in regulation. This has led to more effective pressure from trustees to secure the benefits of scheme members. The net result has been a sharper focus on protecting the rights and interests of scheme members, just as sponsoring employers have had to lower the costs and risks they face in meeting these commitments.

All of this has set the scene for existing insurers and a number of dynamic new entrants to enter the market and provide a wider range of solutions for employers, trustees and scheme members alike. By offering a variety of innovative and increasingly competitive solutions, this thriving 'new' market is now able to help employers to reduce or even eliminate the risks they face more effectively than ever before.

Although arguably the buy-out market is still in its relative infancy, it is already showing significant growth. Some commentators had suggested that the UK buy-out market could reach £12 billion in 2008, but the growing global financial crisis has done much to dampen this optimism, at least temporarily. Indeed, the final outcome for 2008 was just over £8 billion – still a huge increase on the 2007 and 2006 totals of £3 billion and £1.7 billion respectively.

One of the reasons that the buy-out sector has such a positive future is the extent to which the solutions being created are genuinely beneficial and effective for all of the stakeholders involved. Employers can radically reduce or even eliminate the risks they face in running their defined benefit schemes. Trustees can fully secure the benefits of their members. And scheme members themselves can enjoy greater peace of mind and confidence that their interests are protected going forward.

The evolution of this market has been supported by numerous strategies and methodologies that have been developed. Although most of the basic pressures that employers and trustees face are common, the precise details of each business and its defined benefit scheme require a flexible solution, mixing and matching appropriate strategies together and over time to deliver the optimum way forward.

The most frequently referred-to option is pension buy-out. This involves the buy-out provider taking on all the liabilities and responsibilities of the scheme by payment of an appropriate premium by the trustees from scheme assets (possibly topped up by a payment from the sponsoring employer). With a full buy-out, both the trustees and the employer pass on all of their obligations to provide the accrued benefits to the provider.

The most popular and arguably safest approach is an insured buy-out, where the provider is an insurance company that secures all future benefits for scheme members through individual insurance contracts. Stakeholders have the reassurance of knowing that the provider is fully regulated by the Financial Services Authority (FSA) – a crucial protection as the responsibilities towards scheme members are transferred from the employer and trustees to the third-party provider.

Partial buy-outs are also possible, where a subsection of the scheme's membership rather than the entire scheme is taken on by the buy-out provider.

Another option which is becoming increasingly popular is a buy-in. This is where the scheme purchases an insurance policy covering a subsection of the scheme's membership (usually pensioners) to secure member benefits, but the employer and trustees retain their responsibilities and the insurance policy simply becomes an additional investment asset of the scheme.

In addition, non-insured buy-outs, structured buy-outs, longevity derivative solutions and risk management programmes including liability management are all being considered by employers and trustees as part of the de-risking process.

The remainder of this chapter explores in more detail the demand-side pressures that have driven employers and trustees to control cost and reduce risk, leading to the widespread closure of defined benefit pension schemes. This is followed by a supply-side review – an exploration of the developments that have led to the creation of the buy-out market that exists today. And finally we take a look at what the future holds for this thriving, competitive and developing market.

2. Factors driving employers and trustees to control cost and reduce risk

2.1 Changes to accounting rules

The most significant of the accounting rule changes was the introduction of Financial Reporting Standard Number 17 (FRS 17). Proposed in 2002 and put into mandatory effect in 2005, FRS 17 made two significant changes to the accounting rules covering defined benefit pension schemes. Firstly, it changed the basis of how the assets and liabilities of these schemes are calculated, and secondly, it put the net results of the new calculation basis on the sponsoring employer's balance sheet.

Replacing the existing Statement of Standard Accounting Practice (SSAP) 24, under which an actuarial basis was allowed for the valuation of assets, FRS 17 prescribes a more consistent approach using "fair and current" market valuations of scheme assets.

FRS 17 requires scheme liability calculations to use an actuarial basis allowing for all contracted obligations and any constructive obligations reflected in the reasonable expectations of staff based on the scheme's past practice and any relevant statements from the employer.

The current market value of assets is then compared with the present value of the scheme's liabilities to calculate either a deficit or a surplus. This figure is then reflected in the sponsoring employer's balance sheet and company valuation.

Many have blamed FRS 17 for the ongoing withdrawal by employers from defined benefit pension schemes, but this is not a fair assessment.

It is true that the introduction of FRS 17 did have the effect of putting pension schemes on the board agenda of all companies operating such schemes, but a number of other factors contributed to making this problematic.

A further prospective change to accounting rules that has attracted much debate is the mooted move to a risk-free discount rate. This tougher regime would add significant further disclosure pressures to defined benefit schemes, with some commentators calling it a further "nail in the defined benefit coffin".

2.2 Changes to the tax treatment of pension funds

Soon after coming to power in 1997, the Labour government made a number of changes to taxation, including the removal of tax relief on dividends received by pension funds. Dividends are assumed to be paid net of tax and, prior to the 1997 change, pension schemes could claim tax relief on these dividends (eg, prior to this removal a dividend paid into a pension fund of £80 would have given rise to tax relief of a further £20).

This so-called 'stealth tax' received little attention at the time of its introduction, but is now cited as one of the drivers of defined benefit scheme closure as it increased the costs of providing these schemes.

In response to this criticism, the government has argued that the move was not as harmful as some claim, as it was counterbalanced by reductions made in corporation tax.

2.3 Falling markets, lower inflation and lower investment returns

Pension scheme deficits and so-called 'black holes' caused by falling stock markets have become familiar in every household due to their frequent appearances in news headlines since the turn of the century.

However, it was not that long ago that many employers running defined benefit pensions schemes were enjoying surpluses and taking contribution holidays. Inland Revenue statistics confirm that in the triennial returns submitted from schemes in the early 1990s, more than £4 billion of contributions were avoided. Wind the clock forward to returns after 2003 and contribution holidays of just £18 million were recorded by a small number of very well-funded schemes.

Much of this turnaround is down to changes in the regulations that have effectively increased scheme benefits and changed the underlying funding approach of scheme managers.

The dramatic fall in equity markets that followed the bursting of the technology or dotcom bubble in 2001 was the first time black holes in UK pensions hit the news headlines.

With most pensions schemes still heavily invested in stocks and shares, the dramatic collapse of stock markets over the three years that followed the peaks achieved around the turn of the century was a disaster for pension-scheme funding.

In the United Kingdom, the FTSE index fell by more than 50% from its peak of just under 7,000 points on the last day of trading in 1999 to a trough of just 3,200 points in early 2003.

Although stock markets did recover over the years that followed, volatility has remained high. Pension schemes have been under pressure to move away from equities to seek more stable returns from gilts and bonds and this has happened to a limited degree. However, trustees have had to compare the increased stability and improved asset liability matching with the likely reduction in returns relative to investing in equities.

Over this time, inflation has stayed at very low levels. This has allowed interest rates to be kept low and the cost of borrowing to be maintained at some of the lowest levels seen for decades. But for defined benefit schemes, low inflation means that benefits cost more to provide in real terms. In the past, inflation eroded the value of benefits, particularly for early leavers. Lower interest rates mean higher liabilities since liabilities are calculated as the present value of future payments – as interest rates go down, the cost of future benefits rises.

Just as the technology bubble burst in 2001, the credit bubble burst in 2008, triggering some of the most dramatic falls in stock market values ever seen. Banks across the globe felt the pain of writing off billions of dollars and pounds in bad debt directly and indirectly from mainly the US sub-prime mortgage market. Unprecedented government bailouts have been required to try to head off a complete breakdown of the financial system.

At the time of writing, government action on both sides of the Atlantic appears to have calmed market nerves to a reasonable degree, but this has been replaced by a downbeat mood from investors coming to terms with the beginnings of a global recession. Stock markets may have stabilised slightly, but corporate bond prices have continued to fall as investors remain nervous about the cocktail of the impact of the banking crisis and the recession that looked likely even without the financial markets freezing up.

Inflation over recent years had been on the rise, albeit from very low levels, and central banks had started to increase interest rates in an attempt to defuse this. However, as the banking crisis has accelerated the impact and likelihood of a recession, there has been unprecedented coordination across central banks to make dramatic cuts in rates to try to stave it off. All eyes are now on both national output figures and inflation numbers to see what lies ahead. Stock markets are likely to remain nervous and bearish, with very few pundits brave enough to call the bottom of this current crisis.

With only limited action taken by many pension funds to reduce their exposure to equities before this latest market crash, defined benefit pension managers have again paid the price. While liabilities have increased with falling interest rates (offset to some extent by the falling expectations of future inflation), assets have fallen, pushing up scheme deficits once again. Pension black holes have returned to the news headlines and the financial pressures on sponsoring employers have intensified.

Uncertain and recessionary times ahead do not provide any reliable prospect of markets bouncing back in a hurry. The economic outlook appears fairly bleak and there is little for those running defined benefit schemes to feel optimistic about on the investment front. Employers and trustees face worrying times ahead and further pressure to explore ways to reduce the risks they face.

2.4 Increased longevity in the UK population

Over the last three decades there has been a sharp increase in the longevity of the UK population.

Twenty years ago, a 65-year-old man and woman, on average, would have lived for a further 15 and 19 years respectively. The latest Office for National Statistics central projections predict these expectancies to increase to 21 and 23 years respectively for a man and woman age 65 today. Looking to the future, the higher Office for National Statistics projections say that by the year 2040, a man aged 65 could expect to live for a further 29 years, to age 94.

These increases and the fact that we can expect them to continue into the future mean that the cost of running a defined benefit pension scheme has and will continue to increase very substantially as the years roll on. In broad terms, every extra year of life typically adds 3% to 4% to the cost of funding a defined benefit scheme.

Along with low interest rates, changes in longevity are arguably the biggest issue facing the future provision of income in retirement in the United Kingdom. As our life expectancy increases and we still want to retire at age 65, then the amount of money we need to save to provide an income once we are no longer working also increases.

For those running defined benefit pension schemes the issue is a serious cause for concern, as these pensions guarantee to pay a certain level of income from a specified retirement date, come what may, and require the employer to fund the scheme accordingly. Employers are faced with not only spiralling costs, but also uncertainty as to how these will grow in the future. The further into the future one projects, the wider the range of possible longevity experience.

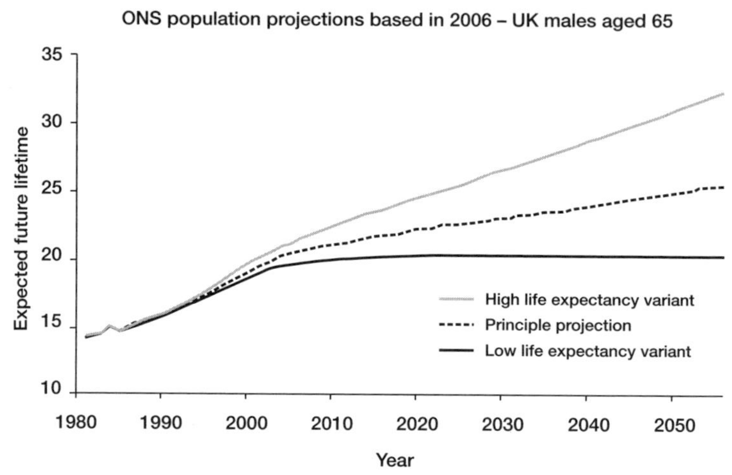

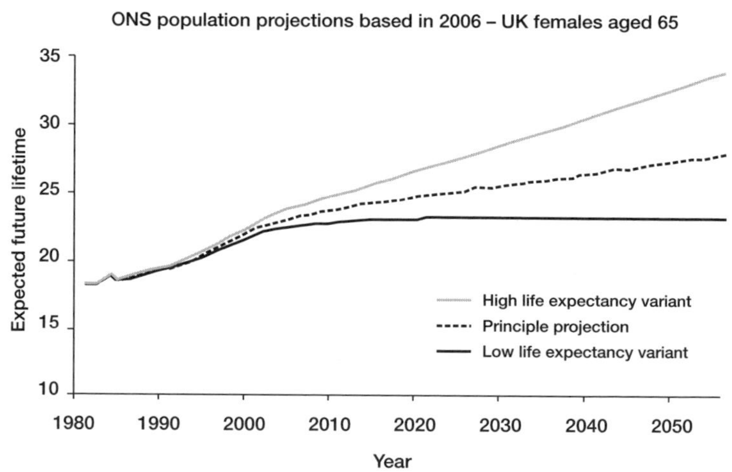

In February 2008, as a result of increasing evidence for continued future growth in longevity, the Pension Regulator (PR) proposed a significant strengthening of longevity assumptions used by defined benefit schemes. These changes would have triggered a formal investigation by the PR where the pension scheme was using less than long cohort mortality assumptions or was assuming that future increases in longevity were tending towards zero.

However, successful lobbying has softened this proposal. Instead, mortality assumptions will not be a primary trigger for a review, but will be investigated in the event of a review triggered by some other issue.

Regardless of the specific actions taken by the PR, increasing longevity is pushing up the costs of running a defined benefit scheme in a dramatic fashion. Looking at scheme returns to the PR from September 2005 to September 2007, Hewitt Associates has recently estimated that on average, pension schemes increased their longevity assumptions by 14 months during that period, increasing their future costs by £40 billion.

These increases in cost and the levels of risk caused by the degree of future uncertainty will continue to be a driver behind employers seeking to close their defined benefit schemes and taking further action to reduce risk.

2.5 Changing employment patterns

The changing face of employment in the United Kingdom has also had an impact on the rate of closure of defined benefit pension schemes.

The country has moved progressively away from the norms and expectations of the 1960s and 1970s. 'Jobs for life' have become increasingly rare, as has the desire of those coming out of school or further education for the single-track career experienced by their parents or grandparents.

In this context, defined benefit pension schemes have arguably become less and less appropriate for both employer and employee. Employees see them as less relevant as they do not expect to be with one employer for their entire career – or even for more than a few years. Whether or not this has driven how they feel, the reality is that most employees do not value the provision of a defined benefit scheme as much as they should. Most are attracted by a higher salary or are equally attracted to a defined contribution pension, despite such arrangements normally being far less generous and secure.

From the point of view of most employers, the fact that defined benefit schemes are less appropriate for modern working practices and undervalued by staff is no bad thing. It has made it easier for them to close existing schemes to new members and to take further steps to reduce the costs and risks they face.

The earnings cap on defined benefit scheme benefits and the increasing mobility of senior management across different employers have also meant that many executives are no longer in a company's defined benefit scheme. This will almost certainly have influenced many companies' decisions (even if only subconsciously) as to whether to maintain their commitment to providing one.

Even where an assessment of the relative costs and benefits in terms of appeal to employees makes the continued provision of a defined benefit scheme the right option for the employer, some have ended up with a scheme that dwarfs the sponsoring employer's business. British Telecom, for example, is effectively a gigantic pension scheme with a telecommunications business attached – a challenging situation for management trying to operate in a highly competitive industry.

The exception to these trends – in terms of both duration of employment with one employer and the presence of an open defined benefit pension scheme – is the public sector. Here, slightly old-fashioned and more paternalistic practices have endured. More powerful trade unions are vocal in support of improved pay and rewards and fiercely defend longstanding, generous defined benefit pension schemes for employees who generally do aspire to stay with that one employer for life.

The most fundamental reason why the public sector pensions situation has become so very different from the private sector is that the real costs of defined benefit schemes in the public sector are not apparent. Schemes are generally funded on a 'pay as you go' basis, which has hidden their real ongoing cost. In addition, most are funded through the opaque context of the tax system – whether local or national – again serving to hide their true cost, even to those footing the bill.

Whether the marked contrast between the generosity of public sector and private sector pension provision remains politically acceptable is one of the more intriguing developments to watch in the wider pensions arena.

3. Drivers to growth and evolution of the buy-out market itself

3.1 Regulatory changes

The Pension Act 2004 replaced the existing Occupational Pensions Regulatory Authority (Opra) with PR. This came into force on April 6 2005.

The government took this action because it believed Opra's powers were too limited and it wanted to see a more proactive, risk-based and flexible regulator in place to deal more effectively with workplace pensions.

In particular, the government wanted to equip the new regulator with greater powers to improve the security of members' benefits. To do this, the PR focuses its attention on finding and dealing with the greatest risks to members' benefits, and works with trustees and scheme managers to raise standards of scheme administration. It also has important additional responsibilities to reduce the risk of situations arising which may lead to calls for compensation from the Pension Protection Fund (PPF).

There is little doubt that since coming into effect in 2005, the PR has made a significant impact and one mainly to the benefit of the security of scheme members, as was intended. The more proactive and 'demanding' approach of the regulator has forced pensions schemes and their trustees to act more overtly in the interests of the security of scheme members. But of course, nearly all of the areas for improvement have – directly or indirectly – served to increase the cost and in some cases the risk to employers of running defined benefit pension schemes.

Specific actions taken by the PR that have served to increase the demand for pension buy-outs and other risk reduction strategies include:

- an underlying pressure for pension schemes to use long cohort mortality assumptions (see section 2.4 above);
- a stern warning issued to pension schemes concerning the need for improved administration practices and standards of record keeping;
- guidance notes issued reflecting the PR's concerns about the impact of conflicts of interest among scheme trustees, professional advisers and pension managers running a scheme;
- the influence that the PR can have on corporate activity such as mergers and

acquisitions because of its power to issue contribution notices and financial support directions to improve or maintain the security of pension scheme member benefits. Before the intervention of the PR, trustees protecting the interests of scheme members have been increasingly influential in improving scheme funding or protection due to threats to the security or support of the scheme from M&A activity. This is all serving to drive increased scheme buy-out activity; and

- new powers in the Pensions Act 2008 which will mean that any company that does anything that turns out to be materially detrimental to the ability of the scheme to pay its members' benefits can, for up to six years following the event, be forced by the PR to make a restorative contribution to the scheme via a contribution notice. This would include events that preceded a merger or acquisition of the company currently running the pension scheme.

While it is right that the PR fulfils its mandate to the benefit of members of defined benefit pension schemes, there is no doubt that as it has pushed for improved standards and the security of members, it has also increased demand from defined benefit schemes for the services offered by the pension buy-out market.

3.2 New entrants and the growth of competition

In the earliest days of pension buy-outs there were only two major players – the Prudential and Legal & General – servicing the needs of schemes being terminated and wound up as a result of employers closing for business.

In those days, business arose only through the enforced requirement for a buy-out where a business became insolvent and action was required to preserve the benefits for members of the defined benefit scheme operated by that employer.

Since then, the various factors described above have conspired to bring about the closure to new members of the majority of defined benefit schemes in the United Kingdom. Many have taken the next step – closing the schemes to further accrual of defined benefit benefits by their existing members.

However, these closures have served only to limit the rate of increase in the costs and risks carried by the sponsoring employer. These businesses continue to hold the responsibility and financial burden associated with the accrued rights and benefits of existing members, even if they are no longer accruing additional benefits.

The need for the solutions now offered by the enlivened and enlarged buy-out market is vast, pressing and, for many businesses, pivotal to their future success or even survival.

Sponsoring employers with closed schemes have been increasingly keen to reduce the risks they still face and, if practical, to pass these risks and responsibilities on to others, subject to fulfilling their responsibilities to their members as represented by the trustees of the scheme.

But it has not just been sponsoring employers. Trustees have faced increased regulatory pressure to secure the pensions promise implied by the employer covenant and have been given additional power by the Pensions Act 2004 and strongly encouraged by the PR to do just that. Even where employers may have been sanguine about the state of affairs in their defined benefit schemes, trustees have turned up the heat by increasing the focus on the scheme's ability to fulfil its promise to its members.

Against this backdrop, a range of factors have combined to attract new players into this market, from entirely new businesses through to large, established insurance companies:

- the sheer scale of the opportunity to offer crucially important solutions to employers offering defined benefit pension schemes;
- the belief that this evolving market offers attractive returns for successful ventures;
- the belief of new entrants to the buy-out market that the assets of these pension schemes could be better managed to improve returns while maintaining the security of benefits for scheme members; and
- the scarcity of other attractive opportunities for insurers.

Up to the end of the millennium, the two original players (the Prudential and Legal & General) enjoyed a comfortable domination of the buy-out business carried out in response to the needs of employers looking to reduce or eliminate risk.

But over the last two to three years in particular, a significant number of new players have entered the market. This influx of new providers – from dynamic new businesses such as Lucida, Paternoster and the Pensions Corporation to large existing insurers such as Aegon, Aviva and Met Life – have not only helped to drive down the cost of buy-outs to trustees and sponsoring employers, but also increased the profile and awareness of the options now available to those running defined benefit schemes.

The buy-out market was worth more than £3 billion in 2007 and twice this volume was done in the first three quarters of 2008. A total figure of around £8 billion is expected for 2008 as a whole. To put these numbers into context – and to give an indication of the buy-out market's ultimate potential value – total private sector pension liabilities in the United Kingdom exceed £1 trillion.

3.3 The Pension Protection Fund

During recent years, the proportion of buy-outs carried out through mandatory closure has fallen rapidly due to the creation of the PPF, although the PPF does still seek trustees to wind up outside the PPF and conduct a buy-out if the scheme assets are sufficient to provide benefits greater than would otherwise have been provided by the PPF.

This new facility, paid for mainly by levies from eligible defined benefit schemes, has provided new protection for members in schemes where the sponsoring employer of an unfunded scheme has become insolvent.

Compensation of 100% is paid to those already in receipt of benefits from the employer's scheme, and for those yet to reach normal retirement age 90% of the benefits earned up to the date of insolvency will be paid from the fund.

Compensation from the PPF is subject to an overall cap – one for those receiving 100% compensation and a smaller figure for those entitled to 90% compensation.

These caps are recalculated each year. Between April 2008 and March 2009, the cap at the age of 65 for 100% compensation is a pension of £30,856.35 per annum, and for 90% compensation it is a pension of £27,770.72 per annum. (At the time of writing the revised caps for later in 2009 had not been published.)

Compensation could also involve a reduction in the rate of any escalation in benefits that is due.

Although creation of the PPF has led to a fall in mandatory buy-outs, this has been more than made up for by increases in the number of voluntary buy-outs being sought by still-solvent employers and their scheme trustees.

3.4 Improved delivery in risk reduction

The core product of insured buy-out providers is the specialist insurance that allows the risks of providing benefits under a defined benefit pension scheme to be transferred to the insurer for payment of a premium.

A buy-in arrangement will leave the employer and trustees with responsibility for the running of the scheme; the insurance policy that provides benefits for the members covered by it simply becomes one of the investment assets of the scheme.

A full buy-out transfers all the risks associated with the bought-out benefits to the insurance provider in exchange for a single premium. Ultimately, the scheme is wound up after the benefits have been converted into individual annuities. This is the most complete shift of risk for the employer and trustees, and offers scheme members the security of individual benefits being guaranteed by a regulated insurance company.

A buy-in and a partial buy-out can target a subset of the scheme membership using age, status, nature of benefits (level, escalating etc), or other criteria to divide the scheme into parts. The full risk inherent in one or more of these groups of members is transferred to the provider via a buy-out.

A buy-in and a partial buy-out can target just those members in receipt of benefits already, whereas a full buy-out will have to handle deferred members still some time from retirement. Given the greater difficulty in predicting longevity over longer time periods into the future, full buy-outs will naturally appear more costly as a greater range of risks has to be covered.

Given this backdrop, different mechanisms and tailored structures and insurances have been created to produce a 'toolbox' of risk-reduction techniques that can be used to create practical, bespoke solutions for pension scheme managers and trustees seeking cost-effective risk reduction.

These include measures such as offering early retirement or enhanced transfer values to encourage deferred members to leave the scheme, commutation of benefits and insurances covering specific risks such as certain groups of members living beyond a certain age.

Alongside buy-ins, there are other investment strategy options including liability-driven investment and the use of swaps to cover inflation, interest rates or longevity risk.

Also of note are so-called 'day one transfers', where the buy-out provider assumes full legal responsibility for the defined benefit scheme on the first day and carries out the buy-out process from that point forward, running the scheme itself until wind-up can be completed.

This range of techniques and methodologies, and the ability to use different approaches over time, mean that risk reduction or elimination has become a far cry from a 'one size fits all', standardised process. Competition and innovation in the buy-out market have meant that increasingly, individual circumstances and preferences of employers and trustees can be met quite precisely and at competitive prices.

A further aspect of recent history has been the emergence of the PR's preference – both implied and inferred – for insured buy-outs versus other solutions. The PR's actions in connection with some high-profile non-insured buy-out activities have shown its determination to ensure clear and transparent protection of members' interests is maintained regardless of the scale, nature or circumstances of the corporate actions being proposed.

This will almost certainly drive more business down the insured route where the protection of members' interests is overt and is further supported by the powers of the FSA.

4. Looking to the future

A further significant factor in the large-scale growth of the buy-out market has been, until recently, the ready availability of capital.

Prior to the 2008 credit crunch, which has threatened the very existence of many of the world's major banks, capital to support growth in pension buy-out business was in plentiful supply.

While this is currently not the case, the net effect has been to concentrate the level of commitment to this market by those remaining. In other words, current market circumstances have led to a number of providers pulling out of the sector, leaving a smaller number of more committed players. We may also see consolidation within the buy-out sector. The scarcity of capital also means that prices have increased somewhat (though levels are still below those of 2005).

Market conditions are also having an impact on the demand side of the pension buy-out sector. Many businesses previously interested in taking steps to reduce risk may feel that they cannot now afford to do so.

Although this may well be true in the short term, the credit crunch has highlighted the issue of the volatility of assets and, if anything, will have increased the desire of employers running a defined benefit scheme to get rid of the liabilities in the long term.

So, looking forward, how is the market likely to develop?

First, we can expect to see further innovation in the design of de-risking solutions and how these are offered to sponsoring employers. It is likely that the market will increasingly move to phased buy-outs, phased premium payment and other methods of de-risking in stages to help make the process more affordable and practical over time.

Although the market has heard a great deal of talk about other products to address pension scheme risk, the reality has been that there is little evidence so far of these alternatives being purchased. Indeed, looking to the future, it will be interesting to see whether the alternatives take hold or whether the current credit crunch makes it impossible to get them off the ground.

In the medium term, it is likely that a new market for longevity risk will emerge, building on the recent, early developments by JP Morgan and others which have already seen a small number of real longevity derivative transactions taking place.

The last few years have witnessed some groundbreaking developments in the buy-out sector. As the United Kingdom adapts to survive and re-emerge from what many believe will be a lengthy and potentially deep recession, there is no doubt that the buy-out arena will develop further and move steadily towards fulfilling its early promise.

The attractions of the current buy-out market

Matthew Preston
Herbert Smith LLP

1. Introduction

This chapter considers the factors in the current market which have been attracting trustees and employers either to buy out defined benefit pension liabilities or to otherwise remove them from the employer's balance sheet, and considers whether some of those attractions were, in fact, overstated in the early days of 2008 as the new buy-out market developed.

During 2007 and early 2008 the principal attraction of the new buy-out market was the realisation that buy-out prices were shrinking. By contrast, defined benefit pension liabilities had been growing steadily and, in the wake of Financial Reporting Standard 17 (FRS 17), had taken root on the employers' balance sheets. In 2007, the number of players in the buy-out market increased from two to more than 10 and the amount of business transacted increased dramatically. Less than £3 billion of business had been written in the whole of 2007, but almost £4 billion was written in the first half of 2008 alone and a total of £8 billion by the end of that year.

Any analysis of the buy-out market must, of course, be qualified by an acknowledgement that market conditions have been changing rapidly since mid-2008 and continue to do so. Certain themes can be identified, but it is not possible to say with any certainty how the market will develop even in the very near future. In particular, the full impact of the credit crunch and the remarkable volatility in the equity markets in late 2008 on the buy-out market will not become clear for some time. In the first half of 2008 it seemed that the credit crunch was barely having any impact on the market at all, but by the fourth quarter business had all but ground to a halt. Nevertheless, despite the rapid changes taking place in the buy-out market, there is no denying that there has been a fundamental shift in the attitude of both trustees and employers towards the possibility of buying out defined benefit pension liabilities since 2007, and that the market is unlikely to return to the way it was before then.

2. Underlying factors: buy-outs became more attractive as running a defined benefit pension scheme became less attractive

The increasing attraction of buying out must correspond to some degree with the fading popularity of the defined benefit schemes themselves. In the period between the passing of the Pensions Act 2004 and the end of 2007, the following factors heightened the awareness of both employers and shareholders of the cost of providing defined benefit pensions or actually increased the (already high) cost of providing those benefits – or, in some cases, did both.

2.1 Increased regulation and governance requirements

The Pensions Act 2004 introduced the Pensions Regulator (PR) and the Pension Protection Fund (PPF) to the world. The increased regulation and governance requirements which they have imposed on trustees and employers have undoubtedly increased the cost of providing defined benefit pensions on a day-to-day basis.

The PR, in particular, has transformed the pensions landscape in the United Kingdom by introducing a new layer of regulation to many aspects of corporate activity and has thus raised awareness of the cost of providing defined benefit pensions. The PR's mandate extends to supervising the effects of mergers and acquisitions, internal group restructurings and dividend payments (among other activities), which many employers had previously pursued without considering pension matters too deeply. Since the PR prefers to be a passive third party, the onus is on employers to determine whether they ought to approach the PR (or whether the trustees of their pension schemes will want to do so) prior to embarking upon any new project. This need to stop and think about the level of the pension scheme's liabilities before embarking upon these activities has thrust pension schemes into the limelight.

No one could argue, post-Maxwell, that if an employer has chosen to provide defined benefit pensions for its employees, it should fulfil the obligation to do so properly. Appropriate regulation and governance in that sense are not unwelcome. However, since 2004, even employers that are acting properly must meet the additional expenses of being seen to be acting properly and of deciphering the new legislation. In October 2008, Hewitt Associates estimated that a single clearance application could easily cost £200,000 once the input of all parties is considered.

2.2 Accounting requirements for pension benefits

FRS 17 was introduced in stages between 2001 and 2005. It brought a realisation for many companies that their pension scheme liabilities were a current problem, not just something for the future. Before FRS 17, finance directors, shareholders and investment analysts had been used to accounting for pension costs under Statement of Standard Accounting Practice 24 (SSAP 24). This required an employer's contributions to a defined benefit scheme and its net exposure to the scheme to be shown in the accounts using the scheme's own long-term actuarial funding basis. As a result, the value of assets and liabilities could be smoothed over the long term and there was no common basis for comparison with other companies' accounts. FRS 17 (and International Accounting Standard 19 (IAS 19)) placed defined benefit pension liabilities on the balance sheet and for the first time required liabilities to be measured using market values. FRS 17 also required all companies to use a standard set of actuarial assumptions for determining liabilities, allowing the balance sheets of different companies to be compared.

In brief, FRS 17 had to be adopted by UK companies for all accounting periods following January 1 2005 (to reflect the requirement for all EU companies to satisfy the terms of the international accounting standard, IAS 19, with effect from that date). While it is an improvement on SSAP 24, FRS 17 is flawed. The FRS 17 assumptions focus on AA corporate bonds, regardless of what is happening in the markets and the scheme in question. In particular, it presents a further problem for employers since it gives only a snapshot of the funding position (surplus or deficit) of the scheme on the balance sheet.

If the FRS 17 snapshot is taken on a particularly good day or a particularly bad one, the figure which appears on the balance sheet for that year may not be truly representative of the overall position of the scheme. As a result, a company which has worked hard to improve the funding level of a scheme over the course of a year is not guaranteed to reap the benefits of its hard work in that year's accounts. Further, few pension schemes will have based their funding plans on the FRS 17 assumptions. In most cases, the trustees and employers of a scheme are now required to agree a set of assumptions which is uniquely appropriate to their scheme (known as the "technical provisions" in the scheme-specific funding regime under the Pensions Act 2004). There will therefore usually be a divergence between the employer's balance sheet and the real level of funding in the scheme as agreed between the trustees and the employer.

To make matters worse, proposals from the Accounting Standards Board and the advent of Solvency II could lead to defined benefit pension liabilities having to be disclosed on an even more conservative basis in future. The Accounting Standards Board has suggested that a 'risk-free' discount rate should be used in company accounts. This would make no allowance for the possibility of pension scheme assets being exposed to investment risk in order to generate returns to meet liabilities in the future. If it were to be extended to private defined benefit pension schemes, then Solvency II would broadly require the reporting of defined benefit scheme funding to be based on the same sort of minimum capital requirements used by insurance companies. This would be significantly more onerous than the FRS 17 assumptions based on AA corporate bonds. At the time of writing, the latest consultation paper from the European Commission suggests that it is unlikely that Solvency II will be extended in this way, but it is an area which employers will continue to view with concern.

In short, changes to the accounting requirements in the United Kingdom from 2001 raised the profile of pension scheme deficits with directors and have pushed the disclosed cost on the balance sheet much closer to the actual cost of buying out. The possibility of removing these liabilities from the balance sheet once and for all in return for a single premium payment thus became significantly more attractive.

2.3 Volatility in the equity and bond markets

Almost all UK pension schemes have some exposure to UK and overseas equities and bonds, and both the equity and bond markets can be volatile. They are vulnerable to high rates of corporate insolvency and 2008 saw this on an unprecedented scale. It seems fair to say that everyone was shocked by the performance of the equity and bond markets when the global financial crisis gripped the UK economy in 2008. As a series of high-profile victims such as Northern Rock, HBOS, AIG, Lehman Brothers, Merrill Lynch and Bradford & Bingley sought assistance from third parties or the taxpayer, or simply became insolvent, every investor was reminded that no investment is absolutely safe and that past achievements really are no guarantee of future performance.

However, it would be incorrect to suggest that short-term volatility in the equity or bond markets automatically makes buying out pension liabilities more attractive. When volatility results in highs in the bond markets, it actually reduces the scheme liabilities on company balance sheets as FRS 17 is linked to the yields on corporate bonds. Also, equities are generally accepted as being risky investments in the short term and a degree of short-term volatility is expected.

Buy-outs become more attractive because both falling asset values and poor returns on bonds will increase the funding deficit in a pension scheme. This in turn increases the demands on employers to pay higher contributions and makes it more expensive to run a scheme on a daily basis. Lower asset values and higher pension scheme deficits also affect company accounts and weaken the perceived financial position of the employers. In addition, when the bond markets are high, buy-out premiums can go down. All of this increases the attraction of a buy-out, which will discharge the liabilities underlying those deficits once and for all.

Even so, the picture is not clear-cut and volatility can also make buy-outs less attractive (at least in the short term). Higher pension scheme deficits also mean that, in order to finance the premium charged by the insurer or other buy-out provider, an employer may need to find more money to top up scheme funding. We return to this point later in the chapter.

2.4 The rise of trustee activism

In the period in question, a variety of factors – not least the increased awareness of the magnitude of pension scheme liabilities and the existence of the PR – have led to increasing levels of trustee activism. More and more employers found that trustees, sometimes in alliance with the trade unions representing employees, were demanding greater security for the employees' pension benefits in case the employer should suffer a catastrophic event of some sort. The PR actively encouraged trustees to act as unsecured creditors (and still does). Increasing numbers of them took to demanding employer covenant reviews, the disclosure of financial information and greater clarity as to the directors' future business plans.

Pension scheme deficits are now such a high-profile issue for some employers that in many cases they can be a distraction from actually running the employer's core business. The cumulative cost in time and money of addressing appropriately the issues raised by active trustees can be very significant. At a rough estimate, three-quarters of UK defined benefit pension schemes are already closed to new joiners. In those cases, management time is being spent on historic liabilities which often relate to only a small number of the current employees (if any). The ongoing cost of dealing with such historic liabilities is one which can be offset, in the minds of the directors, against the premium charged by a buy-out provider.

2.5 The Pension Protection Levy

The principle behind the PPF, in simple terms, is that successful employers must pay for unsuccessful employers' pension scheme deficits. Those employers whose pension schemes would, if the employer were to suffer a qualifying insolvency event, be eligible to enter the PPF must pay an annual levy. The amount payable by each employer is substantially based on the potential insolvency risk which it represents and the funding deficits in its own defined benefit scheme. The levy payable by each employer is, therefore, tailored to its circumstances to some degree. Nevertheless, it is an unwelcome additional burden in the short term and in the long term represents a significant risk as the PPF's capital requirements increase and the number of contributing employers shrinks. The levy offers no direct benefit to the employer paying it unless it becomes insolvent. The amount of the levy is another expense which can be offset against the buy-out premium by the employer, making that one-off payment more attractive.

2.6 Improvements in longevity

The key reason for the increase in the cost of providing pensions is that they must now be paid for longer. As with the other factors considered in this section, the direct result of improvements in the longevity of employees from an employer's point of view is higher contributions to meet the increase in the projected future cost of the pensions. In 1975, the rate of increase in life expectancy was around 0.75% per year. Between 2000 and 2008, the rate of increase has been closer to 4% per year[1] and these increases have forced trustees to ask for higher and higher contributions. Further pressure comes from the PR, which indicated in a consultation paper in October 2008 that it would take particular interest in mortality assumptions when conducting its investigations.

The mortality tables produced by the Continuous Mortality Investigation, which try to anticipate future increases in life expectancy, have been updated in recent years, but it should be noted that these tables flatten out the mortality experience of the population as a whole and take a fairly conservative base as their starting point. They are, therefore, inevitably inaccurate for any given scheme. Actuaries use these tables to advise trustees on what assumptions they should make about the future cost of pensions in order to determine how much the employer should contribute to the scheme. However, life expectancy depends on many different factors which affect different groups of people in different ways. An employee's job, salary, postcode and eating, drinking or smoking habits, as well as the amount of pension received upon retirement, are all relevant to determine life expectancy. Even within a single city, life expectancies can vary greatly from one area to another.

The most accurate way to assess the likely mortality rates for the members of a particular scheme is to look at the actual mortality experience within the membership of that scheme, rather than the population of the country as a whole. Creating specific mortality tables for a scheme does, of course, require quite a large number of members to provide meaningful results, so only large schemes are likely to do this. In most cases, a buy-out provider will require as much evidence as possible relating to the scheme's specific mortality experience before determining the premium for buying out the scheme's liabilities. The attraction of passing this inherently uncertain expense to a buy-out provider can only have grown as the true rate of the increase in life expectancy has become clearer to employers and trustees.

---

1 Paternoster, "Guide to Bulk Annuities", *Professional Pensions*, June 2008.

2.7 The role of the press

Finally, in recent years, pensions have become front-page news. There has been an exponential increase in the number of headlines concerning the sizeable funding deficits in both the public and private sectors. Headlines have also drawn attention to any employers that have tried to control their costs by terminating the accrual of defined benefit pension entitlements for future service or closing their defined benefit schemes to new joiners. The press has, therefore, raised public awareness of the very high cost to companies of providing defined benefit pensions and has, to some extent, contributed to the growth of the buy-out market by bringing the true scale of the problem to the attention of more employers.

3. Why did buying out become more attractive?

While the factors discussed above made running a defined benefit scheme much less attractive in general, they do not tell the whole story. Buying out has become more attractive in its own right because the purchase of a bulk annuity policy has become both more affordable and, to some extent, easier to achieve.

3.1 Factors affecting affordability

The circumstances of the individual scheme will determine whether a buy-out solution is actually affordable. The principal issue for most employers in considering a buy-out is the gap between the value of the assets currently held by the pension scheme and the premium quoted by the insurer. During the early period of growth in the buy-out market, bond yields were increasing. As a result, the gap became narrower for schemes where the trustees had followed a conservative investment strategy and held lots of corporate bonds and gilts. In relation to the £700 million buy-out of the Rank pension scheme by Rothesay Life, for example, the employer did not pay a premium. In fact, Rank expected to collect £20 million when the deal completed because of the surplus in the scheme.[2]

During the same period, the insurers also seem to have benefited from higher bond yields. Higher yields allowed them to make better returns on the investment portfolio which they used to match the defined benefit liabilities following a buy-out, so they were able to reduce the premiums which they charged for buying out.

As discussed above, the increasing cost of running a pension scheme may also have reduced the perceived cost of the premium in the employer's mind. It is worth noting that the cost of the PPF levy was revised upwards in 2007 amid concerns that the PPF may not have been raising enough income. Among all the costs associated with pension schemes, the relatively new, uncertain and volatile movements of the PPF levy appeared to many employers to be another uncertain liability which could be removed or reduced through a buy-out.

More significant than bond yields or rising costs, however, was the explosion in the number of providers in the buy-out market and the fierce competition between them. By 2008, there were more than 10 companies that were prepared to offer a variety of solutions to remove defined benefit pension liabilities from employers'

---

2 Source: *The Times* online, February 29 2008.

balance sheets. The likes of Paternoster and Lucida had stepped up alongside Legal & General and the Prudential and, although they had no history in this field as companies, they brought a wealth of experienced personnel and the necessary capital to do business quickly. Some existing companies, notably multi-line insurers such as AIG, Norwich Union and Aegon, also threw their hats into the ring. A number of other companies also decided to offer alternatives to buy-out policies. Pension Corporation, CitiGroup and Rothesay Life (backed by Goldman Sachs) all developed alternative ways to unburden employers of their pension liabilities by acquiring or replacing the sponsoring employer of the pension scheme.

Competition between all of these different companies drove the price of bulk annuity policies down rapidly in the short period of time during which they were all attempting to chalk up their first major deals. In many cases the return on capital may have been very low, but it was not long before the cost of failing to do business, even with such low returns, was revealed. In November 2008 Synesis, having written no business itself, was acquired by Pension Corporation.[3] The effect of this competition on pricing appears to have been a short-term phenomenon and by the end of 2008 there were already signs that the pricing of some liabilities, for deferred pensioners in particular, was rising as both the number of companies in the market fell and the initial need to be seen to be doing deals faded. It is instructive that, having done one deal each, CitiGroup and Goldman Sachs appeared to withdraw from the market altogether. Their credentials established, they perhaps found that higher returns could be made on their capital elsewhere until prices in the buy-out market rose once again to profitable levels. In some cases, it may be that future price rises will also be fuelled partly by the need to improve the insurer's overall return on capital and make up for the cheap policies issued in late 2007 and early 2008.

3.2 Factors affecting practicality

Traditionally, a buy-out occurred only at the end of the scheme's natural life, following the insolvency of the sponsoring employer and a winding-up period that could last many years. The PPF has effectively rendered this market obsolete. As at the end of May 2009, it had already taken on 101 pension schemes. In the new buy-out market, transaction times are no longer a matter of years, but can be a matter of months for large schemes and, in some cases, a matter of weeks. Lower pricing and competition between the different providers clearly influenced this – if employers do not have to find quite so much money and want to lock in good prices while they are available, everyone will move faster. In addition, the conservative investment portfolios favoured by many trustees (as discussed above) have made it easier to conclude transactions quickly. Insurers like bonds, gilts and cash, and so the fewer the equities in the fund, the quicker it is for the trustees to assemble a portfolio of assets acceptable to the insurers.

However, buying out has also become easier in practice because 'one size fits all' is no longer the order of the day. There is now a great variety of innovative solutions available for the various problems experienced by trustees and employers in trying

3 Pension Corporation press release, November 18 2008.

to buy out. For example, significant delays can be avoided if all of the data cleansing and equalisation risks (including guaranteed minimum pension equalisation) do not have to be resolved by the trustees in advance, but can be passed over to the insurer on day one. This has been possible, in return for an increase in the price of the buy-out policy, in a number of cases. Previously, such issues could take years to resolve. The Emap buy-out, one of the early cases handled by Paternoster in 2007, was completed in only two months. All risks were swiftly transferred to a subsidiary of Paternoster through the simple expedient of making it the sponsoring employer of the scheme, so Emap was able to escape the problems presented by a lengthy data cleansing exercise. At the time of writing, almost one year after the date of the transaction, Paternoster still has not been able to issue individual annuities to the members of the scheme. In the past, this transaction could simply not have occurred and the liabilities would have remained with Emap until all of the data cleansing issues had been resolved.

Other innovations include phased buy-outs, liability reduction exercises and 'profit-sharing':

- In a phased buy-out the mortality and investment bases are fixed on day one, but the premium is paid in instalments over a long period.
- A liability reduction exercise involves inviting employees to take enhanced cash equivalent transfer payments, which is likely to be cheaper than issuing them with annuity policies.
- Depending on the terms, profit-sharing may prove attractive to an employer which is concerned that it has over-estimated its employees' life expectancy. The insurer will give some cash back if the employees expire more quickly than expected.

Another high-profile innovation is the introduction of security and collateral arrangements which have enabled some very large schemes (eg, the Friends Provident pension scheme) to enter into buy-in arrangements despite concerns about the effect of a default on the policy by the insurer in question.

It is worth noting that all such innovations come with an additional cost. In some cases, it may be worthwhile for the employer to pay that cost. For Friends Provident, as an FSA-regulated insurer, the Financial Services Compensation Scheme (FSCS) is not such an attractive safety net, since Friends Provident is one of the very companies which would have to pay higher levies to the FSCS to compensate the pension scheme if the insurer providing the buy-in policy became insolvent. So, while other FSA-regulated employers which are considering buying out their pension liabilities may also wish to consider collateral, it will not necessarily be right for all employers to do so. Insurers are generally opposed to the idea of collateral. Their business model is to pool assets and risk, not to sub-divide it. They claim that their obligations under the FSA's 'treating customers fairly' regime mean that they cannot treat some customers better than others. The insurers are also already obliged to maintain set levels of capital and reserves which are determined by the FSA. It seems likely that in many cases, the insurer's covenant will be stronger than the employer's, even without any collateral arrangements. However, the case of Friends Provident shows that in the right circumstances, collateral arrangements are possible and deals can be done.

When they were an expensive means of securing individual annuities for pensioners, buy-outs held little interest for most employers. Once the cost of buy-outs fell to something much closer to IAS 19 levels, they became much more useful to employers for a variety of reasons. Emap shifted the pension liabilities off its balance sheet in very short order and M-Real offloaded a pension scheme so that it could sell the sponsoring employer unencumbered by its pension liabilities. Buy-outs are much more attractive as a tool for achieving a multitude of corporate purposes and interest in buy-outs seems likely to remain high in the future.

4. Further developments affecting the buy-out market – what might the future hold?

Although they are difficult to measure, it is clear that buy-outs have become less attractive again. At the start of 2008, some commentators had predicted that buy-out business worth £15 billion would be written during 2008.[4] However, even before the results for the third quarter were in, these predictions were being scaled back despite a number of deals being announced during the third quarter of 2008 and bond yields remaining high.[5] Most notably, the first £1 billion buy-in was completed for Cable & Wireless in September 2008.

The predictions were scaled back because the market volatility in the latter half of 2008 started to affect the buy-out market directly. It seems that when less cash is available in the future, buy-outs will be less attractive and employers will be reluctant to transact. This trend can be identified from the following factors.

First, short-term falls in equity values increase the amount of money that an employer has to contribute to the scheme to allow the trustees to pay the buy-out premium, even if that premium has not changed. So, in the course of the credit crunch, buy-outs became less affordable at a time when few companies had cash to spare. With the rate of inflation falling and the likelihood of a period of deflation during 2009, there seems little scope for pension schemes' assets to improve sufficiently to make buying out attractive again (at least in early 2009).[6]

Second, insurers normally quote a premium and hold it for two or three months to give the trustees time to realise the necessary funds. At the time of writing, however, it seems that they are no longer willing to do this. The markets are so volatile that they are not confident of their pricing even over such short periods of time.[7] This is clearly a serious practical impediment to transacting business.

Third, the FSA requires certain minimum levels of capital and reserves before an insurer can write any business. Insurers meet these capital requirements using investment-grade credit. As the spreads on AA-rated corporate bonds rise and the risk of defaults increases, the insurers' ability to meet these capital requirements has actually been weakened. Even if they do not wish to borrow cash themselves, the

---

4 *Financial Times*, October 20 2008.

5 Jonathan Bloomer, speaking at the Westminster and City Pension Buy-outs, Buy-ins and Derisking Solutions Conference, October 1 2008.

6 Mark Wood of Paternoster in *Scotland on Sunday*, December 21 2008.

7 Richard Jones of Punter Southall in the *Financial Times*, October 20 2008.

value of their existing capital is being eroded by the credit crunch and, if the rate of defaults increases, some insurers may be left with insufficient capital to meet the FSA requirements. As a result, some may be reluctant to over-extend themselves by completing further deals at a time when it would be very difficult to raise more capital either as credit or from investors. In the longer term, capital requirements for insurance companies may become higher still with the introduction of Solvency II. This is likely to be another factor driving up the cost of buying out in future.

Finally, it seems that the initial rush to write business ended some time in the third quarter of 2008. The acquisition of Synesis provided the first major sign of the consolidation of the market into a smaller number of larger insurers and others may follow in due course. The initial competition between the insurers to do business and, perhaps more importantly, to be seen to be doing business seems to have faded around the same time, evidenced by the fact that it became more difficult for small schemes to obtain a range of buy-out quotes.[8] Reduced competition in the market is likely to force premiums back up to more realistic levels and, therefore, further reduce the attraction of buy-outs.

5. Is it always attractive to buy out?

We have seen that since mid-2007, both the number of insurers and the variety of innovative products available have increased greatly. However, the only pensions liabilities being secured are liabilities relating to the pensioners, because they represent the lowest risk category of scheme membership.[9] Their pensionable service and final salaries are known and the volatility of their life expectancy is generally lower than that of the younger deferred and active members. Prices in relation to those other categories have not fallen as far; nor are they likely to do so.

As discussed above, longevity presents a very serious risk to pension scheme funding. The younger the members, the greater the potential risk. Therefore, actives present the greatest problem, followed by the deferred members. Closing schemes can eliminate some risks such as salary inflation and the actives' continuing accrual of benefits, but a closed scheme does not eliminate the other risks presented by inflation and longevity. It should be attractive, therefore, to buy out both groups, but employers and trustees have tended in most cases to offload only the pensioners. The reason is simply that the same longevity and inflation risks also make actives and deferreds less attractive for an insurance company which is essentially running a closed scheme of its own and is, therefore, exposed to the same risks itself. The insurance companies charge higher premiums for buying out deferreds, and employers and trustees have generally decided that those premiums are simply too expensive. Depending on the rate of increase in the deferreds' life expectancy, however, some may find in hindsight that they would have preferred to retain the pensioners' liabilities and pay the higher premium to offload the deferreds.

However, just because the prices for buying out pensioners seem low, it will not be the right answer for every scheme. The question for employers is whether it is the

8 "Buy-out Market Watch" from *Pension Capital Strategies,* October 2008.
9 The exception, of course, is where the whole scheme is wound up.

most efficient way to fund their liabilities. It stands to reason that the insurers are interested in the pensioners because they are most likely to make a profit in relation to them, but in some cases there may be a strong argument for continuing to manage the liabilities of the scheme so that this profit can accrue to the pension scheme. Few employers will wish to operate their own core businesses and run a life insurance business, in the form of the pension scheme, on the side. However, in some cases, managing the liabilities will ultimately be cheaper than buying out. Broadly speaking, the pensioners within a scheme balance out the overall mortality experience of the pension scheme and gains made by the scheme in relation to their shorter and less volatile life expectancy can weigh in against the volatile costs relating to the deferreds and actives. The employer must be prepared for the long-term funding commitment involved, but it should not necessarily be dismissed as an alternative to buying out. It is worth also noting that if the pensioners remain in the scheme, there are various methods available for reducing and managing liabilities (eg, liability reduction exercises and liability-driven investment strategies).

6. Conclusion

In conclusion, it seems fair to say that the wide variety of views held by employers and trustees on a number of issues has led to the rapid growth of an innovative and wide-ranging suite of products within the buy-out market. The traditional buy-out, on winding up an entire scheme, is now only one part of a very large range of options available for trustees and employers to use in managing their long-term pension liabilities. It is worth remembering, however, that other options for managing such liabilities exist outside the buy-out market. Trustees and employers should be careful not to be blinded to these other options by the light of the new buy-out market. Liability reduction exercises, liability-driven investment strategies, employer insolvency insurance and longevity insurance products are, or will soon be, available to assist the hard-pressed trustees and employers of the modern defined benefit pension scheme community to manage their liabilities and, ultimately, ensure that employees receive their pensions in full.

Other methods of eliminating defined benefit pension scheme liabilities

Jill Clucas
Penny A Pilzer
Lovells LLP

---

1. Introduction

Buy-out is, of course, the ultimate vehicle for transfer of pension risks, but the cost and the concentration of resources needed to ready a scheme for buy-out may make it impractical for many. However, a number of alternative or partial solutions are available. Some of these alternatives rest on the proposition that the employer will continue to act as backstop regarding some or all of the liabilities, or require continuing involvement in the management of the scheme. That said, deployment of alternative strategies can reduce management time and cost, balance-sheet volatility and risk to more manageable levels.

We begin by briefly discussing why an employer or the trustees may want to buy out pension liabilities and wind up the scheme and the impediments to doing so, before going on to explore the alternatives available.

2. Is buy-out the right choice?

2.1 Why buy out?

On a buy-out, all accrued pension liabilities are transferred from the scheme to an insurer in exchange for the payment of a premium. The pension scheme is wound up and is no longer the responsibility of the employer or the trustees.

(a) Employer view

Changes in the law and in the accounting treatment of pension liabilities over the past five years have made employers more aware of pension costs and have increased the role of pension trustees in corporate transactions. This has concentrated the minds of management on pension costs and pension responsibilities, and many have decided that the costs outweigh the benefits. Buy-out is most likely to be considered where a scheme has been closed to accrual or to new membership and is no longer important to the employer's human resources strategy.

Often, the immediate impetus for an employer is a desire to sell or reorganise a business unit and this activity will be complicated by pension issues if any of the affected companies sponsors a defined benefit scheme. Even in the absence of a contemplated transaction, it may be considered worthwhile to remove defined benefit scheme liabilities (and associated volatility) from the balance sheet.

Sometimes, especially where the scheme is relatively well funded, the employer may believe that it would be more efficient to redeploy management time spent on administration or eliminate the need for ongoing contributions.

(b) ***Trustee view***

Trustees will find buy-out attractive because it usually represents security for members. On a full buy-out, members will have individual annuity policies written in their names and insured by an insurance company that is subject to a stronger solvency regime than is required under an occupational pension scheme. The policies will be protected through the Financial Services Compensation Scheme (FSCS), which will insure 100% of the first £2,000 of loss and 90% of the remainder (although at the time of writing consultation has taken place to replace this regime with one in which 90% of the whole value is insured). This will be much more than is available under the Pension Protection Fund (PPF) for many members, especially in relation to higher earners. Trustees will be particularly interested in buy-out where the employer's covenant is weak or difficult to evaluate, or where there are concerns that a strong employer could be affected by a reorganisation or purchase.

2.2 Why not buy out?

(a) ***Employer view***

Mitigating against the factors above is the expense that buying out all liabilities entails. Although there is more competition in the market than was the case even a few years ago, buy-out entails a premium over the cost of simply running out a pension plan. Some put this premium in the neighbourhood of 40% of the cost of continuing to pay the pensions from the scheme.

For a time, it looked as though the cost would come down considerably. The combination of price competition among new entrants to the provider market and changes in bond rates made buy-out particularly attractive in late 2007 and 2008. However, much of the price competition was due to a desire by new entrants to achieve 'critical mass' by taking on enough business to be seen to be credible. This activity is now more subdued and the cost of buying annuities for members remains considerably higher than it would be to provide pensions through the scheme in run-off, even when administration costs are taken into consideration.

For some, the expense may be a lesser issue than the cash-flow impact, given the likely need for an upfront cash injection that a buy-out will often entail. In addition, the upside presented by favourable markets in the future is forgone on buy-out, as the pricing is dependent in part on current bond returns and will reflect economic conditions at the time of purchase. In the current financial climate, it may be difficult for an employer to evaluate whether this cost is worthwhile. Indeed, as of early 2009, providers have been unwilling to hold their quotes for more than a few days, making it difficult to compare bids and negotiate terms.

(b) ***Trustee view***

The trustees will need to be on board. They often have power under the rules to administer or defer buy-out and therefore will have a good deal to say regarding whether, when and how to buy out. However, it is not unusual for the employer to suggest buy-out, conditional on use of a certain provider or one of a list of providers. Trustees may have concerns about the provider favoured by the employer. While the employer may focus on cost, trustees must act in the best interests of the members.

Trustees will need to evaluate carefully any provider under consideration for financial strength, ability to manage the transition and proficiency in communication with members. The reputation of some of the new providers is still to be earned and buy-out specialists may not present a sufficiently diversified risk portfolio to ensure that the insurer will have the base from which to withstand unexpected events. Indeed, after the tumult of 2008, trustees are requiring that household names disclose information sufficient to evaluate their financial strength and diversified risk portfolio. Systems for administration, risk control, experience (and reputation) in the transition from scheme to provider management and communication tools should be subject to due diligence by the trustees.

(c) *Other considerations*

Buy-out takes a good deal of time and effort. The records of the scheme must be put in order; contracted-out benefits must be reconciled; historic benefits, especially the approach to normal retirement date, must be understood and recorded; deferred members must be located; notice must be given (at least to members with guaranteed minimum pensions); and systems must be cleaned. To the extent that there are any questions regarding the benefits owed to members, the premium will be higher (or it may be difficult to find a provider willing to quote at all). If the postcodes or ages of deferred members are unknown, providers may make unfavourable demographic assumptions.

In the wake of recent court decisions regarding faulty equalisation of benefits between men and women, employers and trustees are likely to be shy of putting the procedures undertaken in the more forgiving 1990s under the microscope of the 21st century. If there are any possible irregularities, the insurer is likely to exclude equalisation claims from the risks it is willing to undertake, in which case the trustees will require an indemnity from the employer in order to buy out at all. At the very least, any lingering questions will be reflected in the premium.

In short, risk will be transferred (at least at a reasonable price) only where it can be evaluated and the provider believes it can make a profit. For all of the above reasons, employers and trustees may be inclined, at least in the short to medium term, towards some of the alternatives to buy-out discussed below.

3. Alternatives to buy-out

3.1 Partial buy-out

Where complete buy-out is impractical, the most obvious alternative may be a partial buy-out, under which the trustees buy policies in members' names in order to remove the risks and responsibilities associated with that group of members from the pension scheme.

Typically, partial buy-out will be applied to pensioners, whose benefits are the cheapest to secure because risk is easier to assess, administration is comparatively easier and the data has been tested. On the other hand, buying out deferred liabilities, or at least some of them, can be attractive. Where the data is more complete or the benefit structure is more straightforward for some groups of members than others, it may make sense to retain responsibility in the scheme for those members who are less attractive to insurers while buying out others (eg, where the scheme for which partial buy-out is contemplated is the result of a merger of several older schemes, some benefits may be more quirky, or less well documented, than others).

(a) Balancing the interests of members

As is often the case with pensions, a partial buy-out comes with its own set of risks, particularly if the trustees are concerned that they will be open to claims that they have unfairly favoured one group of members over another. Trust law does not require trustees to treat all beneficiaries in the same way. However, where one group is being taken out of the trust altogether, the issues become more acute.

Trustees will be aware that the benefits of members who are being bought out are likely to be more secure than those of members who remain. The trustees' concerns may be somewhat alleviated where the buy-out is of pensioners only, because the scheme rules will typically provide that pensions in payment receive higher priority than deferred benefits, at least once PPF-level benefits are paid.

Even in this situation, should the scheme wind up without enough assets to pay all benefits fully or fall into the PPF, a claim could be made that had resources not been diverted to pensioners, assets would have been distributed more equitably among all members. Partial buy-outs of pensions in payment could also give rise to age discrimination allegations, as pensioners are likely to be older than deferred members.

Equally, members who have been bought out may be disadvantaged, because they will no longer be eligible for discretionary increases or other improvements that may be available to those remaining in the scheme. This may not be a concern in the present economic environment, but if changes to the scheme or benefits under the scheme that would result in uplifts to accrued rights are contemplated, it may not be the right time for a partial buy-out.

The issues that arise when some, but not all, deferred members are bought out can be even more fraught and the trustees must ensure that they are treating the membership as a whole equitably. As a result, trustees will not only demand an additional contribution sufficient to cover the cost of the buy-out, but also require that funding for those who remain is at least as good as was in place prior to the buy-out.

(b) Replication of benefits

Where benefits are being secured through buy-out, replication is often a major stumbling block. Providers generally have a standard range of benefits that their systems are capable of calculating and paying. Non-standard commutation or indexation factors or unusual dependants' benefits may be difficult to accommodate.

When this happens, benefits that cannot be replicated must be valued and replaced with benefits that are at least equivalent and can be paid through the provider's systems, having regard to any scheme rule amendments and the requirements of Section 67 of the Pensions Act 1995.

In order to make a detrimental modification to a member's accrued rights – and such rights may extend to benefits owed a deferred member on ill health – the member's consent must be obtained or a benefit that is of an actuarially equivalent value must be put in place. Otherwise, the change is voidable.[1] In addition, the trustees would be vulnerable to a claim of breach of trust if a modification reduced accrued rights. In practice, it is usually not practicable to obtain consent from a deferred member, so the benefit will need to be reconfigured so that the trustees are satisfied that it represents an equivalent, or more likely better, benefit.

(c) ***Compliance***

A number of legislative requirements apply where pension obligations are being transferred to insurance policies. Chief among these are the requirements found in the Occupational Pension Schemes (Preservation of Benefit) Regulations 1991. Where a short service (deferred) benefit is being transferred, the regulations require that the annuity contract contain restrictions on assignment, surrender and commutation; provide increases for pensions in payment in accordance with the Pensions Act 1995; and provide for a guaranteed minimum pension to be paid where appropriate.

So far, so good – but more often than not the benefits will not have been completely replicated, in which case the buy-out of deferred benefits will relate to 'alternative to short service benefit' and additional restrictions will apply. Only those members who have left pensionable service more than 12 months previously may be included; the trustee must be content that it is 'reasonable' to effect the buy-out without the member's consent (if consent is not sought); the benefit under the policy must be of equal value to the deferred benefit in the scheme; and 30 days' notice must be given to the member.

Contracted-out rights are subject to slightly different requirements. A guaranteed minimum pension (ie, contracted-out defined benefits earned prior to April 6 1997) may be bought out subject to the same restrictions that apply to the buy-out of an alternative short-service benefit without consent. In contrast, Section 9(2b) rights (contracted-out defined benefit earned on or after April 6 1997) are subject to additional requirements regarding the form of benefit. There is no provision under the statute for buy-out of protected rights (defined contribution benefit attributable to contracting-out) without consent unless the scheme is winding up.

(d) ***Discharge***

A statutory discharge is available to trustees on buy-out as regards short-service benefit, guaranteed minimum pension and Section 9(2)(b) rights, as long as the above regulations (and statutory conditions in Section 19 of the Pensions Act 1993)

---

1 Section 67 of the Pensions Act 1995.

are followed.[2] Whether discharge of the trustee is available in relation to a long-service benefit is not entirely clear.

A statutory discharge, while desirable, is not necessary – the trustees would probably be in breach of their duties if they obstructed a buy-out that was advantageous to the members on the basis that they could not obtain a discharge. Some are doubtful that a statutory discharge is particularly valuable. However, it would be helpful if the situation regarding the process required to obtain such a discharge were clarified in legislation. At present, the regulations relating to discharge raise more questions than they resolve.

(e) Vesting agreement

Partial buy-outs that cover pensioners are sometimes accompanied by 'vesting agreements' under which the insurer will agree a basis for providing policies for current deferred and active members as they retire. This prevents the scheme from re-developing a rump of pensions in payment that need to be administered from the scheme after a partial buy-out. Where part of the reason for the buy-out is a desire to cease administration of pensions in payment, such an arrangement will be advisable.

3.2 Buy-in

'Buy-in' is the purchase by the trustees of a bulk annuity policy in respect of all or some (eg, pensioner liabilities) of the accrued benefits which they hold in the trust as an investment of the scheme. The trustees and sponsoring employer will remain liable to members in the same way as they were prior to the buy-in. However, the benefits paid out under the policy should very nearly match the liabilities to, or in respect of, the members whose benefits are bought in.

Under a buy-in policy, trustees usually retain responsibility for administering the scheme and paying out the pensions, so the policy represents an income stream to them for some of their liabilities. However, it is possible to purchase policies under which the insurer agrees to take on certain administrative tasks, including pension payroll, or agrees that it will do so if requested (and for a price).

Buy-ins have become an increasingly popular option because the investment and longevity risk is for the most part underwritten to match the scheme's risks, but at a lower cost than under a buy-out. This is largely because the risks relating to benefit description – historic issues such as equalisation and future changes in the law – remain with the trustees, as does, in most cases, administration of the benefit. The provider will still require a data cleanse regarding the demographics of the members being covered in order to make accurate mortality predictions, but may be less concerned about misdescriptions of benefits, because they will pay only the benefits described in the policy. If the member turns out to be due a better benefit than that purchased, this will remain the responsibility of the trustees.

Buy-in arrangements are also often favoured over partial buy-out policies, especially in relation to non-pensioner members, because providers are increasingly willing to agree to reconfigure benefits payable under certain circumstances (eg, in

---

2 See the Occupational Pension Schemes (Discharge of Liability) Regulations 1997.

the event that the scheme winds up in deficit or falls into the PPF, in order to accommodate the priority order of the scheme rules or the PPF). This means that the trustees will not be as concerned about favouring one group of members over others in a buy-in as they are in a buy-out. Of course, the trustees will want to look at the terms under which a reconfiguration would take place. In practice, most buy-in policies allow for the secured annuities to be re-spread among the membership (including deferred members) on wind-up, although this is often treated as a part surrender of bought-in benefit by the insurer, which can be very disadvantageous to the trustees.

(a) *Due diligence*

Entering into a buy-in contract is an investment decision and ultimately for the trustees. Proper due diligence will include a sophisticated evaluation of the provider's administrative capabilities and financial strength. Indeed, for large buy-ins it is not unusual for trustees to demand a great deal of financial information (subject to maintaining confidentiality, where appropriate). The entrance of new providers, coupled with the financial instability of the last quarter of 2008, has made it abundantly clear that all FSA-regulated entities are not equal and that a prudent customer must look at all the nooks and crannies.

The potential insurer should be willing to provide substantial financial information, including information concerning the value of assets in its UK life fund, the extent to which its risk portfolio is diversified and how this is being accomplished, and any financial backing that the provider has in addition to minimum regulatory requirements. Trustees will want to keep in mind that a monoline insurer may be less stable than one which provides other types of insurance. Sometimes, it will be appropriate to request a guarantee from a parent or member of the wider group to which the insurer belongs in respect of the insurance promise.

(b) *Security*

One way of addressing insurer credit risk is for the insurer to grant security in favour of the trustees. This has featured in several large buy-ins in 2007 and 2008. Under these arrangements, the security becomes enforceable by the trustees if the buy-in contract is terminated early because the insurer becomes insolvent or its reserves drop below a certain level, or for some other specified reason. It can take the form of a floating charge over the assets of the insurer, usually over a specified securities account into which the premium is paid, although other arrangements are possible.

A UK-regulated long-term insurer is permitted to grant security over its long-term insurance assets.[3] However, the mechanics of the segregation of assets add considerably to the expense of the transaction. In addition to the implementation cost, these arrangements reduce the degree of diversification and flexibility which the insurer may achieve by pooling all of its assets, so would be expected to increase

---

3 See Rule 1.5.31 of the Prudential Sourcebook for Insurers (INSPRU), which forms part of the *FSA Handbook of Rules and Guidance.*

the premium payable by the trustees. An insurer concerned about fairness to its other policyholders may also require the trustees to accept subordinated status in respect of assets of the insurer that are not secured. In some scenarios, this may work out unfavourably for the trustees.

Trustees and employers looking into such arrangements in the wake of the publicity accompanying the Cable & Wireless and Friends Provident buy-ins have not found insurers receptive to similar arrangements in any but the largest transactions. Nonetheless, trustees looking to invest a significant portion of the assets of a large fund with an insurer are justified in believing that it is only prudent to put some safeguards in place against the failure of the insurer.

Factors which trustees should consider include:

- how much protection is available from the PPF and the FSCS (see below) if the insurer fails;
- how important it is for the trustees to recover particular assets (rather than cash) if the buy-in contract has to be terminated early; and
- how quickly will the trustees need to be able to recover the assets if the contract has to be terminated early. Properly documented security should permit full and prompt transfer of a particular pool of assets.

Any security package must also be considered in the context of the early termination clause in the buy-in contract, which must clearly specify the circumstances in which the trustees are permitted to terminate the buy-in contract and how much they are permitted to recover from the insurer if they do terminate.

(c) ***Insurance***

A small cloud of doubt has hung over the level of Financial Services Compensation Scheme (FSCS) coverage of buy-in contracts, because, among other things, the employer remains liable for benefits payable from the scheme if the contract fails. In December 2008, to the relief of many in the pensions industry, the FSCS was reported to have confirmed that it will cover buy-in contracts as long-term life policies and that any compensation payable will go to the scheme.

Under the current regime, less funding of the members' benefits will be provided through the FSCS in respect of a buy-in than a buy-out, because of the way policies are written. On the insolvency of an insurer, the FSCS will first try to find another provider to take over the contracts. If that proves impossible, it will currently insure 100% of the first £2,000 lost under a long-term life insurance policy and up to 90% of the remainder. This means that in a buy-out, the first £2,000 of each individual's loss is fully insured and the rest of the benefit will be paid to the individual member at 90%. In contrast, buy-in trustees will be fully insured only for the first £2,000 of their policy, although the policy typically will run to tens or many hundreds of millions of pounds in value.[4]

---

4 It is probably worth noting that the FSCS has not been tested in any major insurer insolvency and so it is difficult to state with confidence how the scheme would work in the event of a worst-case scenario (eg, where the entire sector is under stress).

The Financial Services Authority (FSA) initiated a consultation in early 2009 concerning FSCS compensation and suggested that the structure be changed so that compensation is capped at 90% for an all-of-life policy.[5] Should this policy be adopted, equal compensation would be available under buy-in and buy-out arrangements. That said, the consequences to the trustees and employer would differ. Under a buy-in arrangement, there is no doubt that the trustees (and ultimately the employer) would be required to make up the difference between the insured amount and the benefits promised. On a buy-out, the position would be less clear. The trustees should have received a statutory discharge for at least some of the liabilities. They may have received consent from all or most members. Therefore, a member seeking recourse against the trustees or the employer would face a high hurdle, assuming that the buy-out process had been approached in a professional and diligent manner, although the position is not entirely clear.

(d) *Contract features*

Buy-in contracts are often used as a step on the road to buy-out. Of course, the buy-in provider is likely to be the only feasible buy-out provider, inasmuch as it has already taken on most of the long-term liability as regards the members covered by the policy. For this reason, the trustees will want the contract to contain an option for conversion to buy-out, subject if necessary to a data cleanse and possible price adjustment if the bought-in benefits turn out to depart substantially from those that will be bought out (or if the insurer is taking benefit risk, such as risks relating to equalisation). Indeed, many buy-in contracts are presumptively buy-out contracts, but operate as buy-in contracts until such time as the data is in shape and the buy-out terms have been agreed.

(e) *Limited term buy-in*

It is probably worth mentioning that some financial institutions, notably insurers, are willing to enter into contracts under which the provider agrees to pay an income stream to the trustees of a pension scheme for pension benefit expenditure over a period of years in exchange for a premium. Under this arrangement, a rump of longevity risk will be left with the trustees, but cash flow is controlled and investment risk hedged for the period at issue in respect of the benefits covered. There has been very little discussion of this lately, but new entrants to the buy-out market were willing to discuss these sorts of arrangement in 2008 as a prelude to full buy-out. We understand that this sort of investment continues to be available to trustees who wish to reduce volatility, but are not in a position to offload all risk in the near term.

3.3 Quasi buy-out

Under a partial buy-out or buy-in, the trustees will remain in place and the employer remains responsible for the liabilities of the scheme. For employers that have well-funded schemes and wish to transfer the liabilities away and quickly, a non-insured,

5 See "Financial Services Compensation Scheme: Review of limits", FSA Consultation Paper 08/15, published October 2008.

so-called 'quasi' buy-out may be attractive. In these arrangements, the members' benefits are not bought out with an insurer, at least at first, but rather transferred to another pension arrangement for which a new sponsor takes funding responsibility.

The mechanics by which pension liabilities transfer from the employer vary. Under one model, a new principal employer is substituted for the original employer or employers under the scheme. A different model involves the bulk transfer of some or all liabilities to a different occupational scheme sponsored by a new principal employer. In either case, the new sponsoring employer will usually be a special purpose corporate entity backed by a bank or other financial institution that is undertaking the transaction as part of its business. The trustees – at least those nominated by the employer – will usually be replaced.

After transfer, the new sponsor is likely to undertake a liability reduction exercise (see below), in which an effort is made to persuade deferred members to transfer their benefits from the scheme. Pensions in payment are typically reinsured or bought out with an insurer. Data cleansing and contracted-out reconciliation, etc are undertaken and it is intended that the scheme will eventually be wound up, with any remaining benefits being bought out.

The advantage of these arrangements to an employer wishing to shed pensions liabilities immediately (eg, in anticipation of corporate transactions that could be impeded by the uncertainty that pension schemes represent) is that a quasi buy-out can be, or at least has been, implemented much more quickly than a buy-out.

Financial institutions are interested in providing this service because they believe that they can more effectively invest the scheme assets and more efficiently mitigate the risks, allowing them to take a substantial surplus back from the scheme when it is wound up. Insurers providing buy-out solutions must comply with the more conservative funding requirements applicable to insurance, but an 'employer' under a quasi-buy-out arrangement remains governed by the funding regime applicable to occupational pension schemes. These require less capital to be pledged to the payment of pensions.

(a) Recent legislation

The Pensions Regulator (PR) has expressed discomfort with these arrangements, although it has given clearance where the backer is sufficiently well resourced and the trustees supported the move. The discomfort is shared by many. After all, the occupational scheme funding regime in the United Kingdom is based on the notion that the employer has an interest in maintaining the benefits of its employees, past and present, and this notion is undermined where the 'employer' has employed a member only notionally (to affect the transfer) and in fact expects to derive a profit from the scheme. It is hard to see why a financial institution running a pension scheme for profit should not be part of the insured regime.

As a first step, the PR issued guidance to trustees regarding how to deal with proposals in which the liabilities or sponsorship of the scheme is severed from the business that once supported them.[6] More recently, the PR's powers to issue

6 See "Abandonment of defined benefit pension schemes", May 2007.

contribution notices have been enhanced with the specific aim of discouraging these arrangements in situations where members' benefits might not be paid.[7] Contribution notices may be issued by the PR to persons connected to, or associated with, the employer and consist of an order to pay funds into the scheme.

Under previous legislation,[8] in order to issue a contribution order, the PR had to show that "the main or one of the main purposes" of an act or failure to act was to prevent recovery of a Section 75 debt (ie, the debt that would be due from an employer to the scheme on wind-up or departure of the employer from participation in the scheme). Now the PR may issue a contribution notice where the act or failure to act is "materially detrimental to the likelihood that the members' benefits will be paid", regardless of the intent of the party.[9] In addition, a defence that an act had been taken in good faith, which had been available in some circumstances, has been removed.

(b) Trustee concerns

Trustees will also be wary of these arrangements, because it is seldom in the interests of the members to be in a scheme that is run for a profit. Unless the backer is very strong (and confidence in financial institutions and the ability to evaluate them has fallen of late), trustees will be concerned that the covenant and commitment of the new employer will not be sufficiently strong to support member benefits should the investment strategy go awry, even if the covenant looks comparatively strong at the outset.

In addition to the quality of the covenant offered under any quasi buy-out arrangement, trustees will want assurances that the administration of the scheme will continue to be of high quality. They will want to be satisfied that arrangements are in place to communicate fully with members concerning the change, and that benefit administration will continue smoothly without delays or confusion.

(c) Future applications

Some of the actors in this market have gone quiet since the autumn of 2008. This may be partly due to the new legislation and partly due to the absence of liquidity in the markets. The more cynical may observe that the hiatus may also be due to the fact that successful backers are finding running a pension scheme more complicated and expensive than they expected. It will be interesting to see whether this model will develop further.

3.4 Liability reduction exercises

The usual liability reduction exercise is an employer-initiated communications programme aimed at persuading members to transfer their benefits away from the scheme or to give up certain benefits (eg, periodic rises in pensions beyond the statutorily required levels) in exchange for an 'inducement'. This sort of exercise is

7 Section 126 of the Pensions Act 2008.
8 Section 38 of the Pensions Act 2004.
9 The PR's Code of Practice 12.

commonly carried out in a quasi buy-out such as those discussed above, but 'real' employers have shown increased interest in promoting these exercises, at least to deferred members.

The inducement offered to the member in exchange for transfer may be an enhancement to the member's transfer value, cash in hand, or a combination of the two. Where a specific benefit is being reduced, the inducement should be an enhancement to a different scheme benefit.[10] Where a transfer is requested, it will almost always be from a defined benefit scheme to a defined contribution plan, usually a personal pension. A financial adviser will often be retained by the employer to advise the members regarding their choices and a personal pension provider will be designated to aid ease of transfer.

These exercises are lawful – a member may consent to a benefit reduction and a deferred member has a statutory right to a transfer from his pension scheme on request until one year prior to normal retirement date. That said, trustees are rightly concerned that members should not be persuaded to agree to a benefit reduction or transfer that is against their long-term interests and the regulatory community provides support for trustee intervention to protect members.

(a) *Regulatory position*

The PR directs trustees to "consider carefully and apply a high level of scrutiny to all inducement offers",[11] pointing out that significant risk may be transferred to the employee and that if the scheme is reducing its liabilities as a result of a transfer, it is mostly because the member is giving up greater value than he is being given. Trustees are advised to make members aware of the importance of independent financial advice and to satisfy themselves that the employer's literature makes this plain. Any financial advice provided through the employer should in fact be independent.

For its part, the FSA has warned financial advisers participating in transfer exercises that it regards most transfers from a defined benefit to a defined contribution scheme as presumptively not suitable.[12] Promotion of the transfer arrangement must be clear, fair and not misleading, and must include the usual required material, such as a comparison of benefits and an explanation of the yield required by the new scheme to beat the benefits promised in the defined benefit scheme.

(b) *Trustee position*

Trustees do not necessarily oppose well-designed inducement exercises. For some schemes, a reduction or a re-jigging of a benefit may bring down risk or volatility to levels more acceptable to the employer, while allowing the trustees to continue to offer members an adequate baseline benefit. For some members, a transfer may be the right option – particularly if they are relatively young and their benefit is relatively small (in which case investment under the member's control may be

10 Section 91(5)(b) of the Pensions Act 1995
11 "Inducement offers", issued January 2007 by the Pensions Regulator.
12 "Final Salary Pension Transfers," *Financial Advisers Newsletter*, issued November 2007 by the FSA.

desirable), or where the member has a reduced life expectancy or will not leave survivors eligible for benefits under the scheme (in which case an enhanced transfer value may be used to purchase an insurance contract that better matches the member's needs).

Usually, the exercise will require a degree of trustee cooperation – at the very least the trustees' consent would be needed to release the names and addresses of members. (Trustees must be mindful of data protection law governing the release of such information.) Often, as where certain benefits are being given up in accordance with Section 91 of the Pensions Act 1995, the rules will need to be changed. This will require trustee approval.

More importantly, where a transfer is being contemplated, the trustees will want to ensure that the enhanced transfers do not deplete the funding available for remaining members and are likely to demand additional funding for both departing and remaining members.

The trustees' position may be more complicated as regards a transfer if they know (or think it likely) that the employer intends to buy out the remaining deferred benefits in the scheme following the transfer value exercise. Members who decline the transfer offer will have their benefits secured and the certainty of defined benefits backed by the insurer. An inducement is unlikely to reflect adequately the value of the enhanced security of a deferred annuity.

The PR suggests that trustees may wish to send a separate communication to members concerning any inducement offers made, especially if they believe that members may not fully understand the risks involved in taking the offer. This could explain the benefits that are being given up, the risks of the transferee arrangement, the security that would be available on buy-out and the tax treatment of any cash inducement.

3.5 Hedging strategies

Most discussion of liability-driven investment has concentrated on hedging against poor investment performance or changes in interest rates. In addition, there are a number of products – notably, longevity swaps – that are being marketed to trustees as an alternative to buy-out that essentially hedge mortality/longevity risk.

(a) Longevity swaps

These have long been used between insurers to diversify or stabilise their risk profile. They are now being offered to trustees of pension schemes and to players in the capital markets that are looking for returns that are uncorrelated with performance equities or bonds.

A longevity swap is a product by which, in return for fixed monthly payments from the trustees, the provider promises to pay actual pension payment outflow over a period of years. The payments are netted out, so that if mortality is higher than expected the trustees will pay the provider, and if it is less than anticipated the provider will pay the trustees. Alternatively, the swap may be based on the performance of a mortality index calibrated to UK lives (or a cohort of lives), rather than the scheme's performance.

Although these instruments have been marketed for some time, to our knowledge only one scheme has purchased a longevity swap to date.[13] Evaluation of the product requires a degree of sophistication that does not generally exist outside the insurance industry and the data provided by the scheme must be of the same quality as that provided on buy-out. In addition, such swaps may complicate the wind-up of a pension scheme. Therefore, many believe that the market among trustees is small, at least for the time being.

(b) Long-dated bonds

A more traditional hedging strategy is investment in long-dated bonds. At the time of writing, investment advisers often believe that bonds with an end date more than 15 years out do not deliver sufficient returns to be considered a good investment. However, larger schemes are purchasing long-dated bonds and there has been some talk that supply may increase in 2009, making these more attractive.

More esoteric products such as long-dated longevity bonds have been discussed and have been offered in one form or another since 2004.[14] These products seek to securitise longevity/mortality risk and are being refined to make them more attractive. They have not taken off as yet due to a lack of transparency and agreement in the market concerning expectations regarding mortality over time.

4. Preparing for buy-out and its alternatives

In order to take advantage of buy-out opportunities or most of the alternatives discussed above, trustees and employers will need to begin preparations well in advance. Preparations will include:

- consulting the scheme rules, particularly the investment and transfer provisions, to ensure that the employer and/or the trustees have the power under existing documentation to take the desired actions – and making amendments where possible if they do not;
- revisiting the scheme's statement of investment principles, revising it if it seems outdated in light of the contemplated strategy;
- cleansing membership data – this includes determining the precise number and identity of members (and beneficiaries or potential beneficiaries), and locating them;
- recording historic benefits – the benefits in place at the time each deferred member left active membership must be catered for and will involve an investigation of former trust deeds and rules and any subsequent amendments;
- reviewing the history of changes to the scheme, including equalisation, to ensure that amendments and intended amendments have been carried out correctly;

---

13 Babcock International Group plc's pension schemes are reported to have purchased longevity swaps in June 2009.

14 See generally Enrico Biffis and David Blake, "Mortality – Linked Securities and Derivatives", Pensions Institute Discussion Paper P1–0901, January 2009.

- reconciling contracted-out benefits – this will require a surrender of the contracting-out certificate and coordination with the National Insurance Services to the Pensions Industry. Ongoing schemes that cannot surrender the certificate may use services offered through Her Majesty's Revenue and Customs to improve confidence that contracted-out benefits are correctly recorded;
- determining an approach to guaranteed minimum pension equalisation; and
- considering approaches concerning discretionary benefits.

Thought should also be given to the manner in which the scheme's assets are invested and whether any of the premiums may be paid by an *in specie* transfer of assets to the insurer. The assets that will be transferable will be the most liquid (eg, holdings of government or UK blue-chip bonds). It may be desirable to begin shifting assets into this category some time in advance of the contemplated transaction to enable an orderly transition. At the very least, the remaining assets are likely to need to be rebalanced as a result of the transaction.

5. Conclusion

The fact that so many alternatives are under active consideration by so many schemes, despite their complexity, is a testament to the extent to which employers are finding the present regime overly burdensome. As of the summer of 2009, we see many of our clients readying scheme data and documents, waiting for the financial situation to stabilise so that they can proceed. It will be interesting to see how the market for alternatives develops in these conditions.

The FSA-regulated market

Mark Wood
Paternoster UK Limited

---

1. Introduction

The growth of the Financial Services Authority (FSA) regulated buy-out market is in part being fuelled by new product innovation, including solutions for full buy-out, partial buy-out (or, as it is increasingly being referred to, 'buy-in'), and phased buy-out. An appropriate solution depends on various factors: the risk appetite and risk management objectives of the trustees and their sponsoring employer; whether the scheme remains open or will be wound up; and the funding level of the scheme. Here we look at some of the common options available for trustees, as well as the process that trustees and their advisers go through, from initial considerations through to initial quotation and then full asset transfer and communications to scheme members.

2. Buy-in

In a buy-in, not all the liabilities in the scheme are insured and the trust remains operational, not least to continue to manage the uninsured liabilities as before. The trust therefore continues to have recourse to the corporate sponsor.

The trustees continue to be responsible for the payment of pensions and the bulk insurance policy remains an asset of the trust rather than being converted to individual policies after the scheme is wound up.

Through a buy-in insurance policy, the pension scheme receives a regular payment from the insurer that exactly matches the sum of the payments the scheme owes to its insured members, regardless of how long they live, the performance of investment returns, rate of inflation etc. This policy is sometimes referred to as a 'super-matched bond'.

From the end of 2008 we have seen the popularity of buy-ins of pensioners increase, with the Morgan Crucible, TI Group, Cable & Wireless and Friends Provident deals. This is because the 'gap' to fund buy-ins for pensioners is much less, while the risks (particularly longevity) for younger members remain substantial.

Pension scheme assets are selected to reflect the projected cash flows which need to be met over time. Deferred members, who will one day claim a pension, can represent a liability of over 50 years. Equities are sometimes considered to be a better long-term investment more suited to matching such liabilities. Correspondingly, fixed interest-generating securities are more appropriate to shorter-dated liabilities and are therefore usually used to support pensioner liabilities. The shorter duration of pensioner liabilities means that the capital an insurer needs to hold has a lower cost than for deferred member liabilities. Pension schemes are not required to hold this capital; therefore, the price differential between a scheme's pensioner liabilities is closer in value to the insurer's premium than for longer-duration deferred members.

Key aspects of a buy-in are as follows:

- All risk to employer in respect of bought-in members is removed;
- Either the scheme must be fully funded or a top-up will be required;
- The scheme avoids being wound up;
- Individual policies may be purchased at a future date by conversion to a partial buy-out (the corporate covenant continues to exist until the buy-out is effected); and
- An investment strategy is retained over remaining scheme assets.

2.1 Case study: P&O

At the time of this transaction, in December 2007, the P&O buy-in was the largest of its type. The trustees insured two-thirds of the scheme's liabilities, transferring more than £800 million of assets to Paternoster. In exchange, Paternoster took on the obligation to fund the 11,000 pensions in the scheme. These pensioners have two levels of security backing their pension: the insurance solvency capital of Paternoster and the covenant of the sponsoring employer, Dubai Ports.

The P&O transaction showed that the application of insurance is not just for distressed pension schemes, but paved the way for large and solvent organisations to consider this as an appropriate way of managing their defined benefit pension scheme liabilities.

The transaction resulted in P&O exchanging the income stream it received from its bond portfolio – which it used to pay the pensions – for an income from the Paternoster annuity policy. At the same time, it allowed P&O pension scheme trustees to retain overall control of the scheme.

(a) Objectives

The objectives of the P&O trustees and their sponsoring employer were as follows:

- Both wished to transfer all financial and demographic risks associated with the pensioner members of the P&O scheme to a regulated insurer.
- The trustees wanted to retain responsibility and control over benefits payable and communications made to scheme members (with the aim of minimising operational disruption for members).
- The trustees wanted to retain the support of the existing corporate covenant, but also to diversify covenant risk to an insurance company that would pledge capital.

(b) Outcome

Assets relating to pensioner liabilities were transferred onto Paternoster's balance sheet through a carefully coordinated process of transition from four fund managers.

Assets were reallocated in a difficult trading environment. Inflation and duration hedging instruments were used to match asset and liability cash flows accurately.

Clear communications to scheme members outlined the decisions made, minimising concerns and articulating the benefits of increased security through the transfer to a regulated insurance environment.

Rita Powell, P&O's group head of pensions at the time of the transaction, said: "This is excellent news for the P&O pension scheme as it now has the added security of a specialist regulated insurance company, and this is in addition to the ongoing support of a strong global company in P&O Steam Navigation."

3. Full buy-out

Full buy-out is, as its name implies, a transfer of all liabilities and assets within a pension scheme from the trust to an insurance company.

Many trustees transfer their liabilities to an insurer through a full buy-out as part of a wind-up of the scheme. During the period in which the trust is wound up, the precise nature of the liabilities will be confirmed through a data/existence verification exercise and benefits paid will be reconciled to scheme rules. This arduous and detail-orientated process can take many months and sometimes stretches over several years. It can result in a recognition that the scheme's liabilities were in fact under or over-stated at the time they were transferred to the insurer.

At the end of the wind-up process, the trust is dissolved, the trustees discharged and the relationship between the members and the sponsoring employer is severed. The pensioners and deferred members become direct policyholders of the insurance company.

Up to this point, the members are beneficiaries of a policy held by the trustees as an asset of the scheme (a bulk annuity policy). The nature of the pension changes from a promise to pay income in retirement, based on the assets within a pension scheme being sufficient to fund this promise (with possibly supplementary payments from the company), to an insurance company which is contracted to make these payments and supports that promise with solvency capital.

A full buy-out has the following characteristics:

- All risk to the employer is removed;
- Either the scheme must be fully funded or a funding top-up will be required;
- The scheme can be wound up;
- The trustees will be discharged;
- There are individual policies;
- The corporate covenant will be replaced; and
- The investment strategy will be managed by the insurer.

3.1 Case study: Emap

Emap plc, the FTSE 250 publishing company, sought immediate and full de-risking of its defined benefit pension schemes (the Emap earnings-related pension plan and the Scottish radio holdings pension scheme) in the context of corporate restructuring. They achieved this as a result of an innovative solution developed by Paternoster whereby Paternoster secured the liabilities within an insurance environment and simultaneously replaced Emap as sponsor of the scheme at the point of buy-out.

The structure released Emap plc from all defined benefit pension risk, including the ongoing exposure to data errors and wind-up expense overrun, thus enabling 'unknown' as well as 'known' liabilities to be transferred off the balance sheet immediately. This was critical given Emap's corporate restructuring plans. The transaction was agreed in a very short timescale to meet Emap's corporate objectives.

(a) ***Objectives***

Emap plc and the trustees of the scheme sought to secure members' benefits in such a way that it severed its connection with the schemes entirely. According to Ian Griffiths, group finance director at Emap plc at the time of the transaction: "Emap had two clear objectives for this transaction – our desire to secure EERPP and SRH Scheme members' benefits in full and, to remove all pension risk for Emap's shareholders."

(b) ***How did it work?***

The tailored solution put together by Paternoster involved:

- an insurance buy-out of the pension scheme liabilities by Paternoster's UK insurance subsidiary, as a result of which all known scheme liabilities and market conditions risk were immediately transferred to Paternoster; and
- a simultaneous agreement by Emap plc to transfer sponsorship of the schemes to Paternoster and to settle the scheme's Section 75 debt.

This resulted in the transfer of all residual risk (including data cleansing, the expenses of winding-up, guaranteed minimum pension equalisation, guaranteed minimum pension reconciliation, delays, tracing, communications costs and missing members) to Paternoster. Paternoster started to wind the scheme up shortly after.

(c) ***What was the outcome?***

- All member benefits are secured in full with Paternoster and the promise to pay pensions is supported by prudent reserving, solvency capital, a conservative investment strategy and a regulatory framework overseen by the Financial Services Authority.
- The sponsor top-up to satisfy the scheme's Section 75 debt was the final payment made into the pension scheme.
- The trustees have no ongoing data risk exposure.
- The trustees retain the ability to oversee administration of the scheme, during the winding-up process with Paternoster.

The Emap transaction opened a new market for the full and immediate de-risking of a company's obligations to its pension scheme. It seems to have been rapidly accepted as the new benchmark for structuring pension scheme buy-outs, particularly where corporate restructuring is taking place. The removal of these liabilities makes a company a more attractive target for bidders. Many companies are more willing to make Section 75 top-up payments to fund a full buy-out with an insurance company when they are confident that it represents the final payment they will make in connection with the pension scheme.

4. Phased buy-out

A phased buy-out fixes the mortality and investment basis at the outset in the same way as a full buy-out. However, the assets and premium are transferred to the insurer progressively over a period of time, sometimes over several years. Pension benefits are secured in full from the outset. In the event that future premiums are not paid, the insurer has the ability to scale back members' benefits and the shortfall becomes a matter for the trustees and sponsor.

Once the full premium for the bulk annuity policy is paid, the pension scheme can be wound up and the process is as it would be for full buy-out.

The benefit of this approach is that the insurer locks in all the assumptions used to price the insurance policy, except those relating to market conditions (because investment risk remains with the scheme). This gives the trustee and sponsor greater certainty of funding ahead of the funds being available.

A phased buy-out has the following characteristics:

- All risk to employer is removed (when the premium is fully paid);
- Either the scheme must be fully funded or a top up will be required;
- The scheme must be wound up;
- The trustees are discharged (when the premium is fully paid);
- There are individual policies;
- The corporate covenant is replaced (when the premium is fully paid);
- The investment strategy is retained by trustees after transfer; and
- Payments are staggered over time.

4.1 Case study: Morrison Bowmore

Paternoster's transaction with Morrison Bowmore, the scotch whisky distiller, is a good example of this structure. Suntory, Morrison Bowmore's parent company, secured the investment expense and mortality basis and, therefore, fixed the uncertain liabilities of the pension scheme. Morrison Bowmore will settle the balance of the premium due over a number of years. The defined benefit pension scheme has 73 pensioners and 260 deferred members with a total of £30 million of liabilities.

(a) Objectives

Morrison Bowmore wished to secure the member benefits in full in respect of what was an under-funded scheme. It needed to spread the cost of insuring the scheme over an extended period while removing volatility.

(b) Outcome

The investment strategy is now with Paternoster, but winding up the scheme remains the responsibility of the trustees. They will ensure a proper process is implemented for data cleansing and the identification of members' benefits which are then committed to. Additionally, they will ensure that the proper legal and administrative processes are followed.

The terms of the deal mean that the financial and demographic assumptions are guaranteed by Paternoster. Morrison Bowmore's minimal exposure relates to data clean- up issues. With a final payment agreed for the end of 2008, the scheme is set to be wound up in early 2009. The buy-out deal means that 100% of benefits are secured immediately.

Brian Howie, human resources director and trustee, confirmed: "It is interesting in terms of how quickly things move. It has been a very positive direction for us so I would certainly recommend that others go through the same process."

5. Mortality only

Under a mortality-only buy-out, a company fixes the mortality basis for the scheme by buying an insurance policy to protect against people living longer than the liability best estimate. In the event that individuals live longer than projected, the pension scheme receives a payment from the insurer to cover the unplanned pension payments. This structure is attractive given the rapid escalation in life expectancy experienced particularly by males, the typical first claimant on a defined benefit pension plan.

The first life covered receives a higher benefit than the second life and therefore the decreasing gap between life expectancy for men and women brings a material increase to liabilities. Under a mortality-only structure, the trustees achieve risk mitigation that is similar to that of a partial buy-out. They also hold an insurance policy, but continue to manage the investment strategy of the pension scheme and have a call on the sponsoring employer for additional funding if required.

A mortality-only swap has the following characteristics:

- Longevity risk to the sponsoring employer is removed; and
- The scheme trustees retain responsibility for the investment strategy.

6. Buy-outs and the impact of market volatility

6.1 A buy-out in practice

The volatile markets of Summer 2008 led into the unprecedented financial conditions of Autumn and Winter 2008, where insurers' views of the split of spread above the risk-free rate, between liquidity and default, resulted in prices moving in a non-uniform manner, with insurers retaining a greater proportion of spread to cover their risks. The subsequent reduction in inflation expectation has resulted in a reduction in buy-out prices.Trustees/sponsoring companies should not wait for ideal market conditions to start work on the issues associated with a buy-out, but should resolve these issues, prepare fully and then be ready to buy out when the market conditions are more favourable. Buy-out firms should provide quotations that fix prices for all variables except market conditions over an agreed period of time.

6.2 The buy-out process

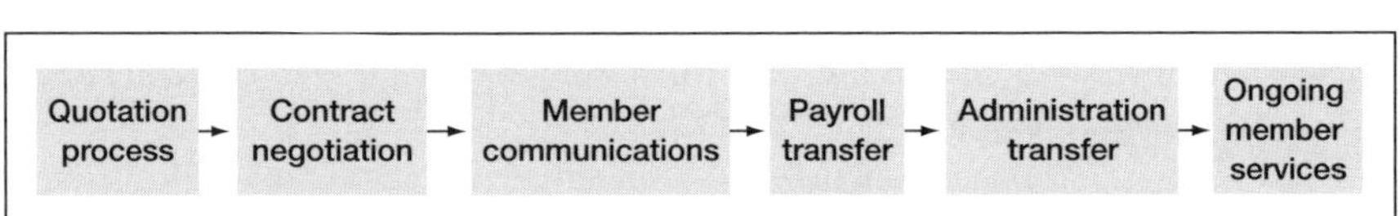

At a conceptual level, the processes involved are easy to understand – contract management, asset management, payroll, administration, etc. The transaction between a company and an FSA-regulated insurance company seems at first sight straightforward.

The detail of the process can, however, differ considerably from scheme to scheme.

(a) *Quotation process*

A quotation process can be run much more efficiently if scheme data is 'clean and complete' and the scheme benefits are clearly outlined. Engaging with insurers at an early stage in the process ensures that the structure developed is designed to meet the specific needs of the trustees and sponsors. Schemes that are looking for quotations for a number of different combinations of scheme members and benefit types, but which have poor underlying data or are still defining their underlying objectives, will usually find it more efficient in the first instance to seek indicative prices rather than a full quotation.

Detailed data about the pension scheme, showing salary or pension, age, gender, address and other factors (eg, increase rates and amounts payable on death) is given to the buy-out provider to enable the production of a quotation. At Paternoster, this is based on an assessment of the mortality of every individual member within the scheme. Examining the data in this level of detail enables more accurate pricing. Actuaries also review the scheme documentation to ensure that every subtlety and nuance is fully understood and that the price quoted reflects this.

The quotation produced is then submitted and reviewed in a competitive tender process. The finance director of the sponsoring company or trustees of the scheme, in collaboration with advisers, will normally look at four or maybe five submissions. Of these companies, two may be shortlisted to produce final submissions, from which one is selected by the trustees and finance director working together to select the buy-out partner.

(b) *Contract negotiation and asset transfer*

Once the quotation is accepted, contract negotiations are finalised and preparation begins for the asset transfer. At this stage the scheme can still be exposed to fluctuations in asset values and interest rates. Often the quoted price is rolled forward to the date to which assets and liabilities settle, with the scheme carrying the risk in the meantime. However, many trustees are anxious to minimise this exposure. This can be achieved by a hedge programme being put in place to adjust the term of the portfolio and cash flows within the portfolio to match the cash flows projected for the scheme as closely as possible. The hedge programme developed to achieve this is subsequently transferred into the name of the insurer.

6.3 Case study: parent company fund deficits for full buy-out

This manufacturing company had been acquired by a multinational organisation in the early 1990s. The parent company, on completing a balance-sheet review, started a restructure of pension arrangements to remove the risk of the defined benefit pension scheme from its balance sheet. The parent company committed to fund the buy-out deficit of the scheme and, having made this commitment, wished to move quickly to remove market risk and to be certain of the buy-out cost. Until the asset portfolio was transferred to Paternoster, the company remained exposed to market movements impacting on its assets and liabilities; it was essential that any mismatch between the asset portfolio (with a weighted average duration of 7.5 years) and the liabilities (weighted average duration 20 years) was resolved as quickly as possible. Pre-transfer, Paternoster put in place a derivative overlay adjusting the duration of the cash flows generated by the portfolio and removing all interest rate exposure. Following transfer, Paternoster ensured that the assets were effectively matched to the liabilities of the scheme, with the result that the payments to pensioners would remain secure throughout the full term of the scheme.

(a) Managing the transition

Although there might be some common trends, generally speaking, a 'one size fits all' approach is not appropriate. Schemes have different numbers of beneficiaries with different benefits under different scheme rules and migration occurs at different stages in the life of a scheme.

Effective project management by the insurer is key: from producing quotations to setting up the payroll. The most important people – the scheme beneficiaries – should not be disturbed by the process.

(b) Communicating with scheme members

Clear communication with pension scheme members throughout the buy-out process is vital. There are three important factors about scheme members which should be taken into consideration:

- Typically, they will not have a full understanding of how their existing benefits in the scheme have been derived;
- They may be nervous or suspicious about what is happening; and
- They will not necessarily be aware that transferring to an insurance environment will ensure greater security than a corporate environment.

Members need to understand what the buy-out means for them. Typically they want answers to the following questions:

- What will I get in terms of benefits?
- What action do I need to take?
- Whom do I talk to when I am concerned?
- Will I talk to a person who can clearly explain the answers to my questions?

In order to ensure that the transaction is viewed positively by the pension scheme members, the combination of communications from the pension scheme trustees and the insurance company providing the buy-out must address all of these points.

(c) Payroll

This ultimately involves the movement of pension scheme member records from the scheme to the insurance company. Once this has taken place and the insurance company has a clear understanding of the nature and structure of the payments (including frequency, currency, etc), then a period of 'parallel run' starts. This is when the projected pensioner payroll is reconciled to the pensions actually being paid by the scheme and discrepancies between the derived payroll and the actual payroll are examined and corrected. The duration of the parallel run will depend upon the size and complexity of the scheme – normally this lasts for no more than two months' worth of payments. Once all parties are satisfied, the scheme stops payments and the insurer's payroll goes live.

(d) ***Transfer of administration***

The physical transfer of administration from the existing scheme to an insurance company should be handled with great care. The benefits that have been bought out need to be clearly understood and re-created in the records set up by the insurance company – remembering that these benefits will not always exactly mirror those in the previous scheme (particularly where the existing scheme is not fully funded). Open lines of communication are important, as is the skill of the insurer to understand how benefits are recorded on multiple IT platforms so that they can be accurately recreated on the insurer's own system.

Until an insurer issues individual policies to scheme members, the trustees are still responsible for how the scheme administration is undertaken. Their options are to:

- transfer administration and payroll services to the selected buy-out provider;
- transfer payroll services only and leave administration as is; or
- leave all administration services as is.

It is standard practice for providers to include the cost of providing all future administrative services in their initial buy-out quotation for insuring a scheme. Trustees can then assess and compare with their current arrangements.

7. Considering the options

While economies of scale may be implicit in how FTSE100 company defined benefit schemes are administered, many medium-sized and small defined benefit pension schemes can benefit from cost savings by transferring their administration to their buy-out provider. Among the transactions Paternoster has been involved in, roughly 80% have transferred at least part of their administration following the buy-out, mainly to enjoy the benefits of our economies of scale. However, changing administration arrangements is an important decision and one which can be made only after a full review of the following:

- satisfaction with the existing arrangements;
- plans for scheme wind-up;
- current scheme administration costs;
- any long-term fixed costs or exit penalties in existing arrangements;
- impact on scheme members;
- any changes likely to take place within the scheme during the next two to three years;

- impact on in-house employees who provide payroll or administration support for the scheme;
- timeframes for administration migration;
- any support required for specific activities such as member existence verification or discontinuance; and
- whether the buy-out provider can work with existing administration arrangements.

Taking the time to consider what is needed from an administration perspective will contribute to defining more accurately the services the trustees will require from the buy-out supplier. It is always useful for the provider to understand the trustees' medium to long-term objectives for the scheme.

8. Other considerations: scheme wind-up

If a scheme has already started to wind up or will do so in the next few years, then it is likely that a plan will have been developed to manage data cleansing, trace members and finalise benefits. The wind-up process can be extremely complicated. Planning the transfer of administration to take place at an appropriate time should be a key factor in the process, as administration records may be a source of data to support many tasks.

If the decision is taken to move administration, it is important that trustees are satisfied with the service being offered by proposed providers. Meeting the people who will oversee the scheme transition and ongoing member services is important to give peace of mind about capability, responsiveness and experience. A proven track record in successful transitions and the delivery of ongoing customer service is essential. Additionally, trustees should be comfortable that a provider has experience of successfully completing transfer and wind-up lump-sum exercises, as well as understanding the importance of relevant pension legislation, scheme funding impacts and member communication options.

8.1 Issuing individual member insurance policies

At any point after the contract is signed and assets are transferred, the trustees of the scheme can surrender the bulk annuity policy that they hold and ask the insurer to issue individual policies to the scheme members. This typically happens where a scheme is approaching the final stages of a wind-up and any contracted-out (guaranteed minimum pension) benefits have been reconciled with the National Insurance Contributions Office. At the point at which the individual policies are issued, the trustees' liability for providing the benefits ceases and the individuals become direct customers of the insurer.

8.2 Buy-out process: key points

A project manager should be appointed by the insurer responsible for the buy-out. The process is complex and without proper project disciplines, timescales will become protracted:

- Scheme members are at the heart of all processes; an early start and subsequently frequent communication with them will reduce the issues which arise during the transition process.

- The buy-out of a pension scheme need not take years – it can be achieved within a few weeks.
- The calibre of the individuals at the insurance company is important. As with all professional work, the experience of the individuals responsible for the transaction is crucial.
- Assets should be locked in at the earliest possible time. The overlay of derivatives to match the post buy-out portfolio structure can remove market risk early in the process and ensure that the transaction is not frustrated by an unexpected shift in markets just prior to assets being transferred.

9. What if it all goes wrong? The Financial Services Compensation Scheme

Individuals and schemes insured through a bulk purchase annuity purchased from an FSA-regulated insurer are protected by the Financial Services Compensation Scheme (FSCS).

Compensation will be paid only when an authorised firm is unable, or is likely to be unable, to pay claims made against it, which is described as 'being in default'. If this is the case, the FSA will carry out an investigation to establish the financial position of the firm.

The FSCS will pay compensation only for financial loss and there are limits to the amounts of compensation it will pay.

9.1 Who is eligible?

The scheme was set up mainly to assist private individuals, although smaller businesses are also covered. Larger businesses are generally excluded, although there are some exceptions to this for deposit and insurance claims.

Individuals insured through long-term insurance contracts are protected by the FSCS unless they are closely connected to the defaulting insurance company or are using the insurance policy to launder money.

According to the *FSA Handbook*, a long-term insurance contract includes life and annuity business and a bulk purchase annuity is a life and annuity contract. There is no distinction between individual annuity policies or bulk annuity policies held as an asset of the scheme – both are covered by the FSCS.

9.2 What are the levels of compensation?

The table overleaf shows the levels of compensation an eligible claimant will receive.

A claimant under a long-term insurance policy will receive 100% of the first £2,000 plus at least 90% of the remainder with no upper limit.

Provision is made for the FSCS to provide continuity of cover and, if the insurer has not become insolvent but is in 'financial difficulties', to transfer the obligation to another insurer.

Type of claim	Level of cover	Maximum payment
Protected deposit	100% of claim	£35,000
Protected contract of insurance when the contract is a relevant general insurance contract	Where the claim is in respect of a liability subject to compulsory insurance: 100% of claim	Unlimited
	Where the claim arises under the Third Party (Rights against Insurers) Act 1930, is in respect of a liability within COMP 5.4.5R(1)(b), and is in connection with an Article 9 default: 90% of the claim	Unlimited
	In all other cases: 100% × first £2,000 90% of remainder of the claim	Unlimited
Protected contract of insurance when the contract is a long-term insurance contract	100% × first £2,000. At least 90% of the remaining value of the policy as determined in accordance with COMP12.	Unlimited
Protected investment business	100% × first £30,000 90% × next £20,000	£48,000
Protected home finance mediation	100% × first £30,000 90% × next £20,000	£48,000
Protected non-investment insurance mediation	Where the claim is in respect of a liability subject to compulsory insurance: 100% of claim	Unlimited
	In all other cases: 100% x first £2,000 90% of the remainder of the claim	Unlimited

Alternatives to a full insurance buy-out

Edmund Truell
Pension Corporation

1. Introduction

Defined benefit pension funds are an increasingly pressing issue for many companies and pension fund trustees.

Trustees find themselves trying to steer a secure course through a sea of investment strategies, taking into account increasing longevity exposure, while keeping a weather eye on the financial robustness of their corporate sponsor. They are required to assess the extent of their dependence on the sponsor and the quality of the sponsor's covenant both at the fund valuation level and when any corporate event occurs.

At the same time, sponsors are often faced with the problem of maintaining a set of financial commitments made in another era, when assumptions and expectations were vastly different. These commitments are difficult to measure, let alone anticipate, and they are entirely dependent on the health and wellbeing of the corporate sponsor of the fund, which is now legally required to underwrite any deficit.

The horizon of success in which most companies operate is at most five or 10 years distant. Yet as their pension funds take a much longer perspective, these corporate sponsors are also charged with maintaining open-ended commitments for a very long period ahead. Some funds will still be paying out benefits in 50 or 60 years' time, depending on the longevity of their members. The knock-on effects for a company's financial statements and cash flow can be significant, potentially lowering profits, increasing leverage and ultimately, impacting on share price.

Management teams, with their primary responsibility to shareholders – typically including other pension schemes as well – have to make necessary decisions that affect the direction of their companies. These decisions inevitably involve taking risks, such as establishing new divisions, closing down old ones or merging with or acquiring other entities. The result is that the shape of the sponsor of a pension fund today may be totally different from that of the company that initiated it.

Pension funds – and the beneficiaries who rely upon them – can be at the mercy of these changes. This can create unhealthy tension and lead to trustees treating the sponsor as little more than the prime debtor to the pension fund. This can be detrimental for all concerned: sponsors may be distracted from their core business and restricted in terms of their corporate goals, ultimately impacting on the funding position of the pension fund.

As well as focusing on its own pension fund, a company wishing to enter into M&A activity has to factor in the health of the counterparty's pension fund because it will take on the responsibility of funding it, even if few of the employees it takes on as part of any deal are beneficiaries of the fund. For their part, trustees may be cautious about potentially new sponsors and can make demands to ensure that their members' rights are fully protected. The projected takeover – which could be in everyone's interests – may be prevented or delayed.

The net result of the increasingly uncertain position in which trustees find themselves is that they are driven to seek additional contributions to achieve 'self-sufficiency' – that is, a level of funding such that little or no reliance is placed on the sponsor.

In fact, UK companies have been forced to increase by a factor of 30 the amount of money that they have put into pension funds to plug deficits since the 1970s. In 2000, they were putting £9.2 billion into their pension schemes. By 2007 that figure had risen to £33.6 billion.

Corporates therefore feel a growing need to remove these large, complex liabilities from their balance sheets so they can reduce earnings volatility and focus on core operations.

Norma Cohen, writing in the *Financial Times*, explained the problem: "Relatively new accounting rules that make clear the extent of scheme liabilities, along with rising life expectancy, have made companies eager to shed risks that are unrelated to the employer's core business and [are] difficult to manage."

So how can responsibilities – to pension fund trustees, to existing pensioners and to future beneficiaries – be maintained?

One answer is to pass the risk and responsibility to a specialist third-party pension solutions provider. By doing this, members gain vastly improved security through a bespoke insurance or corporate pensions solution, while the sponsor company removes future pension uncertainties from its balance sheet and commercial radar. Alternatively, insuring just the longevity risk may be more appropriate for a pension scheme and its sponsor.

The safety and security of the promised pension are the critical factors for every trustee of a defined benefit pension fund. These benefits may have to be paid many years into the future. If the fund is well resourced, the trustees and sponsor may feel that the best way to provide for this security is through an insurance buy-out.

Increasing numbers of trustees are using this method to significantly remove risk, leading to substantial growth in the UK pension insurance market. In the 12 months to December 31 2008, approximately £8 billion of new pensions insurance business was written, compared to a total market size of approximately £2.9 billion in 2007.

2. Insured solutions

As is covered in greater detail elsewhere in this book, a pension insurance buy-out is a bulk annuity policy secured with an insurer that ensures that all benefits are met in exchange for an upfront premium. Buy-out, followed by a scheme wind-up, is a tried and tested method of attaining a complete liability discharge for the sponsor and trustees. The only risk remaining for the members is that of insurer default and this should be mitigated due to insurance regulation, risk management and the mandatory provision of prudent reserves to protect solvency.

Historically, this route had been used as part of insolvency procedures or in the case of wind-up. Healthy, ongoing companies have been able to run under-funded pension schemes precisely because their operating businesses are perceived to provide security for the promise of future contributions. In contrast, insurance companies, with no such operating assets, need to hold assets and regulatory capital in excess of the International Accounting Standards (IAS)/Financial Reporting Standards accounting liabilities. This partially explains why pension insurance buy-out costs are higher than pension liabilities on an accounting basis.

With the arrival of new and dedicated insurers in the pension buy-out market, innovations to the standard model of bulk annuities have become more common. For example, phased buy-outs, staged payments, profit sharing, risk sharing, tranching and enhanced transfer exercises to manage the liabilities down before the buy-out and buy-in of annuity contracts are all now routinely available.

We have seen the increasing rise of the pensioner insurance buy-in contract, where the pension fund takes advantage of the difference between funding levels calculated using gilt yields and buy-out levels (generally calculated using AA credit spreads) to buy an insurance contract which matches their pension in payment liabilities, but actually releases assets to fund the obligations of the rest of the scheme. This pension insurance contract then sits within the portfolio of the fund, rising or falling with the value of the liabilities against which it was written. The asset is held in the fund, written in the name of the trustees and not technically tied to any specific pensioners.

Alternatively, some companies want to keep running their pension fund, but – in an effort to keep their members' benefits secure – are concerned about the longevity risk caused by an ever-increasing life expectancy. Quite simply, the longer that beneficiaries live, the longer they draw a pension and the greater the overall cost to the fund.

Over recent years, the trend has been for life expectancy in the United Kingdom to increase steadily (as the quality of living standards improves). It is estimated that an increase in life expectancy of one year increases a pension fund's liabilities by approximately 3.5%.

The latest longevity models provide little comfort for trustees. It has been reported that by 2050, a 65-year-old UK male might live, on average, to 97. The consensus view is that life expectancy will be up from 83 years today.

The good news for trustees is that insurance companies and the capital markets are able to offer longevity risk transfer solutions; where this cover is taken on, the pension fund can continue to pay its pensioners, but at reduced risk of longevity improvement. This chapter will look in more detail at longevity risk transfer options.

3. Non-insured solutions

The drive to reduce risk for all schemes has also given rise to the creation of alternatives to the traditional insured buy out and buy-in models. Many sponsors that cannot immediately buy out without a significant cash injection – the majority, as there is no requirement to fund to the insured level – nevertheless want to reduce the risk of the scheme and in particular its volatility on the balance sheet.

Shareholders are likely to share this view: continued contributions to a defined benefit pension fund may not be in their interests, particularly if the investment situation subsequently improves and a surplus becomes trapped in the scheme. Similarly, paying additional contributions into a fund without removing risk is an unpalatable option for many sponsors and shareholders. After all, investment conditions may change adversely or legislation may increase the price of the pension promise, requiring even greater contributions from the sponsor in the future.

By comparison, further contribution from a sponsor – when combined with a risk transfer to a specialist provider – provides greater certainty to the sponsor and shareholders, while still improving security for scheme members. When compared to making an open-ended commitment of additional contributions, this can also be a more judicious use of shareholder funds.

Demand for non-insured solutions can also be driven by pension funds themselves if a fund has a real or perceived deficit which can be made up only over some years, as any form of buy-out often exceeds the available assets. In this situation, trustees are relying on an unsecured debt that they hope will be paid by their corporate sponsor in due course. This depends on the continued prosperity of their sponsor. Faced with the situation where this may be in doubt, pension fund trustees will want to explore all options.

However, the market has been slow to accept the non-insured pension risk transfer model which has been offered by providers such as Pension Corporation and Citigroup (although the latter has now exited the market), as it is sensitive to accusations of regulatory arbitrage. Many pension schemes are not sufficiently funded to be able to protect themselves adequately from the major risks to their members and often lack the skills and quality of advice to identify and quantify such risks accurately. Key risks such as longevity, duration, inflation, currency, counterparty and systemic risks are often not sufficiently understood, resulting in excessive emphasis being placed on investment risk. Imperfectly hedged, the recent downturn in the global economy and financial markets means that many schemes that were slowly pursuing a path towards an insured buy-out will never get there.

As a policy matter, the tax-free status accorded to pension funds contrasts with the taxable nature of insurance companies and adds to the perception of 'regulatory arbitrage'.

However, the concept has distinct merits compared to the only alternative for many pension funds of falling into the Pension Protection Fund (PPF). A non-insured pension risk transfer can take place in a number of different ways and is often designed in a bespoke way, dependent upon the situation of the sponsoring company and the wishes of pension fund trustees. There can be transactions where either the sponsor (with pension plan attached) is purchased; or an acquirer becomes the new sponsor directly. The government has said that it welcomes new innovation in the management of pensions risk, noting that "responsible solutions can be of great value to sponsor employers and scheme members".[1]

1 Government response to the consultation on the powers of the Pensions Regulator.

It is key to ensure that the non-insured solution provides additional security for members and is not abandonment. Indeed, the Pensions Regulator (PR) has been urging trustees to be wary of proposals that could lead to the 'abandonment' of pension schemes. However, a non-insured pension risk transfer where the transaction actually increases the value of the sponsor covenant avoids this dilemma, either by replacing the sponsor with a stronger sponsor or by the addition of assets contingently or directly to the pension fund.

It also has a higher chance of being cleared by the PR, which will look at each proposal on a case-by-case basis. In any case, it seems unfeasible that the trustees, let alone the regulator, would approve any transaction in which the pension fund's security was decreased. Hence, the phrase 'corporate pension scheme adoptions' might be more appropriate for non-insured pension risk transfer transactions.

In practice, the non-insured or corporate pension risk transfer solution fills the middle ground between corporate sponsors that are strong and can afford pension insurance and sponsors where the corporate covenant is very weak and of concern to the PR and the PPF over how best to secure the members' pension obligations. Small operating firms with large legacy pension schemes attached to them may also be potentially attracted to this form of pension risk transfer, particularly if the scheme is well funded or is part of a bigger company or conglomerate from which funding is available to remove the costs, governance and volatility increasingly associated with defined benefit pension schemes.

4. Other options

In the cases discussed above, companies can fully remove their pension liabilities. However, some sponsors are looking only at the immediate road ahead and are not concerned at this stage with the complete journey. Since the market for bulk annuities took off in 2006–2007, a plethora of products have been offered by a variety of players to help trustees reduce the risks associated with running a defined benefit pension scheme, without severing the link between the sponsoring employer and the pension scheme.

Not all of them have been taken up by trustees. Some of the more interesting, but less commercially successful, have included exploring the possibility of providing an insurance policy to stabilise the balance sheet as reported in the employer's accounts. Under this mechanism, the scheme gives up some (or all) of the potential for improvements in the scheme's balance sheet in return for protection against the downside risk. The assets are transferred to the insurer and the employer pays an annual premium. In return, the insurer meets all the payments to scheme members as they fall due, meaning that the insurer shoulders the longevity risk during this period. At the end of the policy period, the insurer returns assets to the scheme to a value equal to the value of the liabilities. However, the insurer will cover only the non-accruing pension scheme liabilities and while no independent benchmark of future longevity expectations exists, there could well be differences between the insurer's mortality assumptions and those of the trustees who retain responsibility for the pension scheme. Finally, the contract lasts for only 10 years, leaving the scheme exposed to changes in longevity after this period.

A twist on this theme was on offer from another provider for a while. The essence of its solution was that at the start of the 10-year period, the trustees handed over cash and securities to the value of the IAS 19 liabilities. At the end of the period, assets equal to the value of the new IAS 19 liabilities were returned. This product differed from the above insurance in that it did not cover any changes in longevity. In the event that longevity increased, the return of the scheme assets would trigger a deficit as the assets would have failed to move in line with the liabilities which would have tracked increases in longevity, significantly reducing the attractiveness of this product.

Yet another player hoped to offer to pension schemes a bond which it described as "economically equivalent to buy-out". In exchange for the scheme's assets plus a premium – likely to be similar to the full buy-out premium, as it protected against the same risks – the scheme would be issued with a bond which had coupons exactly matching the outgoing benefits.

All three of these products failed to gain traction with trustees and the solution providers that offered them have since left the market.

In contrast, one product which has gained traction is longevity risk transfer.

5. Longevity risk transfer

The first bonds issued with a mortality element were issued by the Dutch in 1670. In 1693, the British government issued its own mortality bonds, 'tontines', to help fund a war with France. However, unscrupulous holders soon realised they could increase the size of their annuity payments if they killed off other bond holders. Fortunately, mortality-related products have since developed significantly over the last three centuries as financial institutions have attempted to make longevity risk a tradeable and less murderous commodity.

Most of the pension insurance solutions available today contain an element of protection against longevity improvements, with pension buy-outs (insured or otherwise) providing the ultimate cover for a scheme sponsor. However, there are now products available which aim to de-couple the longevity risk from the investment risk for those pension funds that wish to retain the assets. This can allow the pension fund to fine tune its risk budget, seeking to make gains in attractive risk fields while minimising risk in areas that provide little upside. Alternatively, longevity solutions can be used as the final piece in a risk reduction process, which, along with investment measures such as liability-driven investment, can allow schemes to be managed with limited volatility.

Longevity is a very real risk. Take the American Civil War Veterans' pension fund, one of the very first pension funds ever set up. Though set up in the aftermath of the Civil War, which ran from 1861 to 1865, the scheme made its final payment in 2004 – nearly 140 years after the war ended. The lucky recipient was a Mrs Alberta Stewart, thanks to the provision for widows pensions. In 1927, Alberta married an 81-year-old veteran at the tender age of 21. Although her husband died soon afterwards, Alberta lived until 2004 and carried on drawing the pension she was entitled to right up until the point she died at the grand old age of 98 – a poster child for increased longevity herself! Of course, she wasn't the only one to do this over the years, so the scheme continued to pay out large sums for many years after all the civil war veterans had died.

6. Longevity swaps and insurance

The principal vehicle for longevity risk transfer proposed by the capital markets is a longevity swap. This allows the scheme to lock into an agreed level of future longevity or to hedge against general trends in longevity experienced by the UK population as a whole. Longevity-only solutions in the form of notes, or offering limited downside protection, or based on a 'longevity index' as seen in JP Morgan's LifeMetrics index which was developed in association with Watson Wyatt and the Pensions Institute at the Cass Business School. Credit Suisse, Natexis and Swiss Re have all developed bespoke mortality swap products. These initiatives are all designed to parcel up mortality, allowing it to be traded and giving pension schemes the opportunity to hedge their longevity risk outside of a buy-out.

Pension Insurance Corporation, the Financial Services Authority (FSA) authorised and regulated business of Pension Corporation, launched the first longevity insurance product in 2008. It is designed to reimburse a pension fund with the cost of any future pension payments that arise from pensioners living longer than expected. In return for this protection, pension funds will pay fixed annual premiums set at the inception of the policy. The comprehensive policy will remain in force until the death of a pension fund's last covered pensioner or dependant, such as a spouse, regardless of future longevity extension. The insurance will be on a swap basis whereby Pension Insurance Corporation pays the pension scheme the actual pension payments due to pensioners and dependants and the pension scheme pays the fixed payments based on a pre-agreed pattern to Pension Insurance Corporation.

Pension Insurance Corporation developed the longevity insurance product in recognition of estimates that an improvement in life expectancy by one year increases the liabilities of the average fund by more than 3% as improving longevity means that pensioners draw their benefits for longer, which increases pension fund liabilities. British men aged 65 can today expect to live 4.5 years and women 3.2 years longer than they did in 1980. This trend is accelerating and currently male life expectancy is increasing by one year every five years.

The longevity insurance product differs from other products in the longevity market because:

- it is an insurance policy from a fully FSA-regulated insurance company;
- it is not a derivative instrument;
- the policy covers the specific longevity risk of the pension fund, rather than the longevity risk of the population at large, as in an index product. This removes any 'basis' risk;
- the policy covers the pension fund for 'whole of life', until the death of a pension fund's last covered pensioner or his dependant; as compared to swap products that provide cover for a set time period, typically for up to 10 years; and
- the policy requires no upfront payment, so 100% of the pension fund's assets remain fully invested and continue to earn returns for the fund.

Such an insurance policy should appeal to pension funds that currently have imperfect hedges on longevity (eg, equities) or those that plan to buy out in the future and want to retain 100% of their assets in the pension fund to generate future investment returns. The insurance does not affect the assets or their management and allows the trustees to retain full flexibility with regards to investment management decisions. Furthermore, the greater certainty of liability cash flows provided by this insurance would allow the pension scheme to pursue a closer interest rate and inflation liability matching strategy if required. Indeed, the longevity insurance could often be the last leg in a pension scheme de-risking process ahead of moving to complete buy-out or retaining the scheme's assets within an in-house fund management unit.

Whether longevity insurance is the first or the last step towards de-risking, removing the longevity risk from a pension scheme reduces its value-at-risk (VaR). The pension scheme is no longer exposed to changes in longevity assumptions, whilst retaining its asset and capital base. All other things being equal, the pension scheme can subsequently allocate the 'freed-up' risk capital (or VaR) to investment management (if desired by the trustees and the sponsor). This can potentially lead to the generation of additional returns for the ultimate benefit of the members and the sponsor.

Longevity insurance will benefit sophisticated pension schemes by:

- eliminating the most significant long-term risk – that of pensioners living longer;
- mitigating the cost of more conservative longevity assumptions that may be required in the future; and
- facilitating a future insurance buy-out where the payments to pensioners are certain.

Importantly, the pension scheme benefits by having an insurance company covenant covering the longest-dated risk of the pension scheme, thereby relieving pressure on the sponsor's covenant.

There are some advantages to pension schemes and their trustees in entering into longevity insurance as opposed to engaging in a (fully insured) buy-out. A longevity swap allows the assets to be retained by the fund, either as part of a proactive policy that believes the trustees can run the pension scheme assets more effectively than a full buy-out (and here we return to one of the key advantages of the non-insured buy-out solution), or it allows the sponsor/trustees to continue to use the pension scheme assets to earn investment returns to take the scheme to a full buy-out.

Importantly, the longevity insurance product does not prevent the pension scheme from entering into a (full) buy-out at a later stage. In fact, the transfer of longevity risk is consistent with making another step along the road to insured buy-out and reduces the cost of any future buy-out. As the pension scheme would have certainty about longevity expectations (ie, those locked in by the fixed leg), the putative pension insurer would not need to hold capital against this risk, which would result in the pension insurer saving the annual cost of that capital, thereby reducing the buy-out premium to the pension scheme. Pension Insurance Corporation believes that the cost of a fully insured buy-out would be reduced as a result of a scheme holding longevity insurance.

7. Case study – Babcock longevity transaction

On May 12 2009 Babcock International Group PLC announced in its annual report that:

> *We have reached agreement in principle with the trustees of two of our defined benefit pension schemes (the Schemes) for them to enter into contracts with an agreed counterparty to cap their exposure to increasing life expectancy.*
>
> *The exposure will be capped by the use of longevity swaps which will apply to current pensions in payment whereby the Schemes have agreed to make fixed payments in exchange for receiving the actual value of pensions due to members, irrespective of how long the members and their dependants live. In return for the Schemes' agreement to enter into this arrangement, the Group has agreed to fund the excess of the swap payment over the funding assumptions adopted by the trustees over a 20-year period. Other than the future benefit of capping the liabilities covered by the swaps, there will be no material impact on the Group's income statement, balance sheet or cash flow as a result of this transaction. This arrangement is designed to ensure for both the Group and the pension schemes that any further financial risk related to improved longevity has been eliminated.*

The deal to hedge £500 million of longevity risk via an over-the-counter (OTC) derivative with Credit Suisse, the investment bank, was significant because it was the first pure longevity transaction, long anticpated by the market.

Under the terms of the deal, Babcock now has certainty around its level of payments, as the swap will cover any excess due should the longevity of the fund members increase faster than expected. By capping the longevity risk, Babcock has removed any possible need for distressed asset sales or the need for any emergency cash injections.

Reaction to it, however, was mixed. *Financial News* wrote that: "Babcock's solution cannot be right for everyone... Insurers are regulated by the FSA and that gives pension scheme trustees much confidence. Signing a swap with a bank requires very different – and very thorough – due diligence."

8. Conclusion

To many, pension insurance buy-outs and their alternatives may be attractive. Corporate sponsors that initiated defined benefit pension funds in an earlier generation may now suddenly find their balance sheets at the mercy of volatile markets. This can have dramatic effects on their share price, their room for corporate manoeuvre and, in the end, the security of the commitments they are pledged to maintain. Trustees increasingly recognise that maintaining the link with the sponsor and securing member benefits for the very long term are no longer necessarily the same thing.

Much of the recent innovation in the pensions field has been devoted towards increasing the safety and security of member benefits, possibly through steps leading to full buy-out. Cost will usually be the critical factor in any decision. It is important to think about each step, from simple asset allocation towards fully insured buy-out, as being on a continuum and ensure each solution is really tailored to the specific needs of the trustees, their sponsoring company and the funding position of the pension scheme.

If complete pension risk transfer and the discharge of all obligations are the goals of both trustee and sponsor, then insured buy-out is the answer and other products will be stepping stones on this path. However, if full risk transfer is not the goal or is not yet affordable, many of these products offer a reasonable solution to the risks faced by pension schemes.

Elimination of pension liabilities – the trustees' perspective

David Archer
Rosamund Lee
Pitmans Trustees Limited

---

1. Initial considerations

1.1 Risk management

A trustee's overriding duty is to act in the best interests of the scheme members – normally this will mean acting in their best financial interests. Ultimately, trustees aim to ensure that there will be sufficient assets within their scheme to pay pension benefits as promised to every scheme member.

Trustees face many inherent risks in managing pension schemes and their role is becoming increasingly complex. Arguably, the most significant risk currently faced by pension schemes is longevity. The significant increase in life expectancy witnessed over the last decade has raised the cost of providing defined benefit pension schemes and for many schemes, the actuarial assumptions used to calculate these future liabilities are only now being brought into line with future longevity forecasts. In recognising this risk the Pensions Regulator has advised schemes that they should now be using a long cohort table with an underpin in order to give them a near worst-case scenario on longevity.

Additional and significant risks that the trustees face include the volatile movement of investment returns that may limit the growth of scheme assets, the impact of inflation, increasing costs incurred through regulatory impact (eg, the Pension Protection Fund (PPF) levy) and the future solvency of the sponsoring employer, an increasing concern in today's worsening economic environment.

(a) The traditional approach

The traditional approach to minimising costs and risk has been to close a scheme to new members, then to stop future accruals and eventually wind up the scheme. While limiting future liabilities and the level of risk by closing the scheme, the risks outlined above still remain.

A more effective way to reduce risk is to commence the winding up of a scheme, with the scheme trustees buying annuity policies which match the benefits which would otherwise be payable under the scheme as closely as possible. In this way the trustees are able to discharge their liabilities and the members' benefits are secured. However, this approach is not totally risk free for the trustees, as a traditional buy-out involves a 'tail' of risk while the wind-up is being completed. Issues such as data cleansing, member tracing and guaranteed minimum pension (GMP) equalisation can be problematic (see section 2 below).

(b) *Recent innovations*

More recent innovations have seen trustees take advantage of rapid transfer solutions before a scheme is wound up.

Here the trustees can achieve the immediate removal of risk, where the financial and longevity risks are transferred to an alternative scheme or buy-out company. In these transactions, the risks that might conventionally be dealt with in the winding-up process are transferred and the trustees are provided with a 'clean break' in that the new scheme or buy-out company takes on all the liabilities. These transfers also offer the advantage that the scheme is commonly replicated under the new arrangement, regardless of whether the scheme benefits are reflected in the scheme data at the time of the transfer.

Irrespective of which solution is sought by the trustees, offloading the scheme risk is not a cheap solution and even though the cost of a full buy-out policy is more affordable than ever, due to increased market competition, the price of a full buy-out option may be beyond the majority of schemes.

When considering a full buy-out, trustees need to evaluate the options available to them with the sponsoring employer of the scheme to ensure that they find the right solution. When selecting an insurer the trustees need to think, say, 20 years ahead with member service and communications in mind rather than simply comparing buy-out deals on price alone. The entrance of new providers of buy-out policies has increased the choice of solutions available to trustees and reduced prices, but the long-term viability of some of these offers has been brought into question.

Margaret Snowdon, operations director of Lucida plc, has commented: "Most buy-out deals come down to price, especially using an auction approach (whether covert or not) and competition in the market is creating some arguably unsustainable deals."

1.2 Partial or full buy-out

The emergence of new policy providers in the buy-out market has led to a greater level of innovation than has previously been seen, with alternative insurance products available to cover scheme cash flow, employer insolvency and longevity. To date, the main types of insured pension buy-out that have become popular are as follows:

- partial buy-outs ('buy-in') to reduce the risk for continuing schemes; and
- full buy-outs, designed to give companies a clean break from their pension liabilities.

(a) *Partial buy-out*

A partial buy-out provides an attractive halfway house for eliminating pension risk at a more affordable price than a full buy-out. In these instances trustees purchase an insurance policy to cover the longevity and financial risk of part of the scheme and the policy becomes another asset of the scheme. The scheme retains the same board of trustees and the relationship with the principal employer continues as before.

However, by opting for a partial buy-out the trustees are effectively changing their investment strategy to reduce the level of risk to the scheme, at a price significantly lower than if they sought a full buy-out. Choosing which member group to be bought out where limited top-up funds are available can be problematic. Whichever group is chosen, the aim must be to achieve the biggest reduction in liabilities and volatility for the scheme.

A straightforward approach is to ensure that pensioner liabilities within a policy exactly match future pension payments from the scheme for current pensioners. A buy-out on this basis removes the longevity, interest and inflation risks from the pensioner members and may be handled in such a manner that the members do not notice any change.

A partial buy-out of this nature is often seen as a way of 'downsizing' a scheme and allows the trustees to keep their options open if they are considering its eventual winding-up. However, simply removing the pensioner members does not remove the more difficult deferred members where the liablity and risk to the scheme is less easy to forecast.

(b) *Full buy-out*

A full buy-out is the transfer of all of a pension scheme's liabilities to an insurance company in exchange for a premium. Arranging a buy-out is complex and probably the most important step in controlling risk. The trustees will have a number of difficult decisions to make before choosing which annuity provider to use and which annuity quotes to accept.

In a full buy-out, the scheme will usually be wound up (although increasingly of late trustees have been considering the full buy-out of part of a scheme's liabilities in an otherwise ongoing situation). As part of the winding-up process the trustees are able to discharge their liabilities by purchasing annuities from an insurance company in the names of the individual members. Any policies originally purchased in the trustees' name will need to be assigned to the individual members, so trustees should check the assignment terms carefully, not least whether the policy is capable of assignment.

Recent innovations in the buy-out market have seen the introduction of solutions that offer schemes an immediate clean break, the buy-out policy eliminating virtually all risk on the date of the agreement.

One approach,[1] as witnessed by the £170 million deal between Paternoster and Emap, saw the participating employers leave the Emap scheme which was replaced by a subsidiary of Paternoster as the principal employer, the departing employers paying cash into the scheme to top up the funding level to full buy-out as required by UK law[2] The scheme was effectively transferred from the Emap group to the Paternoster group fully intact. Paternoster then took responsibility for winding up the scheme and bore the risk of additional liabilities being uncovered during the wind-up process.

---

1 See Mark Wood's chapter in this publication for further details.
2 Sections 75 and 75A of the Pensions Act 1995.

An alternative method by which a pension scheme may be transferred to a scheme run by a buy-out company was the £700 million transaction between Rank and Rothesay Life, the insurance subsidiary of Goldman Sachs. In this transaction Rank, in essence, 'sold' its pension scheme by transferring the scheme's assets and liabilities to a new sponsor as part of a bulk transfer process. The use of the phrase 'sold' in this context is a misnomer, as the transaction involved the transfer of the scheme assets and liabilities to a new pension scheme established by Rothesay Life. The original pension scheme was retained by Rank, albeit as an empty shell, with the trustees left with the relatively straightforward task of winding up the scheme.

The trustees must ensure that if there is a change of sponsor to a pension scheme, instigated by a corporate transaction or restructuring, the 'covenant' of the new sponsor is as strong as the sponsor it replaces. This should be notified to the Pensions Regulator. If the trustees do not receive sufficient assurance that the covenant strength is not materially worse and/or that pensions will continue to be paid to members as promised, then they may be forced to exercise any powers that they may have to impede the arrangement, including refusing to agree to the substitution where their consent is required.

In both of the examples above, the trustees and members of the respective schemes had the comfort that the pension benefits were secured in full by a regulated insurer. The trustees also had the added assurance that in the unlikely event that the insurer were to become insolvent they were *potential* beneficiaries under the terms of the Financial Services Compensation Scheme (FSCS) and 90% of the scheme benefits would be covered. However, to qualify for compensation the trustees would need to be eligible under the FSCS rules, which are made by the Financial Services Authority (FSA). What is clear is that the FSCS will deal only with claims against authorised firms (those regulated by the FSA) that are unable to pay claims against them. Until very recently it was less clear who would be eligible to receive compensation, with the rules stating that the FSCS can help private individuals, some small businesses and all policyholders of compulsory insurance policies. Fortunately, this appears to have been clarified, with the FSCS confirming that it does offer protection to both members and trustees of pension schemes where there has been a buy-out, or buy-in respectively, involving an insurance company. However, the regulator has expressed concern about some of the new innovations offered to the market and with this in mind the minister for pensions reform introduced an amendment to the Pensions Bill 2008 to allow the regulator to appoint trustees where "reasonable" in order to protect members. This will further extend the power of the Pension Regulator, which recently intervened in the recent acquisition of Telent by the Pensions Corporation by appointing three independent trustees to ensure that undue pressure was not being placed on the existing trustees. In this instance the regulator was approached by the trustee of the scheme, Stanhope Pension Trust Limited, in relation to the proposed takeover of the principal employer (Telent) by the Pension Corporation. The trustee was concerned that the Pension Corporation's primary aim in purchasing Telent was the management of the scheme's investment strategy and to obtain a profit for itself. The scheme was particularly attractive due to the existence of a fund of £514 million held in escrow that could be released to the principal employer if annuities were not purchased to safeguard members' benefits.

It was the view of the regulator that Pension Corporation's interests and the interests of the beneficiaries of the scheme were not aligned in all circumstances and that there were potentially acute and pervasive conflicts of interest in relation to investment strategy in particular. In recognition of these concerns, the Pensions Regulator Determinations Panel agreed that three independent trustees should be appointed to the Telent pension scheme under a special expedited procedure set out in the Pensions Act 2004.

The willingness of the regulator to use the wide-ranging and flexible powers available to it under the Pensions Act 2004 will no doubt provide comfort to trustees of schemes where a 'non-insured' buy-out is considered and act as a deterrent to any company that may see an easy way to releases a scheme's surplus or contingent assets. The regulator's powers are also in the process of being enhanced by the Department of Work and Pensions with the proposal that the regulator will have power to issue contribution notices where the effect of an act is materially detrimental to a scheme's ability to pay members' current and future benefits. As of October 20 2008, there are a number of circumstances in which the regulator may expect to issue contribution notices. These include:

The severing of employer support for the scheme so that employer support is removed substantially reduced or becomes nominal.

The transfer of liabilities of the scheme to another scheme or arrangement which does not have sufficient employer or is not sufficiently well funded.

A business model or the operation of the scheme in such a way that is designed to create a financial benefit for the employer or some other person from the scheme, but where inadequate account has been taken of the interests of the members of the scheme, including where risks to members are increased.

(TPR – PN08–25)

The aim of this and the other powers that are presently being reviewed by Parliament is to ensure that pensions remain secure, promises are kept and pension liabilities cannot be offloaded to the PPF. The regulator has generally welcomed the proposals to increase its powers as some of the business models which have evolved in recent years, due in part to increased market competition, have caused concern and highlighted the need for further protection for members.

1.3 Solvent or insolvent employer

As outlined above, any decision to proceed with a full or partial buy-out, whether traditional in style or more innovative in nature, may have been actioned due to the winding-up of a scheme or as a means to avoid risk.

The solvency or insolvency of the sponsoring employer will undoubtedly affect any buy-out decision. If a solvent employer winds up its pension scheme on or after June 11 2003 and the date of calculating and verifying any debt due under Section 75 of the Pensions Act 1995 is on or after March 15 2004, the debt must be calculated on the full buy-out basis and, if necessary, the trustees must enforce it as a statutory debt. The employer must therefore meet the shortfall required to secure all members' benefits in full by purchasing annuities.

In the case of an insolvent employer, if the date of winding-up and the date of calculating and verifying the Section 75 debt are on or after February 15 2005, the debt must be calculated on the full buy-out basis. As the employer will be unable to make up the deficit, the benefits purchased by the buy-out policy will have to be scaled back as the assets available to the trustees will be insufficient to secure full benefits.

Subject to the nature of the insolvency event and its timing, an eligible pension scheme may be entitled to compensation from the Financial Assistance Scheme (FAS) or entry to the PPF. In both circumstances the future benefits paid to active and deferred members will be reduced and it may be necessary to reduce pensioner payments in line with the FAS or PPF levels of scheme benefits.[3]

2. Practical considerations

2.1 Membership data and administration

When buying out benefits, trustees must ensure that all the members and other beneficiaries of the scheme are identified and that they all receive their proper benefits. Poor data and the time taken to reconcile it are often the cause of serious delay. This can be made more time consuming by an insurer's requirements that data be presented in the insurer's preferred format rather than in the way in which it is held by the scheme.

The Pensions Regulator has recently issued guidance on winding-up which sets out good practice guidelines to assist trustees in managing schemes through the winding-up process, with the aim of completing the key activities as soon as reasonably practical and certainly within two years. Some aspects of the guidance are also directed at ongoing schemes, in particular issues relating to administration and membership data: if good practice is adopted while a scheme is ongoing, difficulties are less likely to arise on a winding-up or buy-out.

In order to verify membership data, it will be necessary to undertake a data cleansing exercise. The extent to which this is required will depend on the particular circumstances of each individual scheme and the trustees should consider this in conjunction with the scheme's administrators. The regulator's winding-up guidance suggests some activities which should be considered as part of a data cleansing exercise:

- using data validation software to check consistency and highlight missing data;
- comparing the benefit structure under the trust deed and rules against historic administrative calculations; and
- ensuring that members are reminded to notify changes in personal details and discrepancies in annual benefit statements.

---

3 Current and deferred members at the time their employer became insolvent will normally receive 90% of their pension under the PPF, subject to a cap that is presently £28,743 per annum for a person aged 65 for the period April 2009 to March 2010. Broadly, the FAS will top up any scheme pension that will be paid (or is already being paid) to 90% of the pension an eligible member has accrued.The combined total of the payments to any one member is limited to £26,000 a year for each scheme.

2.2 Equalisation

One of the most important matters that trustees will need to consider before benefits can be bought out is whether equalisation has been properly implemented. Although *Barber v Guardian Royal Exchange* (1991), Article 141 of the EC Treaty and Section 62 of the Pensions Act 1995 require benefits accrued after May 17 1990 to be equalised for men and women, many schemes have failed to do so correctly.

Following *Barber*, it was established that employers and trustees were permitted to equalise benefits 'upwards' (eg, by raising the normal retirement date (NRD) from 60 to 65). However, this can be done only in respect of benefits accrued after the effective date of the amendment involving the change. Until an amendment is correctly implemented, benefits for both men and women must be based on the more favourable NRD (which will generally be the female NRD of 60). The period running after the date of the *Barber* judgment (May 17 1990) and ending with the date of an effective amendment is commonly known as the '*Barber* window'.

(a) Dubery

Equalisation has recently been given greater importance following the Court of Appeal's ruling in *Trustee Solutions Ltd v Dubery* (2007). In *Dubery* the Court had to decide whether there had been a valid rule amendment to equalise NRD at 65 and if not, whether an estoppel had arisen to preclude everyone affected by the increase in NRD from arguing that they were entitled to retire at 60 because they all believed that their NRD was 65.

The scheme's amendment power required alterations to be effected by deed executed by the principal employer and the trustees, or by any writing effected under hand by the principal employer and the trustees. The alteration purporting to equalise NRD at 65 with effect from October 1 1991 was in fact made by a memorandum dated May 15 1992 addressed to all members and an announcement to female members dated July 1992, both of which were unsigned. The court held that as the strict formalities of the amendment power had not been complied with, the scheme rules had never been validly amended.

Although revised booklets were issued to members referring to the new NRD of 65 in 1992 and 1999, they both specified that in the event of any doubt, the provisions in the scheme rules would prevail. The court noted that the overwhelming majority of cases which had considered booklets containing such provisions had been decided on the basis that this did not, of itself, give rise to an estoppel. It was held that overall there was insufficient evidence to prove that all members had understood that their NRD was 65; consequently no estoppel arose.

Dubery also has important implications for applying benefits under Section 73 of the 1995 act (which governs the priority order on winding-up) for final salary schemes. In *Dubery* the scheme was winding-up and at first instance the court held that male members who had accrued benefits in the '*Barber* window' and who had reached 60 before winding-up started were entitled to be treated in the higher pensioner category in respect of all their benefits since at the time the Inland Revenue would not permit pensions to be paid in part. However, on appeal, the court held that the overriding nature of *Barber* and European law meant that the requirements of the Inland Revenue should be overridden to allow payment of benefits in different tranches. Consequently, it was only the *Barber* window benefits which counted in the pensioner category, with the remainder counting in the deferred category.

Following *Dubery*, trustees may need to take legal advice to ascertain whether benefits have been equalised correctly. If they have not, it will be necessary to instruct the scheme actuary to recalculate the benefits.

(b) *Guaranteed minimum pensions*

Between April 6 1978 and April 5 1997, final salary occupational pension schemes could contract out of the State Earnings Related Pension Scheme if they provided their members with a pension that was not to be lower than a specified minimum – the GMP.

GMPs accrue at different rates and are payable from different ages for men and women, resulting in unequal benefits.

Although there is no doubt that GMPs will result in differential treatment, it is arguable whether there is a legal requirement to equalise them. Case law is also unclear on this point. For schemes winding up, however, trustees must consider whether GMPs should be equalised before the winding-up can be completed.

The Pensions Regulator has recently addressed issues relating to GMP equalisation in its guidance on winding-up. It does not take a view on whether trustees should or should not equalise GMPs or on the method of equalisation. Instead, it recognises that a range of approaches could be taken depending on the particular circumstances of the scheme.

The guidance emphasises that the Pensions Regulator does not endorse any particular approach and recommends that trustees consider the options available in consultation with their advisers. The regulator does, however, discourage trustees from creating unnecessary delays in deciding how to deal with GMP equalisation.

The guidance gives some examples of approaches used by trustees:

- Decision to equalise –
  - Compare pension at NRD with the pension which would have arisen had the member been of the opposite sex and provide the greater of the two;
  - Compare the overall actuarial value of the benefits with the value of the benefits that would have arisen if the member had been of the opposite sex and increase non-GMP liability as necessary;
  - Prepare a year-by-year comparison of a member's actual benefits with those which would have been provided had the member been of the opposite sex and provide the higher benefit;
  - Pay state scheme premiums where contracting-out ceased before April 6 1997 – trustees will still have to consider whether to equalise the remaining benefit; and
  - Offer to equalise, provided members agree to pay for the cost of calculating their entitlement.
- Decision not to equalise –
  - If a surplus allows for improved benefits to be paid which are higher than

the increase resulting from GMP equalisation, trustees will conclude that equalisation is not in the interests of the members as a whole.

In summary, trustees are under an obligation to consider whether to equalise GMPs when securing members' benefits. If the scheme funding position will not support equalisation, the costs are high and the potential additional benefit is small, it may well follow that no action is taken. However, if the employer is solvent or there are surplus funds, then there may be more grounds for equalising.

2.3 Contracting-out certificate

If a scheme is winding up, it will be necessary to surrender any contracting-out certificate and reconcile all contracted-out liabilities. As the reconciliation exercise with the National Insurance Services to the Pensions Industry (NISPI) can take a long time, the surrender should take place as soon as possible.

Discrepancies between the amount of GMPs or protected rights held by the scheme and NISPI can occur, for example, where there are differences in the level of contracted-out earnings recorded, or in the start and end dates of the contracted-out period. The regulator's winding-up guidance emphasises that all reasonable steps should be taken to calculate GMPs or protected rights correctly after consideration of the most proportionate approach that provides the best value for money to the members.

2.4 Missing members

Trustees are protected from personal liability for any missing, untraceable or unidentified beneficiaries who fail to receive benefits following a winding-up when benefits are secured with an insurance company, if they have placed a legal notice under Section 27 of the Trustee Act 1925. The notice asks for any potential beneficiaries of whom the trustees have no knowledge to come forward and make their claim. If they do not do so within the timeframe stipulated in the notice (at least two months), but subsequently bring a claim, the trustees are protected. The notice should be placed in the *London Gazette* and in a newspaper circulating in the area(s) where the members were last known to be employed.

In addition to placing a Section 27 notice, trustees may wish to use other member tracing methods. The cost will be a key factor and the trustees will need to consider whether this is a proper use of scheme resources. Some of the tracing methods available are:

- the Department of Work and Pensions tracing service;
- the National Fraud Initiative;
- a professional tracing service; and
- online directory enquiries.

Trustees should still buy out the benefits of any members who cannot be traced in order to provide themselves with protection against any possible future claims.

2.5 Choice of buy-out provider

The options available in today's marketplace in respect of both regulated insurance companies and non-insured alternatives have been covered elsewhere in this book. Trustees will need to seek competitive quotes from several providers before making their final decision. In drawing up a shortlist of possible providers, trustees will need to take advice from their advisers, particularly consultants with buy-out experience. Factors which determine the selected provider include:

- financial strength and creditworthiness – if necessary, specialist advisers can provide an up-to-date assessment of an insurer's financial strength;
- administrative capability, including the ability to install data – again, this can now be assessed by specialists;
- the availability of compensation in the event of provider insolvency; and
- cost.

Timescales should be agreed with providers both for giving the initial quote and for subsequently accepting a quote. Careful review should be undertaken to ensure that the chosen quote and finalised buy-out contract accurately reflect the benefits being bought out. In particular, the contract should only allow benefits to be paid that are authorised under the new Post-A-Day tax regime.

2.6 Investment

Trustees will need to review all the scheme's investments in the run-up to a buy-out to ensure their investment strategy is appropriate. In particular, the length of time to complete the buy-out will be critical in determining a strategy, as will making any decision to liquidate assets into cash. The process of transferring scheme assets to the insurer is vital and trustees need to carefully review their investments in the two or three months before the transfer. Specialist advice should be taken and any statement of investment principles reviewed.

2.7 Member communications and options

Trustees will usually provide members with options on how they can take their benefits, particularly if the scheme is winding up. However, it is not always necessary to do this as in certain circumstances benefits can be bought out without obtaining members' consent (see section 3 below).

Under the disclosure legislation, if members are provided with options on a winding-up they must be given three months to make their selection, although in practice this may take longer if quotes and financial advice are required. In addition to the choice of having their benefits bought out or selecting a transfer value to an alternative scheme of their choice, if appropriate, members may be given the option of commuting their benefits for triviality.

If a scheme is winding up, benefits may be commuted for triviality up to the new Post-A-Day limit of 1% of the standard lifetime allowance (ie, £17,500 being 1% of the lifetime allowance of £1.75 million for the tax year 2009–2010), provided that the member is under 75 and the employer undertakes to Her Majesty's Revenue & Customs that it will not make any ongoing pension provision in respect of the member in question in the following 12 months. This requirement applies only to the current employer at the time benefits are commuted and not to any previous employer.

On winding-up, the triviality limit is calculated only by reference to the scheme in question: there is no aggregation with benefits from other schemes. Twenty-five percent of the trivial lump sum is tax free, with the remaining 75% being taxed as income.

Benefits may also be commuted for triviality on a member's death in a winding-up situation, provided that the lump sum is paid to a dependant who qualifies under the Post-A-Day regime.

If a scheme is ongoing, benefits may also be commuted for triviality up to the same limit as on winding up, provided that the member is 60 or over and under 75. However, in an ongoing situation, the triviality limit is calculated by reference to the value of all the member's benefits under all registered schemes. Dependants' pensions may also be commuted for triviality and taxation is the same as in a winding-up situation.

3. Trustees' protection

3.1 Exoneration and indemnities

When buying out members' benefits, trustees need to take proactive decisions and be mindful of the possibility of challenges for breach of trust. All steps should be taken to maximise protection for the trustees.

(a) The Trustee Act 1925

The Trustee Act 1925 contains two possible defences for trustees under Sections 30 and 61. Section 30 provides that a trustee "shall be answerable and accountable only for his own acts, receipts, neglects or defaults, and not for those of any other trustee ... nor for the insufficiency or deficiency of any securities, nor any other loss, unless the same happens through his own wilful default". In *Re Vickery* (1930) it was held that 'wilful default' was restricted to cases where the trustee "knows that he is committing and intends to commit a breach of his duty, or is recklessly careless in the sense of not caring whether his act or omission is or is not a breach of duty". This is a very narrow interpretation which may cast doubt on the strength of Section 30 as a defence.

Under Section 61 of the Trustee Act 1925, the courts have the power to excuse a trustee from breach of trust if the trustee has acted honestly and reasonably and ought fairly to be excused. However, this is a discretionary remedy and the general consensus is that it should be viewed as a last resort.

Although the Trustee Act 1925 may prove useful in a breach of trust action, trustees will need to have the benefit of other resources to obtain better protection, such as an exoneration, indemnities and insurance.

(b) Exoneration clauses

The scheme rules should be checked to see whether they contain either or both of an exoneration clause and an indemnity for the trustees. Rules will generally contain the former, but may not necessarily provide the latter.

An exoneration clause excuses trustees from personal liability. It will usually specify that the trustees are liable only for loss attributable to their own fraud or wilful default. It has been argued that exoneration clauses are against public policy. The Law Commission was asked to look into this, but it concluded that no change was necessary. Furthermore, this was rejected by the Court of Appeal in *Armitage v Nurse* (1997). (It should, however, be noted that this was not a pensions case.) There are differing views on the extent to which exoneration clauses will provide protection and case law, and the Pensions Ombudsman has given varying decisions.

Following *Royal Brunei Airlines* (1995), it must be questionable whether a court would accept an exoneration clause which protected a trustee from personal liability where he is found to have acted dishonestly. Additionally, a higher standard of duty and care is expected from a professional trustee and it is most unlikely that an exoneration clause would protect a professional trustee from negligence. Furthermore, the courts have shown that any doubts regarding an exoneration clause will be construed against the trustee seeking to rely on it.

(c) ***Indemnities***

An indemnity may be provided by the pension fund, by the employer or both. If the indemnity is provided by the fund, the Pensions Act 2004 prevents trustees from indemnifying or reimbursing themselves from scheme assets for fines and penalties imposed by the regulator. Also, under the Pensions Act 1995, it is not possible to exclude liability for failing to exercise due care and skill in the performance of the trustees' investment functions.

Trustees will generally seek to obtain an indemnity from the employer in addition to any indemnity that may be provided from the fund to obtain greater protection. The main problem with an employer indemnity is that it is only as good as the creditworthiness of the employer: if the employer becomes insolvent, the indemnity is worthless. Additionally, if the scheme is winding up and the employer is solvent, the trustees should seek confirmation from the employer that its indemnity will survive.

Changes introduced by the Companies Act 2006 with effect from October 1 2007 have impacted on the granting of indemnities in relation to corporate trustees. It is now permissible:

- to exclude the liability of a corporate trustee which is a company in the same group as the principal employer in respect of its work as a trustee; and
- for the principal employer to indemnify a corporate trustee which is a company in the same group.

Difficulties arise, however, with indemnities for directors of corporate trustees where the director is also a director of the principal employer and the companies are associated. The position is as follows:

- The principal employer *cannot* indemnify a director of the corporate trustee against liability for criminal fines or regulatory penalties, or against any liability incurred by the director in defending criminal proceedings in which he is convicted.
- The principal employer *can* indemnify a director of the corporate trustee

against liability to third parties which he may incur in relation to his work for the corporate trustee, provided that this excludes the matters in the first point above.

- The principal employer *can* indemnify a director of the corporate trustee against liability to the corporate trustee, provided that this excludes the matters in the first point above.
- The principal employer *cannot* indemnify a director of the corporate trustee against liability to the principal employer where the two companies are associated. (One possible solution may therefore be to establish an unassociated corporate trustee.)

It is not clear whether an existing indemnity which is now replaced and updated to cover the 2006 act will in fact qualify for the new provisions or whether it will remain subject to the law in force when it was originally granted.

The granting of an indemnity may involve a conflict of interest, both in relation to directors of trustee companies who have interests as scheme members and/or as officers or employees of the scheme employer, and directors of employer companies who may have conflicting interests if they are also trustees.

With effect from October 1 2008, the Companies Act 2006 imposed a duty on company directors to avoid situations in which they have, or could have, interests which conflict, or which may conflict, with the interests of the company. However, this duty is not infringed if the situation cannot reasonably be regarded as likely to give rise to a conflict or the matter is authorised by the non-conflicted directors. For private companies incorporated before October 1 2008, authorisation can be given by the board only if the shareholders have resolved (by ordinary resolution) to do this.

A practical approach could involve amending the company's articles of association to provide a 'safe harbour' (eg, by setting out the circumstances in which the duty will not be breached).

(d) Insurance

It is possible for trustees to purchase indemnity insurance. The scheme rules should be checked to see whether there is power to purchase insurance and whether the premiums should be payable by the employer or met from scheme funds. This can be a vexed issue, although it is arguable that paying premiums from scheme funds is justifiable on the basis that it is in members' interests to protect them from the risk of loss to the scheme caused by the acts of the trustees. The Pensions Act 2004 prohibits trustees from recouping insurance premiums from scheme assets in respect of insurance covering fines and penalties imposed by the regulator, although this does not prevent the scheme employer from indemnifying the trustees against any such fines or penalties from its own resources.

Trustee liability insurance is expensive and the terms of any policy need to be carefully checked to ensure the required risks are covered. A policy will typically cover a fairly wide range of matters, including breach of trust, negligence, errors and omissions and mis-statements. In the case of a winding-up, insurance can be extended to cover missing beneficiaries who may make a claim for benefits several years after the winding-up has been completed. Insurance will generally exclude all liabilities in respect of equalisation and may not extend to former trustees.

Generally speaking, if the employer is solvent and has provided an indemnity, and the trustees believe that the employer is and will continue to be strong enough financially to be able to honour the indemnity, insurance is often seen as an expensive luxury.

3.2 Statutory discharge

When buying out members' benefits, the trustees will need to ensure that they are fully discharged from all further liability. The scheme rules should be checked to see whether they provide an express discharge for the trustees. If they do not, a discharge is available under overriding legislation as considered below.

(a) Section 74 of the Pensions Act 1995

Where a final salary occupational pension scheme commences winding-up on and after April 6 1997, Sections 74(2) and 74(3)(c) of the Pensions Act 1995 give trustees a discharge if they secure members' benefits by purchasing one or more annuities which satisfy prescribed requirements from one or more insurance companies.

Regulation 6 of The Occupational Pension Schemes (Winding Up) Regulations 1996 specifies the arrangements with which the trustees must comply to obtain the Section 74 discharge. In particular, the trustees must give the member a 'discharge notice' informing him that they are proposing to discharge their liability to the member. This must clarify whether the member's consent is required and, if it is, the notice must give a period of at least three months for consent to be given. The notice must also specify how the trustees propose to discharge the liability if the member does not consent.

Consent is required if the trustees intend to discharge their liabilities by transferring benefits to a personal pension scheme. It is not necessary to obtain consent where benefits are bought out by annuities or in the event of a bulk transfer to another occupational pension scheme where the requirements of the preservation legislation contained in Regulation 12 of the Occupational Pension Schemes (Preservation of Benefit) Regulations 1991 (the Preservation Regulations) are satisfied.

The discharge notice must give details of any options available to the member (eg, taking an individual transfer), and must explain that if the member wishes to choose a different option he must give written notice to that effect to the trustees within a period of three months from the date of the discharge notice. Additionally, where the trustees intend to purchase annuities, the discharge notice must give details of the relevant provider and where details of the terms of the contract can be obtained.

A discharge notice is treated as having been given if it is sent by post to the member's last known address. Notices need not be sent if the trustees do not know the member's address or if correspondence sent to the last known address has been returned.

(b) ***Preservation requirements***

If the scheme is not winding up or is not a final salary scheme, it is possible for trustees to obtain a discharge when buying out members' benefits under the preservation legislation, principally Sections 19 and 81 of the Pension Schemes Act 1993, the Preservation Regulations and the Occupational Pension Schemes (Discharge of Liability) Regulations 1997 (the Discharge Regulations).

Regulation 9 of the Preservation Regulations specifies that scheme rules may provide for benefits to be secured by insurance policies or annuity contracts in accordance with Section 19 of the 1993 act and the Discharge Regulations. It is unnecessary to obtain member consent to the purchase of such policies or annuity contracts if:

- the scheme is being wound up;
- the member has less than five years' qualifying service; or
- the trustees consider that, in the circumstances, it is reasonable to purchase annuity contracts without member consents.

The policy or contract must permit the member to assign or surrender it in accordance with the Discharge Regulations. Additionally, if points two or three apply, the following requirements must be complied with:

- The member's benefits must not include protected rights;
- The policy or contract must be taken out more than 12 months after the member left pensionable service;
- The trustees must give the member at least 30 days' written notice of their intention to purchase the policy or annuity; and
- There must be no outstanding application by the member for a cash equivalent transfer.

In practice, trustees may be more comfortable if members are told of their transfer options and informed that their benefits will be bought out in default of any transfer instruction from the member received before the expiry of a period, usually three months.

(c) ***Cash equivalent discharge***

If members are given the choice of transferring their benefits to an alternative arrangement rather than having an annuity purchased for them, the trustees will receive a discharge from any further liability to the member once this transfer is paid in accordance with the cash equivalent legislation contained in Chapter IV of Part IV of the 1993 act under Section 99 of that act.

Elimination of pension liabilities – the employer's perspective

Marcus Fink
Ashurst LLP

1. Introduction

The buy-out process can be instigated by either the trustees (eg, where scheme assets are sufficient to purchase an annuity for all members) or the scheme sponsor. In recent years, there has been a rise in the number of employers instigating the buy-out process and providing the necessary funds to bridge the gap between the value of the scheme assets and the cost of buying out benefits.

This chapter examines the considerations from the perspective of the employers instigating a buy-out and its role when the trustees instigate the process. Key considerations for the employer in relation to buying out benefits are also examined, such as whether a buy-out is the most appropriate method of removing risk from the balance sheet, choosing the most appropriate method of buying out benefits and choosing an insurer.

Cost will invariably be a key driver for the employer, so possible cost-saving measures before buying out benefits are also considered. Finally, the chapter looks at the protections that should be included in an annuity contract in order to safeguard the employer's position.

2. Is buy-out appropriate?

There are a variety of reasons as to why an employer may consider buying-out all or a proportion of the benefits of its defined benefit scheme. However, the employer needs to ask itself whether, given its specific circumstances, buying out benefits is the most appropriate method of achieving its risk reduction objectives. Could risk be controlled in other areas of the business more effectively? Would other practices, such as diversification of the business practice or tighter control of its revenue streams, achieve the same purpose but at less cost? Conversely, would buying out pension scheme benefits require employers to take risks elsewhere in the business to cut costs? If this is the case, the employer must ask itself whether such risks are acceptable.

Throughout 2007 and the first financial quarter of 2008, competitive pricing was, for many employers, a key driver to buying out benefits. Before 2005, Legal & General and the Prudential were the only buy-out insurers in the market. Since then, there has been a rapid expansion of the number of insurers in the market and, combined with changes in bond rates, it was perhaps inevitable that prices would be driven down by the new entrants while they attempted to establish themselves. Arguably, the economic downturn has made competitive pricing in this way unsustainable given the substantially increased investment risk, in addition to ever-increasing life expectancy.

Have employers missed the boat? They must consider the extent to which pricing will become cheaper in the future when the global economy stabilises. Furthermore, the employer must seek to establish whether any buy-out quotes which have been provided are in fact competitive. At a simplistic level, this would involve obtaining indicative quotes from a number of insurers. Building upon this, assessing 'true' competitiveness would involve a careful examination of scheme-specific factors such as the funding position of the scheme, the membership profile and a detailed longevity assessment (preferably based on key factors such as job type and postcode) to yield as accurate a result as possible.

It is important that employers carefully consider the alternatives available. For example, would it be preferable, given the circumstances of the scheme, for the employer and its group to choose a buy-in policy? This could achieve risk reduction for a cheaper price and provide flexibility against adverse events in the future (eg, if the policy allows the payments made under it to be reconfigured in the event of the scheme sponsor's insolvency).

If buy-out pricing is uncompetitive, it could be that retaining a well-funded pension scheme on an employer's balance sheet and adopting a quasi-insurance company approach by eliminating risk over time could achieve the employer's aims at a substantially reduced cost to buying-out benefits. In the case of a whole scheme buy-out, an employer would be paying a premium and allowing any future profits which a well-funded and adequately de-risked scheme could generate to pass to the insurer instead of back to the employer.

Every finance director will have a price at which he or she would be happy to transfer pension liabilities to an insurer. It is likely that in the current economic environment, that price will be substantially lower than prices available in the current market. This is perhaps reflected in the lower volume of buy-out deals carried out in the latter half 2008 as opposed to 2007. An employer must therefore look very carefully at the reasons for buying-out benefits and question whether, in doing so, risk is simply being shifted from one part of the business to another.

3. What type of buy-out?

Alongside the rapid expansion of the number of insurers in the buy-out market has come a bewildering array of buy-out products and options. Some of the main options are as follows.

3.1 Phased payments

This involves a gradual transfer of the scheme's liabilities over a fixed period of time, with pricing agreed either in advance or at the point of transfer. This approach can be made dependent on the scheme reaching certain funding targets.

3.2 Staggered payments

Liability is transferred to the insurer at the outset, but the scheme sponsor is permitted to make payments over a defined period. The insurer is likely to build an additional risk element into the premium and require protection against the default of the sponsor.

3.3 Tranching

Liabilities relating to different classes of member are bought out over time, with prices being fixed either at the outset or at the time each of the tranches are transferred. A common approach would be for pensioners to be bought out first, followed by deferred members approaching retirement age and then younger deferred members.

3.4 Profit sharing

Here the insurer shares the actuarial profits arising from the period following the transfer of liability to the insurer. Profits shared may include those generated from better than anticipated investment returns or scheme-specific mortality experience, and reductions in liability arising from a large number of members opting to take pension commencement lump sums or choosing to transfer their benefits to another arrangement instead of receiving an annuity from the insurer.

3.5 Risk sharing

This applies the same principle as profit sharing, but instead losses are shared. This option would reduce the overall cost of securing benefits with the insurer, but would not provide the clean break which, for many employers, is a key reason for buying out benefits in the first place. Losses arising from areas such as longevity and adverse investment market movements could be shared. Again, the insurer is likely to insist on protection against employer default.

3.6 Data risk

Many schemes suffer from poor data which prevents individual benefit entitlements from being accurately ascertained, therefore posing a risk to the insurer. Here, the insurer agrees to take on the risk of inaccurate data (usually in return for an enhanced premium). A data risk transfer will assist the 'clean break' principle and speed up the buy-out process as the trustees need not reconcile any inaccurate data before the transfer.

3.7 Transfer of liabilities to another scheme

Here the insurer accepts a transfer of all scheme liabilities into a scheme sponsored by itself or an entity within its group as an intermediate step before all benefits are annuitised with the insurer. This type of arrangement could speed up the buy-out process and also allow the insurer to reduce scheme liabilities (eg, by commuting trivial benefits and/or running an inducement programme).

In general, it is important for the employer to analyse the various products available on the market and assess each product's suitability, given the specific circumstances of both the scheme and the employer.

4. Choosing the right insurer

In addition to the long-established insurers such as Prudential and Legal & General, in the past few years a number of 'monoline' insurers which offer only pension-related products, such as Paternoster and the Pension Insurance Corporation, have entered the market. The number of insurers has made buy-out market extremely competitive. However, with so many players in the market, what considerations should an employer take into account when choosing an insurer? Where the buy-out process is driven by trustees, is it possible for the employer to have a say in which insurer is chosen?

4.1 Employer-driven process

In general, most insurers will offer broadly the same products. This makes differentiating between them difficult. The fundamental product offered by each insurer is an annuity contract regulated by the FSA for each scheme member which matches the benefits accrued under the employer's scheme. The obvious differentiating point between the insurers is price, which will undoubtedly be a key concern for the employer. However, there are a number of other elements which the employer should consider.

(a) Financial position

The high-profile collapse of Equitable Life and the US government bailout of the insurance giant AIG show that even top-rated, household-name insurers can fail. While price may be the key driver behind an employer-instigated buy-out, the preferred insurer must be of sufficient financial stature to enable the scheme trustees to form the view that members' benefits will be adequately safeguarded.

Although each insurer must meet minimum capital reserve requirements set by the Financial Services Authority (the FSA), the scheme trustees are likely to look beyond this and will derive comfort from an insurer with capital reserves which exceed the minimum thresholds. The FSA typically requires capital reserves of approximately 15% of the overall amount of the insurer's technical provisions (namely, the insurer's liabilities), which some trustees may feel to be inadequate. The employer should therefore request details of the insurer's capital reserves.

Losses on a bulk insurance policies or individual policies underwritten by an insurer may be covered by the Financial Services Compensation Scheme (FSCS). Levels of compensation are broadly 90% of the members' entitlement that existed before the FSCS took responsibility for payment.[1] Furthermore, the provision of benefits from the FSCS is not guaranteed in the event of the insurer's insolvency. For example, an independent actuary appointed by the FSCS can reduce compensation levels if the actuary deems that the benefits provided by the defunct insurer were excessive. In this instance, the benefits provided previously would have to be excessive to the extent that no reasonable insurer would have provided them at the time that the policy was entered into, with particular reference being made to the terms of the policy, most notably the premium.

---

1 The FSCS provides 100% of pension payments up to £2,000 and 90% thereafter.

The FSCS would also be available in relation to buy-in policies provided by an insolvent insurer, subject to the same compensation caps and the provisions relating to excessive benefits set out above. The scheme may, however, face cash-flow issues in the period before FSCS compensation is paid if it has insufficient assets to pay benefits covered by the buy-in policy.

The employer should investigate the creditworthiness of the insurer as determined by rating agencies such as Moody's and Standard & Poor's. Credit ratings will vary among providers, with providers such as Legal & General and the Prudential operating their buy-out business through AA+ rated subsidiaries, while other insurers predominately use subsidiaries with AA- credit ratings.

(b) ***Are benefits matched?***

Some insurers may be more willing to match members' benefit entitlements more accurately than others. If the scheme which the employer is looking to buy out is a mature scheme with various benefit platforms, underpins and categories of member, an insurer may not be willing to match the benefits for each member exactly due to reasons of complexity. Furthermore, the insurer's systems may be unable to cope with non-standard indexation or commutation factors. Insurers may therefore be reluctant to offer the same options to members as the scheme itself.

The insurer must value any benefits which cannot be replicated and replace them with other benefits so that the equivalence test under Section 67 of the Pensions Act 1995 is met. However, any resulting benefit changes could make the communication process more difficult and result in employee relations issues.

A point to note, especially in the economic climate at the time of writing, is the impact of deflation on pensions in payment provided through an insurer. Benefits payable under occupational pension schemes are generally protected by having a minimum pension increase set out in the scheme's trust deed and rules. Many trustees and employers assume that benefits bought out with an insurer will be subject to similar provisions. In many instances, this is not the case. Unless contractual provisions are included to the contrary, insurers could be within their rights to reduce pensions in payment should deflation occur. Where this is the case, the employer and the trustees could be exposed to claims by members for loss of benefits.

(c) ***Adequacy of insurer's administration system***

Given that, following a buy-out, the insurer will be undertaking to provide and administer scheme benefits to members for a potentially long period of time, the employer should check that the insurer has adequate systems in place. Such a check should include due diligence in relation to the payroll system used by the insurer for the payment of pensions, together with an analysis of how secure the data is. Although the insurer will ultimately be liable for any payroll and/or data protection issues, complaints by former employees are likely to refer to the members' original employer or the scheme sponsor and could cause employee relations issues and possibly reputational damage.

(d) *Further issues*

Employers should also consider the position of the intended insurer – is it an established player which has previously underwritten other large buy-outs? Alternatively, is it a new entrant to the market which has underwritten little or no previous business? An important but difficult factor which the employer should consider will be the future intentions of the insurer. Is it still likely to be around in 10 or 20 years' time? If not, it is likely that the employer and trustees will have little or no input into what would happen if the insurer were to exit the market and sell its business to a competitor? In this instance, it is fairly safe to assume that the insurer will be looking to obtain the best price and will therefore not pay as close attention to the considerations set out in this section compared with the employer and trustees. In this scenario, there could to be a reputational risk for the employer.

(e) *Position of the trustees*

One would have thought that trustees would be happy accept an employer-driven buy-out, especially where the employer is willing to meet the funding shortfall between the scheme assets and the cost of buying out benefits with an insurer. This may be true in some cases, but given the increasingly stringent requirements placed on trustees by both legislation and the Pensions Regulator (PR), trustees as a whole are becoming more reticent. Trustees may be initially sceptical about buying-out with an insurer which is anything less than a household name and, if this is not possible, may feel more comfortable carrying out a de-risking process themselves. It is therefore important that, in an employer-led process, the employer has satisfied itself that the considerations set out above have been met to an appropriate level by the insurer in order to provide the trustees with sufficient comfort for the process to proceed.

After the initial approach, the employer should therefore provide the trustees with as much information as possible on:

- the intended insurer;
- the reasons why that particular insurer is preferred over others in the market;
- the principles which will govern the contract between the trustees, the employer and the insurer; and
- if possible, a draft contract.

An initial meeting between the preferred insurer and the trustees would be useful at the exploratory stage of the process to answer any questions/concerns which the trustees may have.

(f) *Trustee-driven process*

If the trustees are in the fortunate position of being able to buy out members' benefits using scheme assets alone, opting to do so is likely to require the trustees to consult the employer, given that buying out benefits is likely to require an amendment to the scheme's statement of investment principles.

Although the trustees would not have to obtain the employer's agreement to proceed with the buy-out, consultation should entail the establishment of a dialogue and an exchange of views with the employer. This process will enable the employer to raise any of the concerns it may have (eg, those set out above). It will also allow the employer to suggest an alternative insurer to that favoured by the trustees if, for example, the trustees are favouring a long-established and expensive insurer when a new entrant to the market would underwrite the liabilities for a reduced cost while still being able to meet the concerns of both the employer and the trustees.

5. Cost-saving measures

Whether the buy-out process is instigated by the employer or the trustees, certain steps can be taken ahead of the actual buy-out itself. These could result in reduced premiums being payable to the insurer.

5.1 Trivial commutation

Many schemes will have significant numbers of members who are entitled to 'trivial' pensions due to short periods of pensionable service. These may be commuted for a cash lump sum, subject to the limitations set out in the Finance Act 2004. This process could be carried out before obtaining a quotation and, depending on the number of pensions commuted, could reduce the overall cost of buying out scheme benefits.

5.2 Inducement programmes

Employers could instigate an enhanced transfer value exercise under which members are offered an enhancement to transfer their benefits out of the scheme. Members are entitled to transfer their statutory cash equivalent transfer value of a scheme pursuant to the Pension Schemes Act 1993 and could be offered an enhanced transfer value, or a direct payment could be provided to the member (or both), with the enhancement or payment funded by the employer. Inducement programmes commonly target deferred members.

Inducement programmes could reduce the overall buy-out quotation on the basis that the cash-equivalent transfer value, plus the enhancement and/or payment to the member, is likely to be less than the retained liability and the associated costs of managing that liability.

A word of caution here – although inducement programmes do not contravene current legislation, trustees are likely to oppose such exercises. Trustee opposition may arise as a result of concerns from a trust law perspective – namely, the trustees' fiduciary duty to act in the best interests of scheme members. The trustees may also have fears over mis-selling, given that the members may ultimately receive a less valuable benefit if they choose to transfer. There may also be data protection issues, as the employer will need to access trustee records to contact the members.

For an inducement programme to be successfully concluded, a detailed and effective communication exercise with members should be undertaken, emphasising the need for employees to take independent financial advice. Employers will often feel it appropriate to meet the cost of providing members with free access to an independent financial adviser, or be required to provide such access by the trustees in return for their agreement to participate in the process.

The PR has issued guidance on the main aspects which will need to be considered before beginning an inducement exercise in which it states that it is "concerned to see members disadvantaged by inducement-led transfers out of defined benefit schemes", but wishes to see "scheme members [retaining] responsibility for their own financial decisions where those decisions impact their defined benefit scheme benefits". The PR emphasises that "members are to be given enough information to be able to make an informed choice about an inducement-led activity".

It is therefore vital that the employer and trustees seek appropriate advice when running an inducement programme. An improperly carried out inducement exercise could expose the employer and/or trustees to mis-selling, negligent misstatement and sanctions relating to the giving of unauthorised financial advice (pursuant to the Financial Services and Market Act 2000), as well as possible sanction from the PR.

5.3 Data cleansing

Insurers will charge extra if scheme records are in a poor state. Employers should therefore consider whether the cost of correcting poor data prior to transferring liabilities to an insurer would outweigh paying a higher premium for the insurer to accept poor data risk. This will also help the employer to ascertain whether the premium for poor data charged by a insurer is fair.

5.4 Investment risk

It could be that an employer goes through the above processes to reduce the cost of a buy-out, only to find that scheme investments move in an adverse direction, resulting in a substantially increased premium. It used to be the case that, following due diligence, insurers would guarantee quotations for up to 30 days. In the economic climate at the time of writing, with decreasing interest rates affecting bond yields and the global reduction in the value of equities, some insurers are refusing to guarantee quotations for more than 24 hours!

Government gilts have also been affected at the time of writing, especially in light of the Bank of England's recent 'quantitative easing' measures introduced in March 2009. These measures involved a £75 billion government investment in gilts in a bid to boost money supply. This cash injection increased the cost of gilts and, conversely, significantly reduced the rates of return. Given that insurers rely heavily on gilt returns to fund annuities, these measures have had a significant impact on buy-out costs.

Employers could reduce the risk of adverse movement in scheme investments by encouraging trustees to reduce investment risk exposure by entering into products such as longevity swaps and derivative products.

6. Process

There are some variations to the standard process involved in buying out benefits which an employer should be aware of in order to determine the process best suited to its requirements. As an alternative to simply obtaining separate quotations from the insurers in the market which the employer and trustees have targeted, the price could be reduced by utilising the competitiveness of the insurers through an auction process.

Auction processes are usually coordinated by consultancy firms which approach the insurers deemed appropriate by the trustees and the employer and provide them with sufficient scheme information for the insurer to provide a quote. These quotes may then be further reduced during the auction process and the lowest quote at the end of the process is the winner. Where two insurers have provided broadly similar quotes, both can be referred to the trustees and the employer to enable them to take account of other factors such as those outlined above.

Advantages of the auction process for an employer include the fact that the insurers know that the employer and the trustees have a genuine desire to buy out, and will therefore offer competitive quotes having carried out due diligence before the auction. Furthermore, auctions tend to speed up the buy-out process (thus simplifying management of the buy-out project).

The downside to the auction process is that the winner is chosen solely on price. As described above, this is not the only important factor when choosing a suitable insurer to buy out benefits. It is therefore important that, in an auction process, the trustees and employer have satisfied themselves that the participants have met the requirements in relation to these factors. If this is not the case, the employer/trustees could be open to challenges by members over their choice of insurer in the future.

Possible variations on the auction model include parcelling up different categories of liability under the scheme (eg, pensioners, old deferred members and young deferred members), and inviting quotes from a pool of insurers in relation to each packaged liability. This may yield a reduced overall premium. Alternatively, the employer and trustees could invite quotes from a number of insurers and stage an auction process in relation to the three 'preferred' providers, akin to the common structure used in competitive corporate sales or government tenders.

7. Key protections

Employers will need to ensure that their position under the bulk purchase annuity contract (BPA) is sufficiently safeguarded. The underlying principle for most employers will be that the insurer will take all risk with effect from a stated date. There are many different moving parts in relation to risk which are considered below.

7.1 Assets

Given that pension schemes hold a myriad of different investments, an *in specie* transfer of assets will take time and assets may be transferred in different tranches. The BPA must therefore be clear as to when asset risk transfers to the insurer. In the current economic climate, insurers may be reluctant to fix the final price until all asset transfers have been completed. Where this is the case, the BPA will be likely to contain 'true-up' provisions for reflecting the cost of adverse asset movements before the transfer into the final price. This mechanism throws up some interesting scenarios (ie, what would happen if adverse market movements in the days leading up to the transfer made the cost of buying out too expensive and necessitated a withdrawal by the employer and the trustees from the process? What would happen if the insurer went into insolvency having received some but not all of the scheme assets?) In either of these scenarios, it will be important to insert a provision in the BPA to allow the trustees to retain title to the assets until the buy-out process is complete.

7.2 Liabilities

As mentioned above, some insurers may not have the capacity to replicate certain scheme benefits in full. The BPA should list all of the benefits to be provided and all their various permutations. This list should then be checked carefully against the scheme documents to make sure all the scheme benefits are provided for under the BPA or, in the alternative, that actuarially equivalent benefits are provided in respect of each member.

There may be liabilities which have not been accounted for, such as in relation to missing beneficiaries (eg, due to poor data) and guaranteed minimum pension equalisation (in the absence of a definitive position on this point from the government). The BPA will need to make it clear what happens in relation to these liabilities (eg, by factoring such possibilities into the final price or providing for a correction price to be paid if and when such liabilities come to light). Employers will invariably favour the former approach which allows for a 'clean break'.

7.3 Data

The issues surrounding data are discussed above. Poor-quality and/or incomplete data will be a major concern for the insurer, given the relationship between the premium and the liabilities which are being taken on. Data issues can therefore have a significant impact on buy-out price. The BPA will need to cover this issue by allowing the trustees to add beneficiaries with genuine claims at a future date. It should also allow for benefits for known beneficiaries to be amended to the extent that the information given to the insurer turns out to be incorrect. Given that the vast majority of schemes will not have 100% accurate data, the BPA should clearly set out a margin for incomplete or incorrect data which, if exceeded, will permit the insurer to demand a supplemental premium. Incorrect data could also lead to the liabilities in a scheme being overstated, so the employer/trustees should consider including a provision for amounts to be paid back to the employer where this is the case.

7.4 Duty of good faith

Inextricably linked with poor data is the general principle of good faith which the trustees will owe to the insurer. This duty can be explained simply as the requirement for the trustees to disclose all facts which the insurer could reasonably deem to be material. The consequences of non-disclosure of a material fact could entitle the insurer to rescind the contract, unless the BPA contains provisions requiring further negotiation between the BPA parties and a lesser remedy.

A fundamental point for employers and trustees to consider is that the insurer is likely to seek to include an accuracy of data warranty in the BPA. Depending on the terms of the warranty, the insurer may have the right not only to rescind the contract, but also to keep the premium (a comparable power to the remedy available to insurers providing home contents or car insurance where the policyholder has provided incorrect statements of fact). It is therefore important that a caveat be inserted into any such warranty limiting its application to the knowledge of the trustees, having made all reasonable enquiries with stated personnel.

(a) ***Indemnity***

If the BPA relates to a full scheme buy-out, it is likely that the employer will want a clean break in terms of liability from the date the policy begins. The employer should therefore seek to negotiate as comprehensive an indemnity as possible from the insurer as to future claims and actions from the beneficiaries which the insurer will undoubtedly be keen to push back on.

(b) ***Buy-ins***

A buy-in contract will need to address other key factors such as what happens if the scheme is terminated (eg, must the buy-in product be used to annuitise stated members or could it be cashed in and value ascribed to the general assets of the scheme?). Also, a situation where the insurer pays an incorrect amount to the scheme administrator may occur. Here the trustees would ultimately have to ensure that the correct benefits are paid and may incur administration and banking charges. The buy-in contract should seek to pass such charges onto the insurer in this and other similar instances of breach.

Other factors, such as what will happen to the buy-in product if the scheme enters into the Pension Protection Fund, will also need to be considered.

8. Conclusion

As can be seen, there are many considerations for an employer to bear in mind before entering into a buy-out contract. In order to achieve a successful outcome, the employer must carefully consider the myriad of options provided by the insurer and the cost of each option. These factors must then be weighed against whether there are less expensive and perhaps more effective methods of de-risking and removing liabilities from the employer's balance sheet.

Once an employer is committed to buying out benefits, the correct choice of insurer and product is not an easy one. The employer will need to show the trustees why its favoured insurer is preferable to others and will also need to ensure that the chosen provider is capable of providing the comfort that a risk-adverse and potentially sceptical trustee body will demand.

An effective and close working relationship with the trustees throughout the buy-out process will be crucial to the success of the exercise. The employer will need the trustees to facilitate any pre-contract cost-saving measures, and will need to ensure that both its concerns and the concerns of the trustees are met in the contract negotiations with the insurer.

Much planning, investigation, time and a fair wind will be required to reach a successful conclusion.

Germany

Tobias Neufeld
Taylor Wessing

1. Introduction

Germany is well known as a country with unfunded pension liabilities due to direct pension commitment schemes. In fact, 56.2% of German pension schemes at the end of 2006 were direct pension commitment schemes with a corresponding pension liability of €243 billion. German legislation has historically favoured the unfunded approach, in contrast to separate funding found in most other countries. With the adoption of international accounting principles such as US generally accepted accounting principles (GAAP), or International Accounting Standards (IAS) together with International Financial Reporting Standards (IFRS), pension risks have become more visible than under German GAAP, where pension liabilities are generally undervalued due to the statutory fixed discount rate of 6% (independent of market conditions) and ignorance of future pension indexation. In addition, the decline in interest rates over the past several years and improvements in retiree longevity have greatly increased pension liabilities, creating concern for plan sponsors.

1.1 Pension scheme funding

Since the early 2000s more and more companies have pre-funded the pension commitments made to employees instead of meeting them directly from company assets. Companies now have been transferring book-reserved pension liabilities to external pension scheme vehicles such as pension funds or pension insurance funds, or setting up contractual trust arrangements (CTAs) to earmark assets for their direct pension commitment pension schemes.

1.2 A different buy-out model

The German buy-out model is comparable to the UK pension buy-out solution only in principle. German legislation does not allow companies to detach their pension liabilities completely. Even if the company has transferred its pension liability to an insurer, the Company Pensions Act provides that the employer will always remain liable towards the employee for at least the aggregate amount of contributions paid to the insurer as a minimum guaranteed benefit. Accordingly, pure defined contribution plans are legally not permitted in Germany. Nonetheless, biometrical and investment risks may be transferred in the course of a buy-out. In addition, German buy-out solutions will likely involve changing a pension scheme's benefit design, whereas a buy-out in the United Kingdom usually leaves the benefit structure unchanged.

2. German pension schemes – an overview

Before discussing the German buy-out market and alternative ways of eliminating pension scheme liability, it is essential to look first at the types and mechanics of company pension schemes in Germany, which – as far as funding and risk transfer are concerned – differ materially from UK pension schemes. The company pension landscape in Germany is extremely diverse, in terms of both the level of provision and the way that companies finance their pension plans. A typical German company pension plan is designed around a considerably lower benefits target than plans in the United Kingdom or the United States. Historically, German pension plans have been mostly based on defined benefits, although the worldwide trend towards defined contribution is also increasingly evident in Germany.

2.1 Legal framework – regulatory

The Company Pensions Act regulates company pension schemes in Germany. It contains provisions for those types of pension scheme allowed in Germany, whether they are internally financed schemes (ie, direct pension commitment schemes) or external schemes (ie, benefit funds, direct insurance schemes, pension insurance funds or pension funds). The provisions of the Company Pensions Act mainly relate to financing, vesting, liability, insolvency protection, type of commitment and the adjustment of benefits.

The employer may give a pension commitment in an employment contract, in an agreement with the works council, in a collective bargaining agreement or by way of collective grant. Depending on the type of commitment, changes to the pension scheme are subject to different and more or less rigid sets of rules. As a rule of thumb, in practice most changes to company pension schemes, such as changing the benefit structure or moving from internal financing to insurance buy-outs, require the consent of scheme members or their representatives (eg, works councils).

The German pensions market has relatively low regulatory barriers, particularly for direct pension commitment schemes where neither a funding requirement nor investment restrictions exist. The latter is compensated for by the generous German insolvency protection scheme, which basically guarantees 100% cover.

2.2 Internal financing – direct pension commitment schemes

In case of a direct pension commitment scheme the employer covenants to pay the employee a pension. Companies then accrue book reserves corresponding to the present value of pension commitments as liabilities in their balance sheets and write off the accruals from their taxable income. For tax purposes, the pension liabilities are calculated using a mandatory discount rate of 6% and standardised biometric assumptions. There is a cash-out in the pension payment phase only. This is a form of funding with an extreme asset allocation, comparable to a pension fund which only holds bonds issued by the sponsoring company. There are no rules governing investment or any statutory supervision of the scheme. As no restrictions are imposed on investment decisions, it is also possible for resources to be invested in an external investment fund. In the event of insolvency, benefits are safeguarded by the Pension Protection Fund.

2.3 External pension schemes – insurance and fund type

Broadly speaking, external pension schemes work as follows. The employer enters into a contractual commitment with the employee to pay the employee a pension. Rather than accruing pension book reserves and paying benefits from the company's assets, the employer establishes or contracts an external pension scheme vehicle to manage the pension scheme and to pay the pension. The employer must allocate resources to the external scheme vehicle. This is not a statutory requirement, but simply a contractual obligation towards the external vehicle.

The Company Pensions Act allows the employer to choose between a benefit fund, direct insurance policies, pension insurance fund and pension fund. All of these are autonomous external pension vehicles. They are, however, not comparable to a UK trust. Benefit funds are not subject to financial supervision and are not required to comply with any investment criteria unless they are reinsured benefit funds which take out life insurance policies for those eligible to a pension. In a direct insurance scheme, the employer, as the policyholder, takes out individual or group life insurance in favour of employees. Life insurance companies are subject to financial supervision. Pension insurance funds are small life insurance companies operated by one or more employers. Employers pay contributions to the fund to finance the pension benefits. Pension insurance funds are subject to financial supervision. Pension funds – introduced in 2002 – are autonomous institutions which operate a funded company pension scheme on behalf of the employer in return for the payment of contributions. Pension funds are also subject to supervision, but they have greater flexibility with regard to capital investment.

3. The German buy-out and risk elimination model

While direct pension commitment schemes are still prevalent, in recent years more and more companies are looking to transfer pension liabilities to external pension scheme vehicles such as insurance companies or pension funds. Companies are essentially 'de-risking' by pre-funding their internal company pension schemes. Although full funding is a desirable goal, it does not, of itself, address the volatility that pension schemes, particularly defined benefit schemes, can impose on the sponsor. This level of volatility can be considerable. Therefore, companies are simultaneously considering or planning to contain their liabilities using measures such as closing schemes for new entrants or changing the benefit structure.

3.1 Direct insurance/pension insurance fund buy-out

Scheme sponsors may transfer pension liabilities to insurance-type external pension scheme vehicles such as direct insurance schemes or pension insurance funds. The sponsor will hold the respective policy, which is an asset of the individual scheme members in whose name it is written. The insurer or pension insurance fund respectively undertakes to pay the pension benefits when due in return for payment of an upfront premium. In addition to the considerable costs of such a transfer, buying out to direct insurance or pension insurance funds will usually trigger tax disadvantages for scheme members as well as – compared to direct pension commitment schemes – a limitation in investment possibilities due to financial supervision of the insurance-type external vehicles.

3.2 Pension fund buy-out

Pension funds are becoming more and more attractive for employers that want to quit the traditional internal financing book reserve schemes. A pension fund allows higher equity investments than are allowed for insurance companies or pension insurance funds. When first introduced in 2002, financial supervision on pension funds was still quite rigid, with the pension fund essentially being treated like an insurance company for regulatory purposes. Recent legal reforms have improved the situation and the appeal of pension funds. The underfunding limit and the actuarial discount rate have been increased. The existing tax and social security restrictions have been removed – at least for partial buy-outs of scheme retirees. As the pension fund may be too restrictive for future service transfers, so far, companies only buy out their past service and pensions in payment. A CTA structure (see below) therefore often seems to be the preferred option for active scheme members, although direct pension commitment plans transferred into a CTA require a significantly higher premium to be paid to the Pension Protection Fund. Unlike a CTA transfer, a pension fund buy-out will provide for a transfer of the related biometrical risks (in particular longevity/mortality) and the investment risk to the pension fund.

3.3 German market

What is the pension fund buy-out market like in Germany? Big German companies such as Siemens, Bosch and RWE have established their own pension funds and more company pension funds can be expected. A few tens of public or commercial pension funds have been established so far, mainly by German banks and insurers. Just recently, a UK bank teamed up with a German insurer to establish a pension fund in Germany. Commercial pension funds also plan to attract small and medium-sized companies (SMEs) to buy out their pension liabilities. The recent legal reforms will finally get the pension fund accepted and the buy-out market will certainly continue to grow. However, one impediment still remains. Pension funds are subject to an annuity obligation for 70% of the funds – they are not allowed to make lump-sum retirement payments to retirees. If this changed it would amount to a major boost to the size of the pension fund buy-out market. In addition, a German pension fund may turn out to be the right tool for multinational employers, as it can be established as a single European pension fund for all members of a group's pension schemes across Europe. However, some of this may be aspirational as the costs of transferring pension liabilities to a pension fund could be a significant restraint. In the past, 130% to 150% of German GAAP liabilities was seen as a yardstick for buy-out premiums to insurers.

3.4 Contractual trust arrangements

CTAs are voluntary, off-balance sheet vehicles that ringfence pension assets against liabilities. This is a complex legal framework that can be created without changing the investment structure or tax treatment of those assets. Contributions to CTAs are considered company assets and do not represent taxable income to employees. The most common type of CTA is a two-sided trust model. Within the framework of a trust agreement, assets earmarked for funding pension liabilities are assumed and managed by the trust. Scheme members are granted legal claims to the trust assets in the event of the sponsoring employer's insolvency. Regulatory asset allocation regulations do not exist for CTAs.

CTAs are recognised as pension funds under IAS/IFRS and US GAAP, but the pension liabilities remain on-balance-sheet liabilities under German accounting standards. With rating agencies closely monitoring German balance-sheet pension schemes, the company's rationale was to better outsource the funding deficit than to have it as a blot on a balance sheet. The main driver has been the introduction of international accounting standards which forced German companies to report the liabilities on their balance sheet as unfunded. The transfer of existing company assets to the new vehicle may lead to the immediate recognition of capital gains (or losses) at the moment of transfer that have not previously passed through the profit-and-loss account. While the CTA buy-out provides for a balance-sheet outsourcing of pension liabilities under book reserve plans, the biometrical risks are not being transferred to the CTA.

Nearly half of the companies listed on the DAX 30 and many German subsidiaries of foreign corporations already have a CTA in place. There are signs that the trend toward CTAs is likely to continue among the larger companies and spread to SMEs. Banks have meanwhile established public CTAs. The rush among companies to establish CTAs is still ongoing. This is where the market still provides opportunities for banks or insurers to help install and manage CTA models, in particular if aimed at medium-sized companies which still have the pension liabilities on their balance sheet but do not want to launch their own CTA.

4. Conclusion

Managing pension liabilities is high on the agenda for many companies in Germany. In recent years, companies have been transferring book-reserved pension liabilities to external vehicles such as pension funds and – to some extent – pension insurance funds, or setting up CTAs to earmark assets for their internally financed direct pension commitment schemes.

Despite the recent emergence of providers dedicated to buying out scheme liabilities and the continuing trend of big corporates towards CTAs, only a limited percentage of SMEs can be expected to outsource their pension scheme liabilities by pension fund buy-outs within the next two or three years. In practice, buy-out is simply an unaffordable option for many sponsors – particularly in Germany, where book reserve schemes often are not funded at all – a situation which would need to be rectified before a buy-out could even be contemplated. The German market could prove attractive from a buy-out perspective, but it is likely to develop more slowly than predicted, not least because of the global financial crisis.

Netherlands

Bas Cammelbeeck
NautaDutilh

1. General

The Dutch pension system, which is widely seen as one of the best in Europe, consists of three pillars:

- a statutory national insurance scheme under the General Old Age Pension Act, providing for a basic old age pension;
- occupational pension schemes; and
- personal pension arrangements entered into with insurance companies.

The national insurance scheme – the first pillar – entitles residents of the Netherlands aged 65 or over to a basic state pension, the level of which is linked to the statutory minimum wage. The amount of pension paid out depends on, among other things, the number of years between the ages of 15 and 65 during which the recipient has resided in the Netherlands and the recipient's family situation. In comparison with other EU countries, payments under the state pension system, which is financed on a pay-as-you-go basis, constitute only a limited part of the overall pension income in the Netherlands.

The second pillar of the system consists of occupational pension schemes offered by individual employers or applicable at an industry-wide level. These schemes are administered by company or industry-wide pension funds or by insurance companies, and provide beneficiaries with a pension which supplements the state pension.

The third pillar consists of personal pension arrangements (eg, annuity plans) that are entered into and paid for by the individual.

2. Occupational pension schemes

Although in principle there is no obligation for employers to enter into pension agreements with their employees, over 90% of employees in the Netherlands participate in an occupational pension scheme. The general rule is the principle of freedom of contract. This applies with respect to, among other things, the nature of the scheme (defined benefit or defined contribution) and the extent to which participating employees contribute to the scheme's costs. The only exception to this general rule is that participation in the pension scheme of an industry-wide pension fund is compulsory if the minister for social affairs and employment has taken a decision to that effect pursuant to statutory law. An industry-wide pension fund is established, in the form of a foundation, by an employers' association and one or more trade unions pursuant to their collective labour agreement for the relevant sector. Representatives of the employers' association and trade union(s) hold an equal number of seats on the board of this pension fund.

3. The Pension Act

Once an employer has entered into a pension agreement with its employees, the agreement must be administered in accordance with the provisions of the Pension Act. On January 1 2007 this act replaced the Pension and Savings Funds Act which, like the General Old Age Pension Act, dated from the 1950s. The pension rights arising from a pension agreement are protected by the Pension Act. The main safeguard is the rule that the rights must be financed on the basis of capital funding, and that the assets covering these rights must be placed with a legal entity that is separate from the employer's enterprise (ie, a pension fund (whether limited to a particular company or industry-wide) or an insurance company). The employer must enter into an administration agreement with one of these three types of pension providers which, in turn, are required to lay down the terms of the pension agreement in a set of pension rules.

3.1 Triangular contractual relationship

From a legal point of view, there is a triangular relationship between the employer, the employee and the pension provider. The base of the triangle is formed by the pension agreement between the employer and the employee. The two sides consist of:

- the administration agreement between the employer and the pension provider; and
- the pension rules, which lay down the contractual relationship between the pension provider and the employee who participates, or has participated, in the employer's pension scheme.

The Civil Code applies to all three contractual relationships. In both their contractual relationship with the pension provider and their contractual relationship with the employer, employees are deemed to be the weaker party and are therefore given extra protection. Employers and pension providers are required to furnish proper information to all participants in, and beneficiaries under, the relevant pension scheme. In order to protect employees, pension rights can be commuted only in a very limited number of cases.

The administration agreement between an employer and an insurance company is in fact an insurance agreement in which the insurance company, against payment of the agreed premiums and for the term of the agreement, assumes the employer's obligations under the pension agreements with its employees. At the end of the term, which is usually five years, the insurance company is entitled to increase its premiums to cover the further accrual of pension rights. If the employer fails to obtain a better offer from another pension provider, it will have no choice but to agree to pay the higher premiums, as the requirement of a separate pension provider continues to apply.

The amount of the contributions payable by employers to industry-wide pension funds is determined by the board of the foundation administering the relevant fund, which in practice accepts the outcome of collective bargaining between the employers' organisation and trade union(s) on the total package of employment conditions in their sector. Pursuant to the Pension Act, an industry-wide pension fund is obliged to set the contributions at a level sufficient to enable the fund to cover its pension liabilities and costs.

The same obligation applies to company pension funds. The precise amount of the contributions payable by an employer to its company pension fund is determined in the administration agreement. The amount can vary depending on the pension fund's funding ratio (ie, the ratio of the discounted value of its pension liabilities to the market value of its assets at any given time).

3.2 Regulator

The Central Bank is charged with supervising all pension providers. Within the appropriate terms established for this purpose, a pension fund is obliged to provide the Central Bank with the periodic statements it requires to properly perform its function, as referred to in the Pension Act. If a pension fund anticipates or can reasonably anticipate that it will no longer meet or be able to meet the 'own funds' requirements set by or pursuant to the Pension Act, it is obliged to report this to the Central Bank and to file a long or short-term recovery plan, depending on the gravity of the situation.

4. Buy-out

As a consequence of ever-increasing regulations and governance requirements, many smaller company pension funds are considering winding up, or have already decided to do so. The cumulative costs in time and money of appropriately addressing the issues raised by external and internal supervisors, as well as by members and their representatives are becoming increasingly burdensome. The main issues for an employer in considering a buy-out of its company pension fund are:

- the lump-sum payment that must be made to the new pension provider (the insurance company or industry-wide pension fund) to cover the gap, if any, between the value of the accrued pension rights transferred and the value of the fund's assets as at the date of transfer; and
- the premium to be paid to the new pension provider as from the date of transfer.

It goes without saying that the employer must pay the gap between the two amounts, because ultimately the employer remains liable for the pension rights of its employees under their pension agreements. In the course of 2008, the global credit crisis caused the gap to increase substantially and it is not expected to decrease any time soon.

The premium quoted by an insurance company will often be higher than the premium paid by the employer to its company pension fund. Pension funds are foundations and so, unlike insurance companies, are non-profit organisations. Furthermore, insurance companies are liable to tax, whereas company pension funds are not.

If a company pension fund intends to transfer all or part of its assets and liabilities to another pension provider, permission is required from both the Central Bank and all employees individually. Tacit approval from employees may be obtained by informing them of the proposed transfer and giving them the opportunity to object. The objection can be overruled if the employee in question fails to demonstrate a reasonable interest.

In addition, the members' council of a company pension fund has the right to prior consultation before the board takes a decision regarding a possible group transfer of assets and liabilities. The employer can influence this decision via its representatives on the board, but does not have the final say. Pursuant to the Pension Act, any provision that gives a veto right with regard to a resolution or intended resolution of the pension fund to a party other than a corporate body of the pension fund is null and void. The ultimate decision rests with the board, which must ensure that all parties having an interest in the pension fund, including the employer, can feel that the decision is a well-balanced one. In the event of a partial buy-out, the board must, among other things, assess whether the buy-out will impair the pension fund's remaining financial support base. A partial buy-out will generally not result in a proportionate reduction of the costs.

4.1 Elimination of pension scheme liabilities through buy-out by insurance company

A pension fund can eliminate its pension scheme liabilities through a full or partial buy-out. This is effected by the pension fund purchasing an annuity from an insurance company for the benefit of the employees and/or former employees covered by the pension scheme by an insurance company (ie, by purchasing an annuity from an insurance company). Such a buy-out does not eliminate the liabilities as such, but transfers them from the pension fund to the insurance company. A full buy-out also relieves the employer of the obligation under accounting standards to include the liability from the scheme and any pension fund deficit in its balance sheet. In practice, the main issue is whether such a buy-out is affordable.

4.2 Reduction and redistribution of pension scheme liabilities and costs

Employers have an interest in ensuring that the cost of their pension schemes remains manageable and that fluctuations in the value of the assets held by their company pension funds do not, as a result of the applicable accounting standards, affect their balance sheet. Two recent cases demonstrate that there are ways in which these goals can be achieved.

Campina is one of the two largest dairy companies in the Netherlands and has its own company pension fund. Several years ago it became necessary for the fund's funding ratio to be increased. Through amendments to its collective labour agreement, it was agreed that Campina would make a one-off payment, employee contributions would be increased and the yearly indexation rate of a maximum of 3% for pensioners would be reduced. After the members' council consented, the board of the pension fund decided to amend the pension rules in conformity with the amended collective labour agreement. Although the pension fund's articles of association entitled the board to do this, the pensioners took the position that they were not bound by the amendments. The Arnhem Court of Appeal ruled against them.

Akzo Nobel is a listed multinational that is subject to International Accounting Standards. Its defined benefit pension scheme is administered by its company pension fund. To avoid the undesired effect of the international accounting standards, it introduced the concept of a collective defined contribution scheme. This concept provides for the payment to the pension fund of a fixed premium whose level is such that the amount of pension benefits to be paid to the members is similar to the amount that would be paid under a defined benefit scheme based on average salary. The trade unions agreed to this concept on the condition that Akzo Nobel made a one-off payment to the pension fund and that its annual contributions would be set at a level higher than the average over the preceding years. By complying with this condition, Akzo Nobel bought off the risk of having to make extra payments to the pension fund in the future if the funding ratio declines. On the other hand, it cannot claim a share of any future increase in the value of the pension fund's assets. With the consent of the members' council, the board decided to amend the administration agreement with Akzo Nobel in accordance with the collective labour agreement. Pensioners objected to this because the amendments enabled Akzo Nobel to shift the risk of disappointing investment results to the members, especially the pensioners whose indexation depends on those results. The Arnhem Court of Appeal declared these objections were unfounded.

5. Conclusion

Under Dutch pension law, it is possible to eliminate the liabilities of a pension fund via a buy-out as well as to reduce and redistribute the pension liability of employers via collective labour agreements. The 'polder model', the popular name for the Dutch practice of policymaking by consensus between government, employees and the trade unions, forms the basis of the Dutch pension system and makes it possible to tailor it to the needs of both employers and employees.

Norway

Peter Hammerich
Klaus Henrik Wiese-Hansen
Bugge, Arentz-Hansen & Rasmussen

1. Introduction

The Norwegian pension system consists of three pillars. The first pillar is the National Insurance Scheme (NIS), which offers benefits to Norwegian citizens, including disability and retirement pensions. The second pillar consists of occupational pension schemes for employees, on top of benefits paid by the NIS. The third pillar consists of private pension schemes, taken out voluntarily and financed by the individual.

Historically, pension schemes offered to Norwegian citizens and employees have been established as defined benefit schemes.

The NIS, the first pillar of the Norwegian pension system, dates back to 1895, when it existed as a public insurance scheme against accidents. In 1959 all Norwegian citizens aged 70 or older were given the right to receive a retirement pension. Today's NIS was established in 1967. The general retirement age was lowered from 70 to 67 in 1973.

Today, the NIS offers a range of benefits to Norwegian citizens, including a disability and retirement pension. It offers, as a general rule, a retirement pension from the current statutory retirement age of 67. The NIS is a defined benefit scheme and is partly funded, partly unfunded. The Government Pension Fund was established in 2006. This has two parts: the Government Pension Fund – Global, which is a continuation of the former Petroleum Fund, and the Government Pension Fund – Norway, which was previously known as the National Insurance Scheme Fund. The overall purpose of the Government Pension Fund, is to facilitate the government savings necessary to meet the rapid rise in public pension expenditures in the coming years and to support the long-term management of Norwegian petroleum revenues. The assets belonging to the Government Pension Fund – Norway are managed by the fund itself and are specifically allocated to the NIS. Large parts of the NIS's liabilities are covered directly by the state through the annual budgets (ie, through pay as you go).

Norwegian occupational pension schemes date back to the 17th century. The State Pension Fund was established in 1917 as a defined benefit scheme which granted a retirement pension equal to 66% of final salary provided that the employee had 30 years of service with the employer (the Norwegian state). All the main features of Norwegian public occupational pension schemes are based on these principles.

Until 2006, most Norwegian private employers were not legally obliged to offer membership of a pension scheme to their employees. Occupational pension schemes had, however, been common for a great many years and by 2006, the majority of private employers had already established some form of occupational pension scheme even though they were not legally obliged to do so. Today's rules were implemented in 2001 and replaced the former regulations of 1968. Private occupational pension schemes date further back than 1968. Until 2001, group occupational pension schemes were permitted to be established only as defined benefit schemes. In order to benefit from favourable tax treatment the pension scheme had to comply with the 1968 rules and had to be funded.[1] In 2001, important parts of the regulatory framework legislation for collective pension schemes were modernised and collective defined contribution pension were allowed for the first time under the Contributory Occupational Pensions Act of November 24 2000. In terms of volume/values, the Norwegian private occupational pension market is still a defined benefit market, even though defined contribution schemes have become increasingly popular over the last few years. It is likely that an increased focus among employers on pension scheme liabilities and how to reduce or eliminate these has contributed to the shift in the Norwegian pension market.

Section 2 of this chapter gives a brief description of the Norwegian pension system and how pension benefits are financed and secured. Section 3 briefly outlines the most common pension schemes in the private sector and how these are financed and accounted for in the annual balance sheets. Section 4 describes how employers can transfer their entire pension liability to a pension provider (ie, an insurance company or another provider (eg, a bank or an investment fund management company) in relation to defined contribution schemes; whereas employers will ordinarily have to book a net pension liability (ie, posting a debt) in the balance sheet related to defined benefit schemes, even if the pension insurance liabilities have been transferred to a life insurance company or a pension fund, due to a difference between the accounting rules and the financing model. The chapter also describes certain models for reducing or eliminating defined benefit pension scheme liabilities in the Norwegian pension market.

2. The three pillars of the Norwegian pension system

2.1 The first pillar – the National Insurance Scheme

The first pillar of the Norwegian pension system is the NIS which, in one form or another, dates back to 1895 when it acted as a public insurance against accidents. Today, the NIS offers benefits to Norwegian citizens, including a disability and retirement pension. It offers, as a general rule, a retirement pension from the current statutory retirement age of 67.

The NIS consists of two tiers regarding retirement pension: a basic pension

---

1 The premiums were calculated according to an annuity model as opposed to today's linear model, which in real terms both lead to a significant increase of premiums in the later stage of the occupational career and in many cases significantly lower pension benefits in case the employee left the employer before having reached the retirement age. The new linearity model targets this 'problem'. (See section 3.2 below.)

scheme providing basic pension benefits for all citizens and a national supplementary pension scheme providing earnings-related pensions. Any person who is a member of the NIS and has had an income from employment that exceeds the basis amount (BA) (as per May 1 2009, Nkr72,881,[2] adjusted annually) of the income year, is entitled to supplementary benefits, provided however that the person has had an income for at least three years.

The NIS is a defined benefit pension scheme. The full pension aims to provide a pension equivalent of 66% of annual income, albeit that this aim is met only for low-income groups. To receive the full benefit the pensioner must have 40 years of membership, with a 1/40 reduction for every missing year. Full supplementary pension depends on the number of membership years multiplied by the member's annual income (the average of the pension points in the 20 years with highest annual salary), capped at 12 BA.[3] There is also a reduced earning of supplementary pension benefits for income between six BA and 12 BA. For these reasons medium- or high-income individuals receive, in relative terms, lower pension benefits (ie, far lower than 66% of the annual income at the time of retirement) from the NIS than low-income individuals.

In 2005, a majority in the Norwegian Parliament entered into an agreement regarding a new public pension system. As a result of this agreement the NIS will be 'modernised', with a gradual implementation of the changes beginning in 2011. There are several changes to the existing rules, which are not discussed here. All aspects of the reform have not yet been passed by the Norwegian Parliament, but the government issued a white paper in early 2008 regarding flexible pensions and earning of pension rights as a follow-up to the earlier coalition agreement. In short, the government suggests introducing a flexible retirement age under the NIS from 62, with a so-called 'duration of life adjustment' in relation to the expected duration of life at the time of retirement. The annual retirement pension will thus increase if the individual chooses to continue working after the age of 62. Further, it has been suggested that there should be increased possibilities to combine pension and work – the individual chooses whether he wants to take out a full or partial retirement pension from the flexible pension age. Furthermore, new rules for earning pension rights have been suggested. If adopted, an individual's income throughout his entire working life (up to a level of 7.1 BA per annum[4]) will count equally towards pension rights in the NIS. Today's rules, which only allow 40 years to earn pension rights and which calculate the retirement pension based on the 20 highest years of income, will be abandoned.

2.2 The second pillar – occupational pension schemes

The second pillar consists of occupational pension schemes for employees, on top of benefits paid by the NIS.

---

2 £6,941 based on an exchange rate of GBP:Nkr of 10.5.

3 The basis amount in the NIS is a calculation factor which is used to calculate the size of benefits from the NIS. It is adjusted annually by Parliament, with effect from May 1 each year.

4 Nkr517,455 per May 1 2009, £ 49,281 based on an exchange rate of GBP:Nkr of 10.5.

(a) *Private employers*

Until 2006 most private employers were not legally obliged to offer membership of a pension scheme to their employees. Even though trade unions are generally considered to have strong negotiatiating powers, the unions had not managed to negotiate a general right to membership in occupational pension schemes for their members. However, by 2006, a majority of private employers had established some form of occupational pension scheme for their employees, without being legally obliged to do so.

In 2005, there were about 1.3 million employees in the private sector. About 600,000 of these were not covered by occupational pension schemes. (About 100,000 would not have been eligible due to age, part-time employment, etc.).[5] In May 2005, the majority coalition government agreed to pass an act that would require employers to establish membership in occupational pension schemes for their employees. The Mandatory Occupational Pensions Act of December 21 2005 came into force on January 1 2006. This meant that by December 31 2006 most employers had to establish occupational pension schemes that met certain qualitative minimum requirements for their employees, backdated to July 1 2006. Employers that already had occupational pension schemes had to adapt their schemes to meet these new minimum requirements. The Mandatory Occupational Pensions Act meant that more than 600,000 employees were now covered by an occupational pension scheme, around half of these being employed within the retail, hotel and restaurant businesses. Companies and other businesses that were established after December 31 2006 must set up a pension scheme to meet the minimum requirements within six months of start-up.

The Mandatory Occupational Pensions Act requires that most employers (except the smallest) offer membership of an occupational pension scheme to any employees above 20 years of age who are working more than 20% of the time, either in the form of either a defined benefit scheme according to the Company Pensions Act of March 24 2000 or a defined contribution scheme according to the Contributory Occupational Pensions Act of November 24 2000. An important element of the Mandatory Occupational Pensions Act is that pension benefits will have to be funded by entering into an insurance agreement or establishing a separate pension fund (in defined benefit schemes under the Company Pensions Act), or by entering into a savings agreement with a pension provider (ie, a bank, investment fund management company, insurance company, pension fund or a so-called defined contribution company) in defined contribution schemes. Hence, minimum pension requirements cannot be offered on a pay-as-you-go (unfunded) basis.

In short, the Mandatory Occupational Pensions Act requires that employers offer at least an annual contribution of 2% of the employee's salary between 1–12 BA (between Nkr72,881 and Nkr874,572[6] as of May 1 2009) if establishing a defined contribution scheme, or alternatively pay annual premiums to a defined benefit scheme of an equivalent level (ie, not less than the costs of offering an annual

---

5 There is some uncertainty surrounding these numbers.

6 £ 6,941–83,292 based on an exchange rate of GBP:Nkr of 10.5.

contribution of 2% of the employee's salary between 1–12 BA). In both cases the employer must take out a waiver of premium/contribution cover to secure continued earning of pension rights in case of disability. The employer is not required to offer either a disability pension or a survivor's pension.

(b) Public employers

In the public sector, employees have been entitled to membership in a pension scheme for many years. Employees of the state and certain other groups of employers are members in the State Pension Fund.[7] This is – mostly – a pay-as-you-go pension scheme, albeit there is a fund attached to it. Membership is mandatory for state employees, whereas certain companies and other entities with a public connection can choose to join. The state covers the employer's premium via the state budget, whereas most employing companies that have joined the fund pay an employer's premium directly to the State Pension Fund. All employees (members) contribute 2% of their annual salary. Together with benefits from the NIS, membership secures a defined benefit retirement pension equivalent to 66% of the employee's final salary at the time of retirement (as long as he has been a member for 30 years at the time of retirement, or 40 years if no longer a member at the time of retirement), with a linear calculation of earnings and a 1/30 (1/40) reduction of benefit per missing membership year. Pension rights are capped at 12 BA. Members of the NIS have reduced pension rights for income between 6–12 BA, so the State Pension Fund, being a gross pension scheme, compensates this reduction securing a total benefit[8] of 66% of the employee's final salary at the time of retirement as long as he has been a member for 30 (40) years. The membership also secures a disability pension and a survivor's pension (a pension for a member's family).

Even though most companies with a public connection are members in the State Pension Fund, and all their employees pay an annual premium to secure pension rights, the State Pension Fund is not a funded scheme. Pension benefits are paid through annual allowances in the state budget. However, most companies and other entities that have chosen voluntarily to join the State Pension Fund have been allocated a fictitious fund which aims to duplicate an actual fund. Through the fictitious fund, the State Pension Fund calculates a fictitious return on fictitious investments, thus enabling employers to benefit from 'invested' assets by way of lower premium payments. It is not possible to transfer a company's pension scheme in the State Pension Fund to another pension provider (life insurance company or pension fund), as no funds have been built up to back future payments. However, companies and other entities can withdraw from the membership of the state pension fund and here, a final financial settlement will take place. If the employing company's pension scheme in the state pension fund is over-financed, an equivalent

7 The State Pension Fund was established in 1917 and is the largest pension scheme in Norway, securing retirement benefits for some 1 million members of a total value of Nkr330 billion (as per late 2007). The fund is neither a life insurance company nor an ordinary pension fund (despite its name), but an administrative body under the Ministry of Government Administration and Reform. The state guarantees any benefits earned.

8 That is, a retirement pension received from the NIS and the State Pension Fund.

payment will be made from the fund to the company (and vice versa in case of an under-financing). The State Pension Fund will continue to pay benefits to the (former) members (employees) of the pension scheme, regardless of whether they have become retirement pensioners (where their membership in the fund continues) or not. In the latter case their membership will cease to exist and the former member will receive a deferred right (which is almost similar to a paid-up policy in a life insurance company, except that it cannot be transferred to another provider). This will secure payment of benefits from the State Pension Fund once the former member reaches retirement age, becomes disabled or dies.

Local government employees (municipal and county council workers, together with employees in health enterprises and corporations in which the municipalities, county councils and/or health enterprises have significant ownership interests – collectively referred to as 'municipal employees') have agreed the right to membership of pension schemes through collective union agreements. The pension benefits are similar to those earned in/paid by the state pension fund, but the benefits are fully funded and cannot be offered on a pay-as-you-go basis. The union agreements also require that the pension scheme be neutral to age and gender to avoid the situation where older employees of one sex (in practice, women) become more expensive due to higher premium payments than younger employees of the other sex. Kommunal Landspensjonskasse (KLP), a mutual life insurance company owned by the policyholders (the municipals), has traditionally been the main provider of life insurance and pension schemes to the municipal sector, as other life insurance companies were not permitted to calculate premiums based on age and gender neutrality until late 2002. Traditionally, KLP has been the sole provider of pension schemes to municipalities that had not established their own pension funds. A great number of municipalities have, however, established their own pension funds to secure employees' pension rights. These offer the same benefits on the same terms to the members of the fund as KLP and the other life insurance companies do to the municipal employees, to comply with the requirements set out in the union agreements. Hence, benefits will have to be fully funded and cannot be offered on a pay-as-you-go basis. Following the opening up of the municipal pension market in late 2002/early 2003, municipals could freely choose (annually) between KLP (the only mutual life insurance company in Norway), a private life insurance company or establishing their own pension fund. As of mid-2006, municipals were also permitted by law to establish inter-municipal pension funds for the benefit of employees being employed by those municipals that agreed to establish (or later join) such a joint pension fund.

(c) *The AFP scheme – across sectors*

An important element of the second pillar is the AFP scheme (*avtalefestet pensjon*, contractual pension). This is an early retirement scheme which gives an employee the right to retire (20%, 40% or 100% of full time) at any time between the ages of 62 and 67.

The employee's right to AFP is always set out in a collective agreement. This implies that employees who are not member of a trade union are not entitled to early retirement benefit from an AFP scheme. For this reason the AFP concept has been widely criticised over the last years as being 'unfair' to those who are not members of a trade union. Further, critics have pointed out the inconsistency of having state-subsidised AFP schemes that lead to a lower average retirement age for large groups of employees, whereas at the same time it is a common political goal to effectively increase the average retirement age to meet the anticipated increase in future public financial liabilities as a result of the rapidly ageing population (hence also the NIS reform).

The public AFP schemes (covering the state and municipal sectors) do not receive state contribution and the financing model differs from the AFP schemes in the private sector. There are four different AFP schemes. This chapter considers only the largest private-sector scheme, *LO-NHO-ordningene*.

As already mentioned, only companies (employers) that are bound by union agreements with their employees may join one of the AFP schemes. These apply to different sectors and employers cannot choose between them (eg, only financial institutions can join the AFP scheme for the financial sector, only public entities may join the AFP scheme for the public sector, etc).

Employees that are covered by an AFP scheme may freely retire (20%, 40% or 100%) at any time between 62 and 67, with a right to AFP. At 20% and 40% retirement, the employee will continue as a part-time employee in the company. AFP pensioners continue their membership in the company's 'ordinary' tax favourable occupational pension scheme and the employer's premium liability to fund the occupational pension scheme thus continues until the employee reaches 67 even if he takes out 100% AFP at an earlier age.[9] In principle, the AFP benefit is equal to the benefit the pensioner will receive from the NIS at 67. Each employee also receives a monthly, tax-free AFP supplement of Nkr950.[10]

AFP benefits are financed partly by the employers, partly by the state. The employer pays a fixed monthly premium to the AFP scheme for all employees, irrespective of whether any of the employees actually have, or will take out, AFP. The employer also pays a 'premium' (own risk) per employee that actually takes out AFP, being 25% of the paid-out benefit to the AFP pensioner (the employee). The state covers 40% of the pension costs of the AFP disbursements to the pensioners after 64. Consequently, the AFP scheme itself covers 75% of the pension costs (through built-up funds and premiums from the employers) between the age of 62 and 64 and 35% between the age of 64 and 67, whereas the employer covers 25% of the pensioner's AFP benefits between the ages of 62 and 67. The employer may not claim employees' contributions.

As regards the accounting of the employer's AFP liability, the 'premium' (own risk) the employer has to pay for employees who take out AFP will have to be treated as a defined benefit obligation in the company's balance sheet. The AFP scheme is an

---

9 See section (a) above and 3.2 and 3.3 below.

10 £90 based on an exchange rate of GBP:Nkr of 10.5. Pensioners within the other AFP schemes receive a monthly AFP supplement of Nkr1,700 (£162 based on an exchange rate of GBP:Nkr of 10.5) per month. This is taxable.

unfunded scheme (pay as you go) and therefore the employer's gross pension liability will in practical terms be equal to the net liability, as the employer has not built up external funds in a life insurance company or similar to cover parts of the obligation. Hence, more or less the entire gross AFP liability will appear as a debt item on the right side of the company's balance sheet.

As the employer must count the AFP liability as a defined benefit obligation, the obligation will have to be dispersed at the time of the disbursement (in the annual accounts) evenly over the employee's period of service. Further, to determine the net AFP obligation, the company has to make certain financial assumptions to book the obligation in the balance sheet according to applicable accounting standards. In this respect the company will have to assume the applicable discount rate, expected annual pay rises, the annual adjustment of the NIS's BA, the adjustment of current pensions, annual turnover in the company and the expected take-out rate of AFP among company employees. The AFP scheme will be reformed as part of the modernisation of the NIS. The changes to the AFP scheme are not examined in this chapter.

2.3 The third pillar – private pension schemes

The third pillar of the Norwegian pension system consists of private pension schemes, taken out voluntarily and financed by the individual.

Until mid-2006, certain private pension schemes were granted certain tax benefits. The benefits primarily applied to life annuity insurances and the so-called individual pension agreement (IPA). Under the former IPA rules, individuals were granted a 28% tax deduction on annual pension savings up to an annual maximum amount of Nkr40,000 (28% of Nkr40,000). In addition, accumulated funds were not subject to net wealth taxation. On the other hand, all benefits payable were taxed as pension income. As regards savings in life annuities, the tax benefit came from the fact that the accumulated funds (ie, the premium reserves) were not subject to net wealth tax.

These tax benefits were removed from the IPA scheme and from life annuities in May 2006. To some extent, this removed the third pillar of the Norwegian pension system as individuals seemed reluctant to allocate assets to pension savings without any tax inducement. Following political pressure, the government reintroduced a tax beneficial model for individual pension savings in 2008. This is very similar to the former IPA rules, except that the annual saving is limited to Nkr15,000, which is tax deductible (28%) in annual income. Hence, entering into this kind of savings agreement would reduce an annual tax bill by up to Nkr4,200. The accumulated funds of the pension agreement will also be exempt from net wealth tax, whereas payments will be taxed as pension income. The assets will be locked in until the retirement age (67, or 62 or later if the individual does not earn an ordinary salary), and the payment period shall be no less than 10 years.

Third pillar private pension schemes are taken out by each individual and usually do not involve the individual's employer. The assets are secured through built-up funds with an external pension provider (life insurance company, bank or investment fund management company, depending on the product). Unit-linked agreements could result in assets being lost due to fluctuating values in the underlying instruments.

3. The most common pension schemes in the private sector

3.1 Introduction

Occupational pension schemes for employees in the private sector can be divided into two categories, depending on whether the pension scheme is tax favourable for the employer and/or the employee. Pension schemes can also be distinguished between individual and collective (group) schemes, and whether the scheme is established as a defined benefit scheme or a defined contribution scheme.

3.2 Defined benefit schemes according to the Company Pensions Act

The traditional pension schemes for employees in the private sector have been defined benefit pension schemes according to the Company Pensions Act of March 24 2000, which came into force in 2001.[11] These rules succeeded the former 1968 rules for tax favourable defined benefit schemes. Provided that the pension scheme complies with the mandatory requirements of the Company Pensions Act, the employer's annual premiums will be tax deductible in the employer's annual income, whereas the employees will not be taxed either for the employer's premium payments or for their proportionate part of the pension scheme's premium reserve or other built-up funds before actually receiving payments out of the scheme. Defined benefit schemes that fall outside the requirements of the Company Pensions Act will not benefit from these tax advantages. Such schemes will in most cases have been established as 'top-hat' schemes and secure pension benefits for the part of the members' annual salary above 12 BA.[12]

The main elements of a tax favourable defined benefit scheme under the Company Pensions Act are as follows:

- The retirement age is 67.
- Unit-linked benefits are allowed.
- The 'ordinary' retirement pension will equal 66% of the employee's final salary, deducted estimated retirement benefits from the NIS.[13] However, both

11 It is also possible to establish defined contribution schemes under the Company Pensions Act, so-called 'one-time paid company pension schemes'. The purpose was originally to allow life insurance companies to offer defined contribution schemes as well. Later on, the life insurance branch developed other models for establishing defined contribution schemes under the Contributory Occupational Pensions Act which also complied with the legislative requirements applicable to life insurance companies. Accordingly, one-time paid company pension schemes did not become particularly widespread. One-time paid company pension schemes shall be accounted for as defined contribution schemes under the Norwegian accounting rules.

12 See section 3.4 below.

13 This is an important difference from the public pension schemes which are gross pension schemes and thus secure 66% of the employee's final salary, including actual payments from the NIS. Should the payments from the NIS be lowered (due to either to a change of rules or financial difficulties in the NIS), the public pension schemes will compensate the reduction and secure that the employees still receive a total of 66%. Defined benefit pension schemes under the Company Pensions Act are so-called 'net pension schemes' and cannot compensate for a reduction of benefits from the NIS. That is why defined benefit pension schemes under the Company Pensions Act make deductions only for the estimated benefits from the NIS, not the actual benefits.

higher and lower retirement pension than 66% is permitted. The benefits are, however, downwards limited to the minimum level secured through the Mandatory Occupational Pension Act and upwards limited to a total benefit (pension benefit from this scheme plus benefits from the NIS) of 100% of the member's salary up to six BA and 70% of the member's salary between 6 to12 BA (0% above 12 BA).

- The benefits are secured by way of annual premium payments to a life insurance company or pension fund. Pension rights are earned on a linear basis (minimum 30 years of service for the right to full benefits and maximum 40 years (albeit calculated from the time of taking employment until reaching retirement age). This implies that a 20-year-old employee must stay with an employer for 47 years to receive full benefits). This reduced the tendency under the former 1968 rules (under which premiums were calculated according to an annuity principle) to produce significant premium increases for employees nearing retirement.
- The premium reserve shall at any time be fully funded, based on the linear principle, implying that annual salary increases to the employees must be fully funded once the salary increase has been made. The linearity requirement, however, also implies that high salary increases to members of the scheme with long periods of service in the company will produce a significant single premium requirement (a one-off payment) to fully fund the new pensionable income level for these employees.
- The premium fund is subject to size restrictions. Any fund in excess of six times the average annual premium for the last three years must be repaid to the company. A voluntary refund is possible if the premium fund exceeds three times the average annual premium for the last three years. Refund triggers taxation of the refunded amount as the company has been granted tax relief on premiums.
- All employees who work at least 20% of full time and are members of the NIS are eligible for membership.
- Pension benefits can be secured only on annual salary up to a maximum of 12 times the BA.
- In addition to retirement benefits, disability and spouse and child's pension could be offered. Traditionally, all benefits have been offered.[14]

Defined benefit pension schemes established under the Company Pensions Act will be accounted for as defined benefit schemes under Norwegian accounting rules.

3.3 Defined contribution schemes according to the Contributory Occupational Pensions Act

As mentioned in section 3.2 above, defined benefit schemes have traditionally been

---

14 However, to reduce premium costs, a number of employers have amended their plans in the last few years (eg, by removing the disability, spouse and child's pension or by amending these benefits to become purely risk benefits without a saving element.

the main pension schemes for employees in the private sector. Until 2001, group occupational pension schemes could be established only as defined benefit schemes. As of 2001, important parts of the regulatory framework legislation for collective pension schemes were modernised and collective defined contribution pension became permitted for the first time through the Contributory Occupational Pensions Act of November 24 2000.

Apart from the fact that that the pension promise according to a defined contribution scheme is conceptually different from that of a defined benefit scheme (in the former the employer promises an annual contribution, whereas in the latter the employer promises an annual pension which is based on a certain percentage of the employee's final salary (eg 66%)), a defined contribution scheme according to the Contributory Occupational Pensions Act will in many ways be similar to a defined benefit scheme according to the Company Pensions Act. The Contributory Occupational Pensions Act is based on the Company Pensions Act.

The legislative framework for pension schemes under both sets of rules is designed to prevent discrimination between groups of employees in the company. Therefore, all employees having more than 20% of a full-time position are eligible for membership and there is no discrimination regarding benefits to be offered.

To comply with the mandatory requirements of the Contributory Occupational Pensions Act (and thus for the employer to be able to deduct annual contributions in the annual income), the contributions are capped at a pensionable level of 12 BA with a sliding scale of annual income between six BA and another sliding scale of annual income between six and 12 BA. Annual contributions cannot exceed 5% of the employee's salary between one and six BA. and 8% of salary between six and 12 BA.

Risk benefits such as disability, spouse and child's pension could not be offered in a defined contribution scheme, but may be secured by taking out separate insurance cover for some or all of these benefits with a life insurance company, under the rules of the Company Pensions Act.

Life insurance companies, pension funds, banks, investment fund management companies and so-called defined contribution companies may offer defined contribution group pension schemes.

Defined contribution pension schemes have become increasingly popular in recent years, particularly following the implementation of the Mandatory Occupational Pensions Act in 2006. A new trend has also emerged: the conversion of defined benefit schemes into defined contribution schemes. This eliminates pension scheme liabilities, cuts administrative costs relating to the follow-up and accounting of defined benefit schemes liabilities and allows the employer to benefit from knowing the cost in advance.[15]

Defined contribution schemes established under the Contributory Occupational Pensions Act will be accounted for as defined contribution schemes under the Norwegian accounting rules.

---

15 See section 4.

3.4 'Top-hat' pension schemes

Many companies offer 'top-hat' pension schemes to some of their employees – normally some (sometimes all) employees with an annual salary exceeding 12 BA, typically senior and/or top management.

Top-hat schemes in the Norwegian market have traditionally been established as defined benefit schemes, in the form of either pay-as-you-go benefits (unfunded, paid over the company's ordinary budgets) or group life annuities. A few larger companies have also established separate pension funds for their top-hat schemes. A group life annuity can be structured as a defined benefit scheme or a defined contribution scheme. However, just a few top-hat schemes have been established as defined contribution schemes. For the employees (members of the scheme), the main advantage of having a top-hat scheme established as a group life annuity is that the benefits are secured (funded) in a life insurance company. Until 2006, an employer could not deduct annual premiums to a top-hat group life annuity in the annual income, but the employees were not taxed for the employer's premium payments or for their proportionate part of the pension scheme's premium reserve (provided that the group life annuity met certain requirements). The members enjoyed tax benefits, whereas the employers did not. These tax benefits were abolished as of January 1 2007. Due to this, most top-hat schemes are now established as pay-as-you-go schemes.[16] To a certain extent, it is still possible to secure the employer's pension liabilities without imposing negative tax liabilities on the members of the scheme. Most top-hat schemes have been established as defined benefit schemes.

The pensionable income level is capped at a certain level in many top-hat schemes (eg, 20 or 30 BA) and it is fairly usual to offer benefits for 10 to 15 years after retirement instead of lifelong benefits. Top-hat schemes are frequently used for early retirement benefits, typically for the top management, and often have a shorter period of membership for the right to full benefits than tax favourable pension schemes (eg, 15 to 20 years of membership as opposed to 30 to 40 years).

Individual top-hat pension schemes (individually agreed and applicable only to the single member) are normally offered as pay as you go, over the company's annual budget. Individual pension schemes tend to vary a lot and consequently, are not discussed further herein. It seems that most individual top-hat pension schemes have been established as defined benefit schemes.

4. Elimination of pension scheme liabilities

4.1 Introduction

As is clear from sections 2 and 3 above, a majority of Norwegian supplementary pension schemes are either externally funded through annual premium payments or the employer's liability to pay pensions to the employees has been transferred to a

16 The life insurance companies issued paid-up policies to the members of the group life annuities which existed as of year-end 2006. Hence, the acquired pension rights as of year-end 2006 were secured with the life insurers.

third-party provider, even if the scheme itself is not funded. The latter applies to pension schemes within the State Pension Fund, which is a defined benefit unfunded (pay-as-you-go) pension scheme, but where companies that have chosen to become members pay annual premiums to secure the members' pension earnings. Thus, the pension scheme is sort of quasi-funded as the future liability rests with the pension fund itself.[17] Larger 'true' unfunded pension schemes exist, though: primarily the AFP schemes and smaller unfunded pension schemes – typically top-hat schemes that apply to one or some employee(s) or smaller groups of employees.

To comply with the requirements under the Mandatory Occupational Pensions Act, employers will have to establish either a defined benefit scheme or a defined contribution scheme under the Company Pensions Act, or a defined contribution scheme under the Contributory Occupational Pensions Act.[18] The requirements imply that private employers cannot offer their employees membership in an unfunded pension scheme for the part of their annual salary up to 12 BA.[19]

However, even if the major part of private employers' pension liabilities have been secured with third-party pension providers (primarily life insurance companies and pension funds), most employers that have established defined benefit pension schemes still have to book a net pension liability in the balance sheets of the annual accounts (the debt side). Under International Accounting Standard 19/NRS 6 (the Norwegian accounting standard), pension liabilities are calculated in a linear manner (from a perpetual perspective) and the employer should account for expected annual salary increases going forward. Even if the pension provider (life insurance company or pension fund) requires annual premium payments that are based on a linear earning of pension rights, these premiums will not take into account expected future salary increases. The employer will normally have to book a deficit (net pension liability – that is, pension liabilities > pension assets) in the balance sheet.

The elimination of defined pension liabilities has attracted a lot of attention among Norwegian employers in the last few years and it seems evident that a clear trend exists in this respect. As employers will not have to book future costs (contributions) to defined contribution schemes in the balance sheets, the discussion is relevant only to defined benefit schemes. There are many ways to reduce future liabilities in defined benefit schemes, but all employers are not permitted to change their pension schemes. Employers in the public sector are as a rule bound by collective union agreements to maintain their pension schemes in the existing form. Further, the AFP scheme cannot be amended unilaterally by an employer and the latter cannot even terminate the connection to the AFP scheme without terminating the entire collective agreement, which in real terms is rarely an option. Employers in the private sector have greater power to change their pension schemes, but will be obliged by the Mandatory Occupational Pensions Act to maintain a pension scheme at a minimum level. However, as the Mandatory Occupational Pensions Act secures only a retirement pension and waiver of premium/waiver of contribution, employers

---

17 See also the state pension fund's system with 'fictitious funds'. See section 2.2.2 above in this respect.
18 See section 2.2.1 above.
19 As per May 1 2009 Nkr874,572.

will normally be free to reduce retirement benefits down to the minimum level or to make certain other changes, provided that they are not bound by a collective agreement in this respect or the employees do not have individual rights to pension benefits at this (unchanged) level. The Financial Supervisory Authority of Norway (FSAN) also serves as the pensions regulator for pension schemes established according to the Mandatory Occupational Pensions Act (pension schemes established according to the Company Pensions Act or the Contributory Occupational Pensions Act), and serves as the financial regulator for Norwegian life insurance companies and pension funds. Hence, the FSAN supervises the major part of Norwegian pension schemes. If it is of the view that an employer's change of a pension scheme's terms does not comply with the prevailing legislation, the FSAN may demand that the changes be corrected. For tax favourable pension schemes, the consequences of not complying with the FSAN's requirement are that the pension scheme in question will not qualify for favourable tax treatment. Provided that the employer complies with the prevailing legislation and has not been bound by a collective union agreement regarding the pension scheme, the traditional view has been that the employer may freely carry out any of the changes mentioned in this chapter. Over the last few years Norwegion unions and/or employees have been increasingly willing to take such changes to the courts and require them to be annulled, based on alleged rights to pension benefits of a certain kind and/or a certain level. Norwegian courts have so far been reluctant to acknowledge these rights.

The purpose of this chapter is to give a brief outline of some frequently used models for reducing or even eliminating employers' accounting pension liabilities relating to defined benefit schemes. Some of the models below are also relevant for the reduction of costs related to defined contribution schemes. Under the Company Pensions Act and the Contributory Occupational Pensions Act, changes cannot be made with retroactive effect, which implies that the employees' acquired earnings up to the time of changes will always be secured with the pension provider.

4.2 Frequently used models for the reduction or elimination of pension scheme liabilities

(a) Termination of pension schemes

The most extreme way of eliminating pension liabilities is to terminate the entire pension scheme. To the extent there is a requirement to calculate premiums in a linear manner and the pension scheme's premium reserve is not fully funded according to the linearity principle, the employer must top up the premium reserve to meet the requirements before the termination can be carried out. So a termination may impact negatively on the employer's liquidity. Due to the requirements of the Mandatory Occupational Pensions Act, most employers will be restricted from terminating pension schemes that fall within the scope of this act without simultaneously establishing a new pension scheme that meets the act's requirements. In these cases the ordinary way of carrying out a termination would be to convert the scheme from a defined benefit scheme into a defined contribution scheme. Termination may, however, be a solution for top-hat schemes as these fall outside the Mandatory Occupational Pensions Act.

(b) ***Conversion of a defined benefit scheme into a defined contribution scheme***

Following the implementation of the Company Pensions Act and the Contributory Occupational Pensions Act in 2001, employers were allowed not only to establish group defined contribution schemes for the first time, but also to convert defined benefit schemes into defined contribution schemes. A 'conversion' in its purest form implies terminating the defined benefit scheme while simultaneously establishing a new defined contribution scheme. None, some or all of the existing members of the defined benefit scheme will then be transferred to the new defined contribution scheme and their membership of the defined benefit scheme will be terminated. The pension provider (life insurance company or pension fund) will issue paid-up policies to the transferred members for their acquired earnings, which will then be secured. There are further details to this concept which are not outlined further here.

Conversion can take place using several different models. For example, the employer can choose to allow the existing members of the defined benefit scheme to continue their membership in the scheme, but all new employees (being eligible for membership under the mandatory requirements) will be offered membership of the new defined contribution scheme. Obviously, this will not result in an elimination or even lower pension liabilities at the time of conversion, but the employer will benefit from lower annual liabilities (though not necessarily lower annual costs) going forward (as the members of the defined benefit scheme will be phased out as they gradually reach retirement age). The most frequently used conversion models either transfer all existing members from the defined benefit scheme to the defined contribution scheme or transfer members under a given age (below 52 or higher) to the new defined contribution scheme, whereas the older members above the given age continue their membership in the defined benefit scheme. New employees are offered membership in the new defined contribution scheme. In the latter model the employer may, depending on the age structure in the company, benefit from eliminating a certain part of the pension liabilities and at the same time protect the older employees who normally lose the most when they become members of a defined contribution scheme in the later stages of their occupational career.

If the employer chooses to convert the defined contribution scheme completely (ie, to transfer all existing members to the defined contribution scheme and to terminate the entire defined benefit scheme), the employer's net accounting liabilities related to this defined benefit scheme will be eliminated.[20]

(c) ***Reduction in benefit level***

Another – and perhaps the most frequently used – model for reducing defined benefit pension scheme liabilities is to reduce the level of benefits (eg, by reducing

20 If the premium reserve is underfunded (ie, not fully funded according to a linear calculation of pension earnings), the employer will have to fund the outstanding part before terminating the scheme. Conversion may thus impact on the employer's liquidity in a negative way.

the retirement pension level from 66% of the final pensionable salary (provided full period of service) down to, for example, 62% of final pensionable salary). If the pension scheme also includes disability or survivor's pension, a reduction of the retirement pension level will automatically imply a reduction of other such benefit levels as well, as these are usually calculated as a given percentage of the retirement pension (the disability pension equals 100% of the retirement pension, whereas the spouse's pension and child's pension frequently equal 55% and 40% (for the first child), respectively, of the retirement pension.

(d) ***Removal of benefits***

Removal of one or more benefits may also be an option to reduce pension liabilities. The Mandatory Occupational Pensions Act secures only retirement pension plus waiver of premium in case of the employee's disability. Thus, many employers have chosen to remove other benefits from the pension scheme – typically survivor's pension (spouse or child's pension), or even disability pension.

(e) ***Removal of the savings element***

Employers can choose to keep the existing benefits, but convert these into pure risk benefits (ie, by way of removing the savings element for the employees/their survivors). In such case (save for already aquired earnings (if any) up to the time of the change(s)), the employees/survivors will have insurance cover against the risk in question (disability and/or death of the member), as long as the employment relationship continues, but not thereafter.

(f) ***Changing retirement pension from lifelong to shorter duration***

Traditionally, retirement pension and spouse's pension have had a lifelong duration (ie, the pensioner receives retirement pension at a given level (typically 66% of the final pensionable salary) until the time of death). The employer can reduce pension liabilities and costs by introducing a shorter payment period for the retirement pension and spouse's pension, albeit not shorter than 10 years from the time of retirement. Several models can be used (eg, to have full payments for the first 10 years, then lower payments for the next five years and then zero thereafter, or even lower payments but lifelong (or a shorter period)).

(g) ***Employee's contribution***

Traditionally, employees' contributions have been restricted to the public sector whereas a relatively low percentage of private employers have claimed employees' contributions. Already the 1968 rules allowed for claiming employees' contributions to a defined benefit scheme and the Company Pensions Act continued this principle.[21] The employer may claim employees' contributions of up to 4% of the employee's annual fixed salary. However, this may not be above 50% of the total premium (excluding administration costs) to be paid for by the employee.

---

21 For no apparent reason this concept was not applied to defined contribution schemes under the Contributory Occupational Pensions Act before late 2005

South Africa

Hunter Thyne
Hunter Employee Benefits Law (Pty) Ltd

At the end of December 2006 assets in South African retirement funds[1] were valued at R1.5 trillion (£107 billion).[2,3] Data obtained from the 2008 Financial Services Board Annual Report states that there were 7,370,436 active members in retirement funds and 1.89 million pensioners, deferred pensioners and dependants for the period under review.

1. Classification of retirement funds

There are three types of retirement fund in South Africa:

- pension funds;
- provident funds; and
- retirement annuity funds.

Participation in pension and provident funds is dependent on a formal employment relationship. Pension and provident funds can exist only if there is a participating employer in such a fund. These retirement funds can thus be classified as occupational funds.

Membership of retirement annuity funds is voluntary. Members of retirement annuity funds have traditionally been individuals who cannot belong to occupational funds (ie, self-employed professionals). The South African revenue authority encourages people who belong to occupational funds to make additional contributions to retirement annuity funds by allowing a percentage of the contributions made to retirement annuity funds, in additional to the contribution made to any occupational fund, as a tax deduction.

The essential difference between the aforementioned funds is the benefit that accrues to a member on retirement.

The Income Tax Act[4] specifically defines the terms 'pension fund', 'provident fund' and 'retirement annuity fund'. The relevant portion of the definition contained in the Income Tax Act for a pension fund is: "that the (pension) fund is a permanent fund bona fide established for the purposes of providing annuities for employees on retirement from employment."

---

1 The term 'retirement fund' is a collective noun for pension funds, retirement annuity funds and provident funds.
2 At an exchange rate of R14:£1.
3 See the Financial Services Board (FSB) Annual Report 2008, p 56.
4 Act 58/1962.

The relevant portion of the definition of 'provident fund' contained in the Income Tax Act reads: "that the (provident) fund is a permanent fund bona fide established solely for the purposes of providing benefits for employees on retirement from employment."

The portion of the definition of 'retirement annuity fund' contained in the Income Tax Act which is of import is: "'retirement annuity fund' means any fund other than a pension fund, provident fund (and) ... that the fund is a permanent fund bona fide established for the sole purposes of providing life annuities for members of the fund."

It is quite clear that when a member retires from a pension fund, the member accrues an annuity. Similarly, when a member retires from a retirement annuity fund, the member accrues a living annuity.

However, on retirement from a provident fund, a member accrues a benefit. In practice, this means that the benefit could be the payment of a lump-sum benefit – the lump sum being equal to the value of assets allocated by the provident fund for the payment of a benefit to the member. As such, no annuity would become payable. Rob Rusconi[5] has concluded that "provident fund coverage is more widespread" in the lower and middle-income groups.

At present, there is no mandatory annuitisation on retirement in South Africa. In light of the risks that a retiree of a provident fund may spend his retirement capital and not ensure it is applied to provide an income, the South African National Treasury is considering amending the accrual laws and prescribing some compulsory annuitisation. This will mean that provident funds will have to amend their rules. It also means that the annuity market can be seen as a growth area for insurers.

The concept of buy-ins and buy-outs is not new in the South African retirement environment. Buy-ins have been used by retirement funds for many years and this is evident if one analyses the premiums paid to long-term insurers. The 2008 Financial Services Board Annual Report states that 47% of the premiums paid (R226.1 billion) to long-term insurers for the calendar year ending 2007 were paid into fund policies.[6] Not all of these premiums would have been paid for buy-in annuities, but a percentage most certainly would have been. As per the definition of 'fund policy', this amount will not include any premiums paid to insurers for buy-out annuities. As the policyholder of a buy-out annuity, it is not a fund – buy-out annuities are categorised as life policies.[7] In the same period 46.2% of the net premiums paid to long-term insurers were paid into life policies.

---

5 "Non-profit annuities: Thoughts on South Africa", Rob Rusconi March 2006, p 29.

6 The term 'fund policy' is defined in the Long-term Insurance Act (Act 52/1998) as: "a contract in terms of which a person, in return for a premium, undertakes to provide policy benefits for the purpose of funding in whole or in part the liability of a fund to provide benefits to its members in terms of its rules, other than such a contract relating exclusively to a particular member of the fund or to the surviving spouse, children, dependants or nominees of a particular member of the fund; and includes a reinsurance policy in respect of such a contract."

7 The term 'life policy' is defined in the Long-term Insurance Act (Act 52/1998) as meaning: "a contract in terms of which a person, in return for a premium, undertakes to (a) provide policy benefits upon, and exclusively as a result of, a life event; or (b) pay an annuity for a period, and includes a reinsurance policy in respect of such a contract."

2. Buy-out annuities in South Africa

2.1 Brief legislative history

Buy-out annuities were initially prohibited in South Africa.

On July 20 1995 the South African Revenue Services issued General Notice GN12/95, which stated that:

(s)ome approved pension, provident and retirement annuity funds are, in terms of the rules of the funds, terminating or relinquishing their liability to pay an annuity on the members' retirement from employment. The rules of the funds provide for a purchase of an annuity at an insurer or other institution after which the funds' liability towards the provision of the annuity is terminated..... not withstanding the rules of such fund, it should be noted that no ongoing approved retirement fund may terminate the aforementioned liability of paying an annuity, neither by virtue of the provisions of Section 14 of the Pension Fund Act nor by virtue of anything else.

General Notice GN12/95 thus expressly prohibited a retirement fund from purchasing a 'buy-out' annuity and thereby extinguishing the retirement fund's liability to pay the retiring member an annuity. With the move from defined benefit funding arrangements to defined contribution funding arrangements, this prohibition made the obligations of defined benefit funds more difficult to meet. How much should the annuity be on retirement? What pension increases should be given so as to not expose the retirement fund to potential deficits? Should the trustees allow the retired member investment choice if the retirement fund ultimately is legally liable to pay the annuity? After retirement, how should the assets set aside by the retirement fund to meet the obligations it has to the retirees be invested? Can the retirement fund segregate its assets into active and retired members and then follow a different investment strategy for each group?

In August 1996 the South African Revenue Services issued General Notice GN18/96, in terms of which it approved the use of buy-out annuities to completely discharge the retirement fund's obligations to retiring members on the purchase of the annuity.

The relevant portion of General Notice GN18/96 reads:

General Note GN12 conveyed the South African Revenue Services requirement relating to the termination of the liability of a pension or provident fund (retirement fund) to provide an annuity on a member's retirement from service. Following upon discussions with representatives of the pension industry, an agreement has been concluded in terms of which retirement funds may terminate their continued liability in respect of a retiring member once an annuity has been purchased for him or her.

The annuities purchased, as in the case with an annuity purchased in the name of a retirement fund or paid directly by such a fund, must be compulsory, non-commutable, payable for and based on the lifetime of the retiring member and may not be transferred, assigned, reduced, hypothecated or attached by creditors as contemplated by the provisions of Sections 37A and 37B of the Pension Funds Act. No retirement fund may purchase a member owned annuity unless its rules specifically provide for the purchase of an untied annuity in the name of a member from a registered insurer and the concomitant transfer of liability to the insurer, and unless the annuity is purchased with the full value of the retiring members' benefit that is available for the provision of an annuity. Retirement funds, are, as a result, permitted to provide an annuity to a retiring member by paying the annuity directly, or by purchasing an annuity in the name of the fund, or by purchasing the annuity in the name of a retiring member. While the aforementioned methods may be provided for in the rules of a retirement fund, a member may only select one of them and not a combination. The approval of a retirement fund which does not comply with the aforementioned requirements will be withdrawn.

2.2 Legal protection afforded to buy-out annuities

Buy-out annuities purchased by the retirement fund must replicate certain of the protection provisions contained in the Pension Funds Act.[8] Sections 37A and 37B[9] of the Pension Funds Act provide specific protection to pension benefits.

Section 37A provides that:

no benefit provided for in the rules of a registered fund (including an annuity purchased or to be purchased by the said fund from an insurer for a member), or right to such benefit, or right in respect of contributions made by or on behalf of a member, shall, notwithstanding anything to the contrary contained in the rules of such a fund, be capable of being reduced, transferred or otherwise ceded, or of being pledged or hypothecated, or be liable to be attached or subjected to any form of execution under a judgment or order of a court of law.

This has led to some interesting debates.

It is clear that the protection afforded to the benefit provided by the retirement fund extends to annuities "purchased or to be purchased by the said fund from an insurer for a member". However, are these buy-in or buy-out annuities? Arguments have been made that the Section 37A protection applies only to buy-in annuities. Another argument is that the money held by the insurer to pay the buy-out annuity is protected in terms of Section 37A, but when the actual money payment is made to the annuitant into his nominated bank account the protection is lost. Once deposited into the annuitant's bank account, creditors can then attach the money in execution of a judgment debt, thus leaving the annuitant destitute.

What is clear is that there has been an intention to protect retirement benefits from creditors and thereby reduce the risk on the South African government to pay

8 Section 24/1956

9 Section 37A and 37B of the Pension Funds Act read:

37A. Pension benefits not reducible, transferable or executable–

(1) Save to the extent permitted by this Act, the Income Tax Act, and the Maintenance Act no benefit provided for in the rules of a registered fund (including an annuity purchased or to be purchased by the said fund from an insurer for a member), or right to such benefit, ..., shall ... be capable of being reduced, transferred or otherwise ceded, or of being pledged or hypothecated, or be liable to be attached or subjected to any form of execution.

37B. Disposition of pension benefits upon insolvency–If the estate of any person entitled to a benefit payable in terms of the rules of a registered fund (including an annuity purchased by the said fund from an insurer for that person) is sequestrated or surrendered, such benefit or any part thereof which became payable after the commencement of the Financial Institutions Amendment Act, shall, ... not be deemed to form part of the assets in the insolvent estate of that person...

a state pension.[10] This was confirmed in the case of *ABSA Bank Ltd v Burmeister,*[11] where the court stated: "(the) effect of s 37A(1) is to establish a general rule protecting pension fund benefits from, inter alia, attachment and execution. Its object is clearly to protect pensioners against being deprived of the source of their pensions."

2.3 Process of selecting buy-out annuities

As the retirement fund is to transfer its liability[12] to the insurer, must the retirement fund choose which insurer is to be used?

What criteria are used to select the insurer?

What is the retirement fund's risk if the chosen insurer does not perform or is dissolved?

In *Muller v The Pension Fund of Nasionale Pers Bpk (Kantoor Personeel)*[13] the then Pension Funds Adjudicator held that the trustees of that fund had fettered their discretion when they made a policy that all retiring members had to purchase their buy-out annuity from a specific insurer. The complainant, in this instance, wanted to purchase a buy-out annuity from an insurer that the trustees had not approved. The then Pension Funds Adjudicator held that the trustees' decision was unreasonable and in excess of their powers.

This case has led many trustees of retirement funds to adopt a *laissez-faire* approach which allows retiring members to select the insurer from which the buy-out annuity is to be purchased.[14] This approach has been affirmed by the opinion that on the purchase of the buy-out annuity, the retirement fund's liability to the retiring member has transferred to the insurer.

Is this approach warranted?

As is discussed later on in this chapter, there are many different types of buy-out annuity, each of which has its own strengths and weaknesses. Given the general lack of financial literacy (and the complex product design of buy-out annuities), should the retirement fund not ensure that a member has enough information to make an informed decision on the type of buy-out annuity best suited for him and which insurer to use?

The issue of retirement fund risk towards buy-out annuities has yet to be tested. What has, however, been tested is the mis-selling of a certain type of buy-out annuity known as a living annuity. In many instances retirement funds (and/or participating employers), mindful of the potential risks described above, require a retiring member to consult with a registered financial adviser.[15] This financial adviser should assess the

---

10 South Africa does not have a compulsory government pension fund from which retirement benefits are paid. Membership is compulsory.

11 2004 (5) SA 595 (SCA).

12 See General Notice GN 18/96.

13 [1999] 10BPLR 188 (PFA).

14 In South Africa there are a limited number of insurers and as such the market is not too large. Rusconi, in his paper "National annuity markets features and implications" (Rusconi, R (2008), "National annuity markets: features and implications", Organisation for Economic Cooperation and Development (OECD) Working Papers on Insurance and Private Pensions, No 24, OECD publishing, Copyright OECD. Doi 10.1787/240211858078 at p 30) states that "the South African annuity market is strongly dominated by five insurers".

15 Registered in terms of the Financial Advisory and Intermediary Services Act (Act 37/2002).

retiring members' financial needs, appetite for risk and then advise them on what buy-out annuity to purchase and from which insurer. The South African experience has been that living annuities have been mis-sold. Retirees who should not be exposed to the vagaries of the financial markets have purchased living annuities and, over time, their real income has decreased significantly due to high draw-down rates or exposure to non-guaranteed asset classes. This has led the Life Offices Association of South Africa (LOA) to issue a Code of Conduct relating to the selling of living annuities.

Chapter 21 of the LOA Code of Conduct is specifically dedicated to living annuity policies. Paragraph 6 of Chapter 21 places a positive obligation on insurers to provide thorough product training regarding living annuity policies.[16] Paragraph 6.1.2 of Chapter 21 provides that the financial adviser must "make the investors (annuitants) aware of the fact that the assets of a living annuity will be subject to market fluctuation depending on the underlying investment portfolio selected".

Paragraph 6.1.3 then states that the financial adviser "must make investors (annuitants) aware of the fact that they must be in a financial position to withstand a reduced income in times of reduced capital or reduced investment returns".

What is most interesting is paragraph 6.1.4 of Chapter 21 of the LOA Code of Conduct. This discourages the purchase of a living annuity where the annuitant's only source of income is the living annuity and where the annuitant requires a pre-tax annuity "of more than inflation plus 2% of the capital at the onset of the annuity". In these circumstances the financial adviser "must inform the investor (annuitant) that he/she should rather select a different type of annuity".

The South African experience has been that many financial advisers are eager to earn the commission on the initial purchase of the "living annuity" (up to 5% of the initial capital) and are thereafter loath to provide any ongoing advice. Paragraph 6.1.5 of Chapter 21 of the LOA Code of Conduct provides that the financial adviser must be aware that ongoing advice should be given – even if no remuneration is paid for that advice. Many a financial journalist has thus concluded that living annuities are attractive only to the sophisticated investor.[17]

With what has been said above, many an annuitant still purchases a living annuity because of the perceived advantageous product design.

2.4 Types of buy-out annuity

There are various types of buy-out annuity on offer to South Africa retirees. These include the following:

- Fixed annuities pay a flat nominal amount for the life of the annuitant. The annuity ceases on the death of the annuitant. The insurer assumes all risk.
- Joint and survivor annuities pay a flat nominal amount for the lifetime of the annuitant and upon the annuitant's death a percentage of the nominal amount to the annuitant's surviving spouse. On the death of the surviving

---

16 See paragraph 6.1.1 of Chapter 21 of the LOA Code of Conduct.

17 See "Are living annuities really so great?", an article prepared by the Actuarial Society of South Africa as a service to the public. April 2002.

spouse, the annuity ceases.

- With-profit annuity (fixed and joint and survivor) pay an initial guaranteed amount which increases over the lifetime of an annuitant by increases declared by the insurer. These increases are determined solely by the insurer, taking the performance of the insurer's assets into account.
- Flexible annuities (also known as living annuities) allow the annuitant to select an income based on the value of assets paid to the insurer by the retirement fund, minus previous income payments plus (minus) market growth on the assets.

In his recent paper Rob Rusconi states that:[18] "one of the most common reasons given by consumers for not purchasing life annuities is they perceive themselves as having incurred a loss should they die soon after purchase. Most immediate annuity products around the world are available with some form of guarantee designed to provide a benefit in the event of early death. The guarantee is most commonly expressed as a guaranteed number or years for which the annuity will be paid whether or not the principle annuitant survives the period".

The opinion expressed by Rusconi above has led to a boom in living annuities. These buy-out annuities are now analysed.

2.5 Living annuities

Living annuities have been marketed and sold by insurers in South Africa since 1996 when General Notice GN 18/96 was issued. Despite nearly 12 years having passed since their advent, there was no statutory definition of a 'living annuity' in South Africa until the Income Tax Act was amended in 2008 and a definition of 'living annuity' was created.[19]

The definition reads:

"living annuity" means a right of a member or former member of a pension fund..., provident fund, or retirement annuity fund, or his or her dependant or nominee, or any subsequent nominee, to an annuity purchased from a person on or after the retirement date ... in respect of which–

(a) the value of the annuity is determined solely by reference to the value of assets which are specified in the annuity agreement and are held by or on behalf of that person for purposes of providing the annuity;

(b) the amount of the annuity is determined in accordance with a method or formula prescribed by the Minister by notice in the Gazette;

(c) the full remaining value of the assets contemplated in paragraph (a) may be paid as a lump sum when the value of those assets becomes at any time less than an amount prescribed by the Minister by notice in the Gazette;

(d) the amount of the annuity is not guaranteed by that person;

(e) on the death of the member or former member, the value of the assets referred to in paragraph (a) may be paid to a dependant or nominee of the member or former

---

18 Rusconi, R (2008), "National annuity markets: Features and implication", OECD working papers on insurance and private pensions, OECD, Doi: 10.1787\240211858078.

19 The definition of 'living annuity' was inserted into the Income Tax Act by Section 2(1)(o) of Act 3/2008.

member as an annuity or lump sum, or, in the absence of a dependant or nominee, to the deceased's estate as a lump sum; and

(f) further requirements regarding the annuity may be prescribed by the Minister by notice in the Gazette.

The attraction of the living annuity is that on death, all is not lost (or paid to the insurer). The remaining value of the assets in the living annuity contract then becomes payable to the deceased annuitants' dependants or estate in the form of an annuity or lump sum. The living annuity therefore overcomes the concerns of many annuitants, as expressed by Rusconi above, and lives until the assets are depleted. This is one of the major selling points of living annuities. As a living annuity continues to pay an income until it is depleted, many insurers expressed concern about the cost of administering 'small' living annuities. The definition of 'living annuities' now allows an insurer to commute small annuities and pay the full value of the assets to the annuitant.

(a) Product design

On retirement from a retirement fund, the fund pays an amount of money (the value of assets) to a registered insurer. The value of assets is specified in the annuity contract.

The annuitant is then able, for the year in question, to draw an income on the value of assets held by the registered insurer at a rate determined by the minister of finance.[20] The annuitant is also able to select the frequency of the income payment (ie monthly, quarterly, annually and in advance or in arrears).

The actual income amount payable to the annuitant is then fixed for that year. By way of example, if at the anniversary date the value of assets is R1 million and the annuitant selects a draw-down rate of 10%, the annuitant will be paid R100,000. If at the next anniversary date the value of assets, despite the previous year's income payment of R100,000, has increased to R1.05 million, then the annuitant can take between 2.5% and 17.5% of R1.05 million – the value of assets.

Once the annual draw-down rate has been selected, the annuitant is unable either to increase or decrease it until the following anniversary date. At each anniversary date the annuitant is able to vary the draw-down rate to best suit the annuitant's income requirements up to the percentage level prescribed by the minister of finance. The percentage is always based on the value of assets as at the anniversary date. This inability to reduce the draw-down rate before the next anniversary date is problematic in a falling financial market. As the annuitant's draw-down amount is determined on the value of assets at the last anniversary date, if this decreases during the period between anniversary dates then the income draw-down will be higher than the determined percentages and capital will be eroded.

On the death of the annuitant, the annuitant's dependants or nominees can continue to receive an income, or can request that the annuity be commuted to a lump sum. Payments will be equal to the value of the assets at the date of death.

As can be seen by paragraph (d) of the definition of 'living annuity', the annuity is not guaranteed. Most insurers allow annuitants to select how the value of assets is

20 Currently between 2.5% and 17.5% of the value of assets.

to be invested. Most insurers allow annuitants to invest the value of assets in collective investment schemes (mutual funds) and across all asset classes (cash, bonds, equities, hedge funds and property).

This investment flexibility provides the annuitant with the opportunity to increase his value of assets through prudent investment selection. The capital growth of the value of assets is tax free. Tax is paid when an income accrues and is paid to the annuitant.

This investment flexibility is most attractive in an upwardly moving market where the value of the assets increases. However, the reverse also applies – if an annuitant (and his adviser) has made a poor investment choice and the value of assets decreases, then the income payable in the subsequent year will be lower.

Some insurers are now offering guarantees within the living annuity. These are usually capital guarantees. This then allows an annuitant to invest a portion of the value of assets in a guaranteed product and the balance in non-guaranteed investment products. Some form of capital protection is thus provided.

It is clear that living annuities do assuage many annuitants' concerns regarding the loss of the capital on death. The South African Actuarial Society[21] specifically records that "the remaining capital is not lost in the event of death after retirement. This is a particularly attractive feature for retirees suffering from poor health".

Despite the attractive features of living annuities, there are also inherent risks, which include longevity, investment and high draw-down. The South African investment community has become aware of these risks and the LOA has issued a specific code of conduct on living annuities. The minister of finance recently reduced the draw-down rates from between 5% and 20% of asset value to between 2.5% and 17. 5%.

2.6 Buy-ins

On July 20 1995 the South African Revenue Service issued General Notice GN8/95 which specifically provided that: "(a) pension fund or provident fund may ... insure a compulsory life annuity at a registered insurer on the member's retirement from service. Such a fund may, however, not insure or pay more than 1 pension for a member on retirement from employment."

This general notice confirmed the established practice of buy-ins.

Buy-in annuities were traditionally used by defined benefit funds which wished to purchase them to ring fence their liability to specific pensioners.

In purchasing the buy-in annuity, the retirement fund does not discharge its obligations to its members. In law, the insurer would pay an amount of money to the retirement fund. The fund would then pay the annuity to the pensioner. If the payment amount from the insurer did not meet the retirement fund's pension obligation in full, then the retirement fund would have to make up the difference. In many instances the annual pension increases, payable by the retirement fund to pensioners, would equal any income increases paid by the insurer to the retirement fund.

What has become clear is that retirement fund trustees must understand the type of annuity policy purchased and the insurer risk taken on by the fund. If the

21 An article prepared by the Actuarial Society of South Africa "as a service to the public", dated April 2000.

insurance policy does not cover the pension risk, the retirement fund would then have to make up any shortfall. This could mean that the retirement fund (if it were a defined benefit fund) may be called up to require the participating employer to fund the shortfall.

The following two scenarios will show some of the risks faced by South African retirement funds and buy-in annuities.

(a) *Scenario 1*[22]

Various retirement funds had purchased a specific 'with bonus' policy from an insurer. The insurer guaranteed the 'capital' value (ie, the premium value), but not the bonus to be declared. Bonuses were declared annually. The quantum of the bonus was determined and set solely by the insurer and based, essentially, on the performance of the assets of the insurer.

Insurers in South Africa are not required by law to separate policyholder assets from shareholder assets. This particular insurer, through internal accounting, mixed the two. Investments made by the insurer were funded using both policyholder and shareholder assets.

On the declaration of a bonus, the full money value of the bonus was placed in a non-vested account. Ten per cent of the total amount in the non-vested account would vest (ie, accrue and become payable) to the retirement fund.

The insurer had contractually reserved the right to not pay out the moneys sitting in the non-vested account if the need arose due to market conditions (ie, a reversionary clause).

Over time, the insurer made certain investments that were not profitable. Policyholder and shareholder assets had been used to purchase and fund these non-performing investments. The insurer was then purchased by another shareholder. In one specific year a 0% bonus was declared.

The new shareholder, on acquisition, went through an exercise where all the insurer's assets were revalued. This revealed that the insurer's assets had previously been substantially overvalued, particularly the property assets. The insurer then exercised the contractual provisions and reversed approximately 10% of the value sitting in the non-vested account (approximately R500 million).

The trustees of the various retirement funds have challenged the declaration of a 0% bonus and the reversal of 10% of the value of assets sitting in the non-vested account. They have also cited several of the erstwhile directors of the insurer in the cases before court claiming breach of the fiduciary duties owed to the policyholders and negligence in the management of the insurer's business. It may be too little, too late as the policy value has now decreased, but the obligations of the retirement funds have not.

The then registrar of long-term insurance[23] has investigated the circumstances

---

22 The facts stated in this example are from a sub judice case that is before the High Court of South Africa (Witwatersrand local Division).

23 See the Inspection Report performed by Merrs-Marx, G and Stander F in terms of the Inspection of Financial Institutions Act (80/1998) titled: Fedsure Life Assurance Ltd, now known as Investec Employee Benefits Ltd. A copy of this report is available at www.fsb.co.za.

surrounding the reversal and the 0% declaration. The inspection report makes certain fundamental recommendations. These include:

- Standardisation of policy documentation – at page 160 paragraph 329 of the inspection report it is stated that "(the) life insurance consumer is inundated with most confusing documentation, fine print, misrepresentations and misunderstanding on the part of the insurers and intermediaries/brokers". The inspection report recommends that the authorities and the long-term insurance industry "initiate (academic) research into desirable and practically feasible standardisation of life insurance and competing financial services products in South Africa. As part of this research, the standardisation suggestions are likely to be determined by policyholder expectations...the research will define and differentiate these expectations to a level that may be used in setting investment and other mandates for the asset management of those portfolios".
- Investigation into bonus policies – the inspection report requested that the Actuarial Society of South Africa "draft guidelines for the product design, investment mandates and termination conditions for... bonus policies, including reversionary bonus policies". Furthermore, it recommended that where there were reversionary clauses in policies of insurance, the policies should not be called guaranteed.
- Separation of policyholders' and shareholders' assets – the authors of the inspection report at page 149, paragraph 294 opine that "a separation of policyholder and shareholder funds would (create) more discipline in weighing the return and the risk profiles of shareholders versus policyholders".

What can be learned from the above? Trustees of retirement funds:

- must understand what policy has been purchased and must be made aware of the limitations of the policy, including any reversionary provisions;
- must be made aware that the retirement fund is taking specific insurer risk; 2008 taught many an investor that even the big can fall and as such, the trustees should annually review whether the retirement fund should own the policy of insurance issued by the insurer; and
- should perform due diligence risk assessments on asset managers and on insurers. The due diligence should be done not just at the inception of the policy, but on a regular basis. The retirement fund trustees must ask specific questions on whether there policyholder assets are separate from shareholder assets and whether these assets are managed differently. Considering the audited annual financial statement of the insurer is essential. This should provide the trustees of retirement funds with some information to assess whether the insurers' assets have changed year on year.

(b) Scenario 2

A retirement fund purchased buy-in with profit annuities from two registered insurers. The inception premium paid to the both insurers was the same money value. One insurer had consistently provided a with-profit bonus which was substantially more than the bonus paid by the other insurer.

In both instances the with-profit bonus was calculated by taking into account the performance of the insurer's assets. On investigation, the retirement fund ascertained that the underperforming insurer had not effectively managed its assets, including key asset management staff leaving the insurer's employ.

The retirement fund has now sought advice as to whether it can claim any damages from the underperforming insurer.

What the above two scenarios quite clearly show is that trustees of retirement funds must be circumspect when choosing to purchase buy-in annuities. Insurer risk, asset management risk and systemic risk must all be taken into account when an insurer is selected. Once purchased, the trustees cannot just hope that the policy promises will be met. Continuous and active checks must be performed on the insurer to ensure that the policy promises will be met.

3. Conclusion

Annuity markets are critically important, for they play a substantial part in determining the well-being of their customers at a time in their lives when their human capital is behind them and the income alternatives are few. These markets will grow in importance as state-sponsored channels and defined benefit occupational plans reduce in significance and as increasing numbers of workers with individual account arrangements reach and pass their retirement age.[24]

Annuities, be they buy-in or buy-out annuities, will remain relevant within the South African retirement industry. With the well-known risks associated with purchasing living annuities, this market will continue to grow because of the perceived lifespan of the living annuity. Product innovation, and more particularly guaranteed products, will be offered to annuitants who purchase living annuities. This will then provide some solace to the annuitant, who will then be able to ensure that their value of assets, or what remains at death, is not lost to the insurer. What will be of interest is how insurers will price the guarantee and, given the current financial malaise, whether those guarantees will, in the end, be guaranteed.

Despite various inspection report recommendations, policy documents remain complex and annuitants (and trustees) find that the product descriptions are full of insurance jargon and complex legal terms. This tends to add some mystique to an already complex product. Oral explanations of the product are often relied upon and, ultimately, to the detriment of the purchaser. Most instances policies specifically exclude oral representation (explanations) and when disputes arise the written (complex) policy document is all binding.

As insurers are the custodians of the retiree's future income, one can only hope that prudence and not irrational exuberance will govern all decisions taken by policy makers. Catastrophic failure at any insurer will bring untold hardship to retirees. The wisdom of Solomon is required.

24 Rusconi, R (2008), *National Annuity Markets: Features and Implication,* OECD working papers on insurance and private pensions, OECD Publishing, OECD. Doi: 10.1787\240211858078 at p 37.

Spain

Juan Alonso
Paz de la Iglesia
Francisco de León
Ashurst

1. Legal framework for external management of employer's pension obligations

Spain implemented Council Directive of October 20 1980 on the protection of employees in the event of the insolvency of the employer by means of Law 30/1995, which introduced an additional provision into Law 8/1987 on pension schemes and pension funds.

The effective date for the entry into force of this provision in November 1995 was, in general, November 16 2002, as different transitional periods were granted in view of the delay in the outsourcing of internal pension funds by many employers.

However, the outsourcing of certain pension obligations contained in different collective bargaining agreements (the so-called 'retirement bonuses' which consist of a single payment to which the employee is entitled once he retires or voluntarily terminates the employment relationship, or just for loyalty to the company, provided that he remains with the company or in the economic sector at the retirement date) off the employer's balance sheet was postponed until December 31 2006. There was considerable concern about the negative economic impact that this could have for small and medium-sized enterprises, whose collective bargaining agreements often contain these pension obligations. With the clear aim of lessening the impact that these obligations could have on employers, the Ministry of Economy and Finance approved Order EHA/3433/2006, dated November 2. This set out special technical terms to outsource this type of obligation.[1]

Credit institutions, insurance undertakings and financial services firms could maintain internal pension funds for any employees with pension rights granted before May 10 1996, provided that the institutions already had internal pension funds and that the employees joined the company before November 16 1999. (To obtain an exemption, these institutions had to apply for authorisation before January 1 2001. In any event, the internal funds had to be supervised by the relevant regulatory bodies of such institutions, under rules that were at least as restrictive as those applicable to external pension funds.) In practice, most of these financial

1 One of these rules allows the hypothetical employment periods of covered employees within the workforce to be taken into account when calculating the insurance premiums or contributions to be made to the group insurance policy or to the pension scheme covering the retirement bonuses. This prevents certain employers from having to pay premiums or contributions if these hypothetical time periods (set out in a table contained in the order, according to different economic sectors) are below a certain percentage.

institutions have already outsourced their pension obligations (as the special regime allowing the maintenance of internal funds applied only to employees who joined before November 16 1999).

The current legal framework on this matter (the outsourcing of pension obligations assumed by employers *vis-à-vis* their employees) is basically contained in the first additional provision of the revised text of the Law on Pension Schemes and Pension Funds, approved by Royal Decree 1/2002 (the Pension Schemes and Pension Funds Law) and the Regulations on the externalisation of pension obligations approved by Royal Decree 1588/1999. Additionally, the Pension Schemes and Pension Funds Law and its Regulations, approved by Royal Decree 304/2004 (applicable not only to employment pension schemes and pension funds, but also to individual and 'associated' schemes – those not sponsored by an employer to cover pension obligations assumed under collective or individual agreements with its employees, but voluntarily entered into by individuals and those sponsored by professional associations or trade unions in favour of their members) and Law 50/1980 on insurance contracts are respectively applicable, on a subsidiary basis, to pension schemes and group insurance policies covering these pension obligations.

According to the provisions set out above, pension obligations assumed by employers must be outsourced either through:

- pension schemes whose assets must be integrated in a pension fund (an 'institution for occupational retirement provision', according to Directive 2003/41/EC on the activities and supervision of institutions for occupational retirement provisions); or
- a group insurance policy entered into with an insurer. These group insurance policies have certain special characteristics, such as restrictions concerning the withdrawals or surrender rights of the employer (although the provisions refer to 'group' insurance policies, it is expressly stated that the policy includes one insured party).

After an amendment dated December 14 2007, a new type of group policy, called an employers' provision scheme has been created as a vehicle for outsourcing (basically, a sub-group of insurance policies whose contributions and benefits have a tax regime equivalent to that of contribution and benefit pension schemes).

Employers seem to prefer group insurance policies, mainly due to the fact that when the funds are externally managed through a group insurance policy, there is no control committee, as in employment pension schemes, where half of the representatives are appointed by the employer or employers or, in the case of pension schemes sponsored jointly by several employers and the other half are representatives of the employers and beneficiaries, the existence of a control committee gives rise to potential operative issues (eg, possible conflicts within the control committee, lack of technical ability in the members of the control committee for the management of investments, lack of rapid response). The new type of group insurance policies mentioned above seems to be, at least theoretically, a good solution to obtain a regime equivalent to pension schemes, but through a formal group insurance policy (the rights of employees and other beneficiaries are protected by the relevant laws and regulations).

Pension obligations are considered to be any of the contingencies which can be covered by means of a pension scheme, according to the Spanish Law and Regulations on Pension Schemes and Pension Funds (eg, retirement, total and permanent disability, death, long-term care), and which are assumed by an employer (either a company, an association or an individual) by virtue of an agreement with the employees (usually through a collective bargaining agreement; but any type of collective or individual agreements applies if it contains 'pension obligations').

2. Buy-ins or buy-outs of pensions

Spanish law and regulations applicable to pension obligations assumed by employers, and to pension schemes and pension funds, provide as follows:

- The employer may outsource its pension obligations through:
  - pension schemes integrated into pension funds;
  - group insurance policies (including employers' provision schemes, which are in fact group insurance policies); or
  - a combination of both types of instrument (pension schemes and group insurance policies).
- In principle, if group insurance policies are used, the Regulations on the outsourcing of pension obligations approved by Royal Decree 1588/1999 state that all pension obligations assumed by an employer must be covered in a single group insurance policy, but it is expressly allowed that different group insurance policies can be used if necessary (eg, if different contingencies and pension obligations exist and are covered under each policy, there are different groups of insured parties with different professional qualifications or other objective factors are accepted in a collective agreement with the employees).
- In practice, different vehicles (a pension scheme integrated in a pension fund plus one or more group insurance policies or several group insurance policies) are used jointly by the same employer. A typical example would be that of the senior executives of an employer: their pension rights *vis-à-vis* the employer can be so significant that it is not possible to cover them through the general pension scheme of the company integrated in a pension fund, since the contributions to pension schemes are subject to an annual quantitative limit (currently €10,000 for most employees and €12,500 for members over 50; those limits apply to the aggregate contribution of the employee and the employer), which can make it impossible for the pension scheme to cope with its obligations. In this context, 'ordinary' employees are usually covered by the pension scheme, while the pension obligations for senior executives are insured under group insurance policies. Other examples are retired employees or the families of deceased employees (eg, widows and widowers, orphans) who are entitled to receive life annuities after the death of the insured employee. These groups are usually 'segregated' from active employees and are covered by different group policies, as the amount of the pension obligations in relation to these groups can be calculated more easily than those for the active employees (where there are continuous leavers, dismissals and new

arrivals, so premiums or contributions have to be constantly adjusted). In this context, it is quite common to see companies where there is a group insurance policy (or a pension scheme) covering the employer's pension obligations *vis-à-vis* the active employees and another policy covering the annuities in favour of retired employees, widows, orphans, etc.

- All the different situations set out above could take place during the life of a single pension scheme or a group insurance policy (ie, where an ordinary employee becomes a senior executive with a higher pension entitlement and then retires, he can be removed from the existing scheme or policy and integrated into the appropriate scheme). These movements are, in general, tax neutral[2] and legal. In a certain sense, these movements could be seen as a buy-out from the existing schemes or policies.
- There are other situations (eg, the employee joins a new employer with its own pension scheme or group policy), where such movements are possible.
- The Regulations on Pension Schemes and Pension Funds, approved by Royal Decree 304/2004 and amended by other provisions (among others, Royal Decree 1684/2007), foresee the possibility for the pension scheme, in respect of defined benefits granted under the scheme or those benefits determined on an actuarial basis, to enter into insurance policies with an insurance company which would cover these benefits. A normal example would be a pension scheme covering, among other contingencies, the risk of death. In this scenario, it is possible for the pension scheme (through its control committee – a body composed of the representatives of the members and the beneficiaries of the scheme and of the employer) to enter into an insurance policy covering such risk (usually these policies are entered on an annual basis and are tacitly renewable every year, which avoids significant deviations in the mortality rates in favour of the insurer). This would be the more typical example of a buy-in.

2.1 Liability in the event of incorrect cover

The following should be noted regarding the risk in relation to pension obligations covered under group insurance policies (either entered into directly by the employer or by a pension scheme):

- If pension obligations have been correctly outsourced (eg, the policy correctly covers all the risks corresponding to the pension obligations assumed by the employer, contains the mandatory provisions restricting the possibility of withdrawal or surrender by the employer), this implies in principle that the employer/policyholder no longer bears any risk.
- If mistakes have been made when calculating the premiums or benefits under the policy, the question of who must bear that risk (the policyholder, the employer, the pension scheme or the insurance undertaking) must be resolved on a case-by-case basis. For instance, if the employer provided

2 Although the change from an insurance scheme to a pension scheme will impact on the personal income tax of the beneficiary in respect of the benefits obtained.

incorrect information about the age of its employees and the premiums paid are not enough to cover the insured risk, then the employer will be responsible for any deficit and will be obliged to make an additional contribution to the insurer. If the insurance company becomes insolvent, in principle, any rights under the policy will have absolute priority over the assets covering the technical provisions of the insurer (according to the implementation of Directive 2001/17/EC on the winding-up of insurance undertakings).[3] If, after liquidation, the pension obligations are not covered, it would arguably be a matter of how the collective agreement from which the pension obligations arose was drafted which would determine whether the employee – or the pension scheme – bears any risk.

Case law in respect of this matter seems to depend on the circumstances of each individual case. According to the Law on Labour Judicial Proceedings, only the labour courts can decide any voluntary social provision system arising from an employment relationship (irrespective of whether the instrument to cover these benefits is a pension scheme or an insurance policy). Existing case law can be summarised as follows:[4]

- The labour courts have considered that the employer must be held liable if:
  - the employer has not entered into a group insurance policy covering the risks set out in the applicable collective bargaining agreement;
  - the insurance policy excludes certain risks or the sum insured is lower than that set forth in the applicable agreement;
  - there is no proper insurance policy covering the pension obligations of the employer, just professional liability insurance; or
  - the insurance policy had not been entered into when the right to the benefit was accrued, the policy has been terminated by means of the surrender right exercised by the employer or the employer has not notified the affected employee of the need to adhere to the new terms and conditions of the insurance policy (if there was a change in the pension obligations covered).

---

3 Spain has implemented the EU Directive on winding-up of insurance undertakings, choosing the option setting out an absolute priority for the credit rights of insured parties and beneficiaries under the policies in respect of the assets which cover the technical provisions of the insurance undertaking. However, under the law there is no specific right over the specific assets covering the technical provisions of a certain insurance policy (ie, all the insured parties and beneficiaries have the same priority over all the assets which cover the technical provisions of the insurance undertaking). Additionally, the *Consorcio de Compensación de Seguros* (a public entity in which not only the Ministry of Economy and Finance, but also insurance companies take part) can be appointed by the Ministry of Economy and Finance as the liquidator of insurers that become insolvent. In such cases appointment of the *Consorcio* implies that bankruptcy proceedings and judicial actions cannot be initiated against the insolvent insurer. This public body is financed by a surcharge on all insurance premiums which currently amounts to three per thousand of the premium (except for life and political risk insurance). It can anticipate the credit rights of the insured parties and beneficiaries (and third parties covered by general liability policies) after it has calculated the net worth of the insolvent company. Although, unlike the UK Financial Services Compensation Scheme no minimum amounts are guaranteed, in practice payments by the *Consorcio* always exceed 90% of the amount of the credit rights of insured parties, beneficiaries and third parties.

4 According to "*Memento Práctico Francis Lefebvre. Previsión Social* 2003-2004", several authors, pages 124 and 125.

- The labour courts tend to understand that the liability must be borne by the insurer if the employer clearly enters into the group insurance policy for the purposes of covering its pension obligations arising from the applicable collective bargaining agreement, based on the fact that the insurance undertaking is a specialised entity, which must be aware of the obligations assumed by the employer under the collective bargaining agreement, the insurer being obliged to adopt the necessary technical measures which adequate the policy to the collective agreement.
- However, this is not the unanimous position of the courts, as there have been certain decisions in which the insurer was not deemed to be liable for the lack of adequacy between the insurance policy and the pension obligations arising from the collective bargaining agreement, as the insurer was not an obliged subject under the collective agreement.
- Finally, it is understood that neither the employer nor the insurer must be held liable if the obligation assumed by the employer is limited and the employee acted in bad faith when he notified the insurer of a medical condition. However, the courts understand that any omission on behalf of the beneficiary can be taken into account, thus excluding the insurer's liability, only if the discrepancy between his statement and the actual situation is evident and does not due to the limited questions contained in the health questionnaire submitted by the insurer. (In other words, as stated in the case law of the civil courts in relation to life and health insurance policies and in accordance with the Law on Insurance Contracts, if the insurer did not ask the relevant question in the health questionnaire or the questionnaire was not submitted to the insured party, then the insured party could not have acted in bad faith when he omitted details about his health condition).

Sweden

Jenny Jilmstad
Ashurst Advokatbyrå AB

1. Introduction

The Swedish pension system is divided into three pillars. The first state mandatory pillar is a pay-as-you-go system, where money collected is used to pay for current pension commitments. The current working population pays the pensions of the retired part of the population through the tax system. The contribution level is 18.5%. The second pillar consists of supplementary occupational pensions based on collective bargaining agreements, which could be regarded as quasi-mandatory due to the Swedish model of industrial relations. The third pillar is voluntary and is made up of voluntary contributions to an individual pension by means of private savings.

This chapter reviews the Swedish pension system and examines how an employer can secure and limit possible liabilities. There are three ways to ensure that pension commitments can be met. They can be secured through the accounting of a pension debt in the balance sheet, through transfers to a pension fund or through paying a pension insurance premium to an insurance company. Pension insurance companies also help to secure the pension commitment in Sweden, but the employer is always responsible for paying the insurance premiums.

The vast majority of occupational pensions derive from collective bargaining agreements. The collective bargaining agreement that applies to each sector sets the level of the occupational pension (ie, the cost for the employer). The collective agreements form the basis of an occupational pension. We also present a brief introduction to the labour market and the Swedish model of industrial relations.

2. The labour market

2.1 Introduction

There are around 4.1 million employees in Sweden and the majority are employed in the private sector. However, over the past few decades the public sector has expanded significantly and up to 40% of all employees are now public employees.[1]

Employees in Sweden are traditionally divided into three groups: manual (or blue-collar) workers; white-collar workers; and professionals (normally university-educated employees). The distinction has no legal basis and no differentiation is made in the legislation between these employee categories. The legislation has sought to remove the differences that exist in collective agreements where white-

1 National Statistics Office (SCB), www.scb.se, August 10 2008.

collar workers and professionals traditionally enjoyed more favourable employment conditions than blue-collar workers.

The division of employees into three categories is today less meaningful, particularly as regards the borderlines. However, these divisions are still upheld in the area of pensions.

(a) *Labour market unions*

The Swedish model is characterised by a high degree of representation, even though trade union numbers are currently falling. This applies to both employees and employers. The trade union movement is divided into three major federations: one for blue-collar workers, one for white-collar workers and one for professional employees.

The Swedish Federation of Unions (LO) represents blue-collar workers. With 1.7 million members (45% of them women), it represents some 40% of all Swedish employees.[2] Historically, unions in private industry were dominant, but over the past few decades a shift has taken place with regard to the growth of public sector employment. LO is based on political foundations.

White-collar workers are organised in the Federation of White-Collar Workers (TCO). This consists of 16 sectoral unions which cover both the private and public sectors. The total membership amounts to some 1.2 million employees (more than 60% of them women).[3] TCO often appears within the White-Collar Workers' Council for Negotiation and Cooperation. TCO has no political affiliation.

SACO represents mostly university-educated employees and comprises 24 different unions. Its total membership amounts to almost 600,000 (about 50% of whom are women).[4] The large number of affiliated unions as compared with SACO's modest membership reflects the fact that most of the unions within SACO are occupational unions, many with quite small memberships. SACO maintains a neutral position in political matters.

Supervisory staff have had their own union since 1905. This was known as the Swedish Union of Supervisory Staff. In 1994, it changed its name to *Ledarna* ('The Leaders').

(b) *Employer unions*

Despite the high degree of representation among Swedish employers, many small employers do not belong to any association. However, many of these non-organised employers actually apply collective agreements and pension schemes for their respective industries.

The regulation of employment relationships in the public sector is basically the same as in the private sector, so it can be safely stated that employment has been 'privatised' in Sweden. Public employers need representation in employment-related matters in the same way as private employers.

---

2 Swedish Federation of Trade Unions membership statistics December 31 2007, www.lo.se, October 8 2008.

3 TCO website, www.tco.se, October 10 2008.

4 SACO membership statistics, December 31 2007, www.saco.se, October 10 2008.

The private sector is dominated by what was formerly the Swedish Employers' Federation (SAF), which in April 2001 merged with the Federation of Swedish Industries, a former trade association, to form *Svenskt Näringsliv* – the Confederation of Swedish Enterprise. The SAF was originally founded in 1902 primarily as a form of defence against the manual-worker union movement. In 2008 its membership consisted of 50 such organisations, one for each branch of economic activity in the private sector. In 2008 the number of companies belonging to these sectoral-level associations totalled around 54,000, with approximately 1.6 million employees. Although the majority are small businesses (some 30,000 companies have fewer than 10 employees), large companies are dominant within the federation.[5]

(c) Self-regulation

Both unions and employers' associations are almost completely self-regulating. They are non-profit making associations and as such are not covered by legislation. Proposals have been made from time to time for statutory regulation of their activities and operations, but these have never come to anything. The unions are opposed to any such legislation and have always been able to fend off all proposals of this kind.

No state or other authority oversees the activities or functioning of the collective organisations. Nor can any authority impose, arrange, conduct or monitor ballots within the unions. They are not obliged to render accounts or otherwise report to any state authority. The absence of legislative regulation means they have considerable freedom to run their internal affairs.

3. Collective bargaining and agreement structure

3.1 General remarks

The collective bargaining system in Sweden's labour market has always been centralised. Few market economies have had a more centralised system. At present, however, a process of decentralisation is taking place. Collective bargaining agreements can be concluded at national, sectoral or local (company) level. Nowadays, the key negotiations usually take place at sectoral level.

Legally binding collective agreements can be concluded at all three bargaining levels. However, at national level neither the trade union federations nor the employers' confederation can sign agreements which are binding on their member organisations. Agreements concluded at this level nevertheless become collective agreements when they are adopted by the respective organisations at sectoral level.

Normally there is a collective agreement for each branch of economic activity. The most important is probably that in the engineering industry – the so-called Engineering Agreement – which often serves as template for other collective bargaining agreements. The Engineering Agreement was concluded between, on the employee side, the Metalworkers' Union, the Swedish Engineers Union and the Leaders and, on the employer side, the Association of Engineering Employers. It was

5 Svenskt Näringsliv website, www.svensktnaringsliv.se, 8 October 2008.

signed for the first time in 1905 and it regulates employment relationships in a large number of key industries.

Notice of the intention to take industrial action can be given at sectoral level. The negotiations are often led by mediators, at least during the closing stage. New rules introduced in 2000 mean that the Mediation Agency is now empowered to initiate compulsory mediation; the process they regulate is still predominantly voluntary in nature.[6]

The final bargaining process takes place at local company level. It is here that much of the scope of pay increases agreed at sectoral level is actually distributed. Bargaining at local level can either be collective or take the form of individual pay negotiations. It is usually subject to the peace obligation (ie, industrial action is not legally permitted).

In the public sector, the bargaining system is still centralised. The Swedish Agency for Government Employers negotiates on behalf of the state sector and the Federation of Local Authorities and Federation of Provincial Councils negotiate on behalf of the local government sector. As mentioned, these two sectors account for almost 40% of employees.

In the private sector the most important collective bargaining agreement regarding pensions is the ITP pension scheme for supervisors and white-collar workers. For blue-collar workers it is the SAF-LO collectively agreed occupational pension scheme for blue-collar workers.

The state pension system is supplemented by different pension schemes established under collective agreements. These are known as collectively agreed occupational pensions.

4. Swedish pension system

The Swedish pension system can be divided into three different parts or pillars.

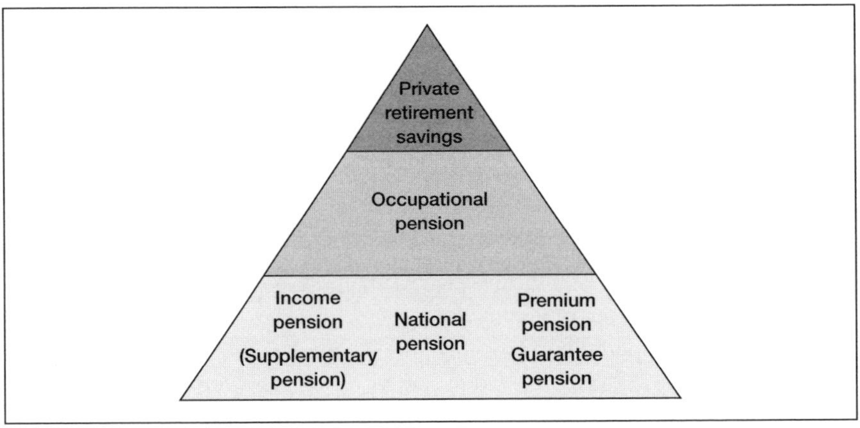

4.1 National pension

The national pension consists of three or four parts. The fourth part is the supplementary pension, which is administered by the National Insurance Office. The pension is primarily based upon the individual's total taxable life income (entitled pension income = before-tax income minus 7%), and has both a maximum and a minimum level. The maximum level equals 7.5 times basic income[7] per year (in 2008, the maximum level equals 7.5 x Skr48,000 = Skr360,000), and any amount exceeding this will not be counted when calculating the national pension. The minimum level, which must be exceeded to have any right to national pension at all, is currently 0.423 times basic income per year – approximately Skr17,343.[8]

There is also an entitlement to a pension amount during periods where no direct income is received (eg, due to military service, pregnancy, or unemployment). An individual in receipt of ordinary social security payments is not entitled to a pension.

4.2 Income pension

This is based on pensionable income, which consists of the earnings from work and/or pension-entitled amounts earned due to pregnancy, unemployment etc. Of the pensionable income, 16% constitutes the pension right for income pension, which is determined and calculated on an annual basis. The right to an income pension depends on factors such as salary, number of years worked and retirement age. Pension rights are accumulated on the individual's pension account. As described above, the income pension system is an indexed system, where the pensions paid to those who have retired are financed by payments of those currently in work (partly by income tax paid by the individual and partly by social security contributions paid by the employer). As the income pension system is an indexed system, the pension rights on the individual's pension account do not correspond to actual money.

4.3 Supplementary pension

This applies only to those born between 1938 and 1954 and the size of the supplementary pension depends on the individual's year of birth. The reason behind the supplementary pension and why it is limited to certain age groups is due to major changes in the Swedish pension system. The new plan resulted in lower pensions for individuals who had already earned pension rights under the old system. The supplementary pension was introduced to compensate those generations. For those born between 1938 and 1954, the national pension consists of an income pension, a premium pension and a supplementary pension. This is calculated based on pension rights earned under the old system. The supplementary pension constitutes a larger part of the total national pension the earlier a person is born.

---

6 The Mediation Agency was founded in 2000. Its main tasks are to mediate in labour disputes, to promote an efficient wage formation process and to provide official statistics on wages and salaries in Sweden. Mediators are not permanently employed by the agency, but are appointed for each individual dispute. Most of them have previously served as negotiators with one or other of the social partners. They are usually veterans with considerable experience in their field.

7 The basic amount is an amount used to calculate various types of contribution and remuneration (eg pensions, social allowances etc). There are three types of basic amount:
- the basic income amount, based on the annual national income index;
- the basic price amount, based on the annual consumer price index; and
- the basic marked-up amount.

The basic income amount for 2008 is Skr48,000; the basic price amount is Skr41,000; and the basic marked-up amount is Skr41,800.

8 The National Government Employee Pensions Board (SPV) website: www.spv.se, October 8 2008.

4.4 Premium pension

Unlike the national pension, the premium pension right corresponds to actual money and is 2.5% of the annual pensionable income. The amount is placed in an individual account administered by the Premium Pensions Authority (PPA). The individual can then choose to invest the money in different pension funds which have been approved and registered with the PPA. An individual can currently choose to invest in some 800 different funds and the supply of funds includes share funds, bond funds, mixed funds, funds targeting certain generations etc. If an individual does not make an active choice, the premium pension money is invested in the *Premiesparfonden*, a global share fund managed and administered by the governmental Seventh AP Fund. Although the premium pension rights correspond to money that is available for investments, the actual premium pension that is paid out once the individual has retired is calculated based on an index. The method for calculating the pension is different from how the income pension is calculated.

4.5 Guarantee pension

The guarantee pension provides a basic security for those not entitled to the income pension, supplementary pension or premium pension due to no, or very low, levels of income. Everyone who has been a Swedish resident for more than three years is entitled to a guarantee pension. In order to receive full guarantee pension, the individual must have been resident for at least 40 years between the ages of 16 and 64. The pension decreases in relation to the number of years below 40 for which the person has been a Swedish resident (thus, a person who has been a Swedish resident for 20 years is entitled to half a guarantee pension). The guarantee pension is wholly financed by taxes and can be paid from the age of 65. The pension equals 2.13 price basic amounts (Skr87,330) for single senior citizens and 1.9 price basic amounts (Skr79,420) for those who are married.

5. Occupational pension

The middle tier of the Swedish pension pyramid is the occupational pension. This is wholly paid by the employer and is regulated by agreements between employers and employees, often through collective agreements, but in certain cases in the individual contract of employment. The pension may be either fee or benefit defined. The former means that the pension is based on premiums paid by the employer which the employee can decide to invest into different pension funds, whereas the latter guarantees the employee a certain level of pension, calculated as a percentage of the employee's final salary. The most important occupational pensions are listed below.

5.1 Government employees

Most government employees are covered by the PA 03 agreement. According to this agreement, employees are granted a combination of fee and benefit-defined pension. Pension rights are earned from the age of 23 to the age of 65 (60 or 61 for certain categories of employee). The fee-defined pension rights are calculated as 2.5% of annual salary up to a maximum of 30 income basic amounts (Skr1.44 million). The employee can choose which pension fund manager (eg, bank, insurance company) should administer the pension capital and how it should be invested. An additional 2% of annual salary is paid by the employer, but this cannot be invested by the employee. It is instead invested in traditional pension insurance with a guaranteed rate of interest. There is also a benefit-defined section in the PA 03 agreement for those with salaries over 7.5 times the income basic amounts (Skr360,000). The benefit-defined pension is earned after 28 and the percentage of the final salary varies between 60% and 65%, depending on year of birth, duration of employment etc.

5.2 Employees within the counties and municipalities etc

As of 2006, employees within the counties, the municipalities, the church and certain companies with operations closely related to the functions of the municipalities and counties are covered by the KAP–KL agreement. The agreement is mainly fee defined but also contains a benefit-defined amount. Employees can start to earn pension rights from the age of 21. For salaries up to 30 income basic amounts, the employer pays between 4% and 4.5% of the annual salary. The employee chooses his or her pension fund manager from among some 20 different insurance companies and how the pension capital should be invested. If no choice is made, the pension capital will be invested in a traditional life insurance. The benefit-defined part of the insurance covers salaries above 7.5 income basic amounts. The rate of remuneration (between 55% and 62.5% of salary up to 20 income basic amounts and between 27.5% and 31.25% for salary between 20 and 30 income basic amounts) varies depending on the employee's annual salary and year of birth. The same flexibility as for governmental employees applies in respect of retirement age, period of payment, etc.

5.3 Employees within the private sector

(a) The LO-area

Employees are covered by the SAF-LO collectively agreed occupational pension scheme for blue-collar workers, a fee-defined contractual insurance. The employer pays 3.5% of the salary, which is then invested by the employee.

(b) White-collar workers

The ITP agreement covers most white-collar workers, supervisors and professionals. For those born in 1979 or later, the pension is fee determined. On April 25 2006 the Confederation of Swedish Enterprise and PTK reached an agreement about the contents of the new ITP Agreement. The new plan came into force on July 1 2007 with retroactive application to most components with effect from January 2007. The plan primarily covers salaried employees born in or after 1979. Salaried employees born in or before 1978 will continue to be covered by the old ITP plan. The new plan is a defined contribution plan and is open to competition through procurement of insurance providers with a decision by the ITP Committee in February 2007.

6. Securing pension commitments – risk elimination

6.1 Introduction

A pension commitment is a part of the compensation that is agreed upon with an employer as reward for the work of the employee. As stated above, in the private sector this is the ITP pension scheme for white-collar workers and supervisors within industry and commerce, and the SAF-LO collectively agreed occupational pension scheme for blue-collar workers.

The pension commitment is a binding agreement for future pension payments, meaning that the employee continuously earns a right to a pension. There are three specifically regulated ways to ensure that the pension commitment will be met on the day the pension is due to commence: through the accounting of a pension debt in the balance sheet; through transfers to a pension fund; or through paying a pension insurance premium. The Securing Pension Commitments Act (531/1967) deals with securing pension commitments according to the first two alternatives. The purpose of the act is to protect pension rights that are acquired through work. It is compulsory and cannot be deviated from. Essential regulations in the act deal with the situation where a business operation transfers from one employer to another and when an employer ceases to trade.

6.2 Securing through the accounting of a pension debt in the balance sheet

The act regulates the accounting of a pension liability as a pension provision on the balance sheet.[9] In general, all kinds of pensions can be accounted for in this way, but normally it is only old-age pensions that are treated as a provision on the balance sheet. The employer will not have to make any actual cash payments until the employee has reached the age of retirement, but transfers to the pension provision will affect the profit and loss statement.

It is mostly the largest corporations that avail of the possibility to account for a pension provision on the balance sheet. The pension liability derives from the agreed pension commitment. The pension provision should at any given time be valued to the present value of the commitment, as agreed between employer and employee or in collective agreements. The size of the pension provision will vary over time, as the employer's commitment increases the longer a person is employed or until he retires. Once the former employee has started receiving pension payments, the pension provision will decrease until it finally disappears once the payments have expired.

A pension provision on the balance sheet will not secure the pensions *per se*. The pension liability must instead be secured by credit insurance. The insurance company Pensionsgaranti FPG (FPG) signs the insurance. FPG insures corporate pension liabilities as a fundamental element of the insurance, enabling the company to post its pension commitments as a liability on its balance sheet. The business pays a credit insurance premium to FPG annually. The level of the premium varies.

Accordingly, pension assets can be utilised as a source of long-term funding,

---

9 Articles 5 to 8 in the act. In addition, there are regulations in the Annual Accounts Act and in the Income Tax Act.

while guaranteeing employee pensions. Regardless of what happens to the company itself, staff will still receive their pensions. If the business becomes insolvent, FPG redeems the pension liability by purchasing pension insurance.

6.3 Transfers to a pension fund

By starting a specific type of foundation, a pension fund, the employer can secure occupational pensions. A pension fund is a foundation/trust established by the employer with one purpose only – to secure the pension commitment to the employees and their surviving relatives. A pension fund is formed in accordance with the Foundation Act and the employer decides the statutes for the pension fund.

Statutes regulate which kind of employees have their pension commitments secured by the pension fund. The fund is administered by a board of directors with equal representatives for the employer and the employees. The board is supervised by the County Administrative Board. The board of directors will administer the capital allocated by the employer for pensions, and ensure that the capital available is invested with a satisfactory yield and that the funds are not used for any other purpose than those stated in the statutes of the pension fund. All employees, current and former, and their survivors can be included by the objective of the pension fund.

The County Administrative Board is basically focused on securing the interests of pension creditors. The County Administrative Board supervises placements and can give advice about them.

The employer decides how much money will be placed in the pension fund. Once the employer has reserved money into the fund, it cannot be paid back to the employer unless it is used to secure pensions. The pensions fund's only purpose is to secure the employer's pension commitments. Pensions are not paid by the pension fund; instead, the employer pays the pensions and receives reimbursement from the pension fund. Under this system the employer gets back the money it paid into the pension fund. Reimbursement could only concern the cost for an employee who, according to the statutes of the pension fund, is comprised of the pension commitment.

6.4 Payment of a pension insurance premium to an insurance company

Pension insurance is a tax-deductible life-interest insurance. Pensions insurance is normally signed either as traditional pensions insurance or as a unit-linked insurance. Traditionally, guaranteed amounts are paid to the insurance holder. In unit-linked insurance, the customer is taking the risk and there are no guarantees that there will be any yields.

An employer that is bound by a collective bargaining agreement to accept the ITP scheme should notify the insurance company when applying for a pension agreement. The employer is the insurance holder and the employees are the insured persons. The pension premium paid by the employer will cover all future payments of pensions. The cost of the pension premium is decided from technical insurance terms such as interest, expected length of life, taxes and operating expenses.

(a) Alecta – an insurance company example

Alecta is a mutual life insurance company (and one of the key players in the pensions insurance market). This means that the company is owned by the policyholders (companies) and the insureds (the companies' employees), and that any surplus in operations is returned to the policyholders and the insureds in the form of a bonus.

Alecta has two product segments: pensions and disability and life insurance. Pension products include the savings products retirement pension, ITPK (a supplementary retirement pension) and a family pension. Most of the retirement and family pension is a defined benefit pension. The retirement pension in the new ITP plan and ITPK is a defined contribution pension, for which Alecta offers the Alecta Optimal Pension.

Alecta is assigned by the collective agreement parties, the Confederation of Swedish Enterprise and the White-Collar Workers' Council for Negotiation and Cooperation to manage the ITP plan. Since July 1 2007, Alecta has been one of five suppliers of traditional insurance in the new defined contribution ITP plan.

The role of the insurance company is largely unchanged with regard to both the retirement pension within the old ITP plan and private sector salaried employees' disability insurance and family cover under both the old and new ITP plan.

Alecta has also been involved in the procurement process for the private sector blue-collar workers' pension plan. The SAF-LO collectively agreed an occupational pension scheme for blue-collar workers and Alecta submitted a tender. The process was broken off at the end of 2007.

Alecta bases its calculations on age and salary. The information forms the basis of the charges on the monthly invoice. Salary changes also affect the cost for every employee. Employees who are the same age and have the same salary can still cost a different amount, as one may have a higher salary or a longer qualification period than the other. This means that one employee has made more pension contributions so the scheme pays lower premiums for him.

Some large companies have chosen to affiliate themselves to FPG/PRI. This means that the company itself has assumed the rule of insurance company towards its employees with regard to their retirement pensions. PRI Pensionstjänst AB calculates the company's pension liability to its employees and pays pensions from the company with the help of Alecta. The pension liability is secured by the company taking out credit insurance with the insurance company FPG.

In the ITP system employees start earning pension rights from the age of 25. The employer pays 4.5% for salaries up to Skr30,000 per month and 30% on any salary exceeding Skr30,000. Fifty per cent of the pension rights are invested in traditional pension insurance; the rest is placed in a pension fund according to the employees' instructions. For those born before 1979, the fee-determined ITP is complemented by the benefit-defined ITPK. The employer pays an annual ITPK premium equivalent to 2% of the employee's annual salary from the year the employee turns 28. This is invested by the employee.

6.5 Transfer of pension commitments

The act enables the transfer of pension commitments when a business operation is being transferred.[10] However, this is possible only if the holder of the commitment consents, a rule that derives from the general principle that a creditor must consent to a change of debtor. The supervisory authority may give its permission to transfer pension commitments without consent if it finds the successor is able to underwrite the commitments. The application for consent need not involve a large number of pension commitments and does not require any consultation with the individual pension holders. Thus, the employer can apply for permission directly from the supervisory authority instead of contacting the individual pension holders. The application can be filed by the assignor as well as the assignee.

The pension commitments of employees who do not continue their employment in the successor's business operation can also be transferred. The act then allows a retroactive service with the new operator. This means that even commitments referring to retired persons and fee policy owners can be transferred.

According to the preparatory work of the act, the transfer of pension commitments can be carried out even if only a certain line of the business operation is being transferred.[11] The government has stated that if both parties to a transfer agreement regarding a certain part of the business operation agree that the buyer will take over the responsibility for the seller's pension commitments, this agreement should be valid according to general legal maxims in accordance with stated law. There is some uncertainty as to how large the transferred part of the business operation must be. It is clear that it needs to be an easily distinguishable operation.

In its Decision RÅ 1997 ref 30 II, the Supreme Administrative Court has accepted that the responsibility for a pension commitment transfers even if the business operation itself does not transfer. However, a prerequisite for this is the consent of the individual pension holder. In case of a transfer of a pension fund, a transfer of the business operation or a part of it is necessary.

The preparatory work accepts that pension commitments are separated and transferred to different business operators in connection to a separation of different lines of the business operation.[12] Regarding pension funds, the legal position has become unclear due to some contradictory decisions. The County Administrative Board of Stockholm does, however, seem to accept the division of pension funds. The board approved the division of the pension funds of Swedish bank SEB, a matter that was fiscally decided by the Supreme Administrative Court in Decision RÅ 2001 ref 45.

When a pension commitment covered by Article 23, paragraph 1 is credit insured by the insurance company Pensionsgaranti, a transfer of the pension commitment is not allowed under the terms of insurance unless the insurance company agrees that the transferee has a credit insurance covering the transferred pension commitment.

6.6 Mergers under the Companies Act

The act contains regulations regarding mergers according to the Companies Act (551/2005) and the Economic Associations Act (667/1987).[13] It states that if any other

10 Article 23, para 1.
11 Governmental bill 1967: 83 pp 166–167.
12 Governmental Bill 1967:83 p 167.
13 Article 23, para 2.

act contains regulations regarding the rights of creditors in mergers, these are to be applied instead of paragraph 1. Furthermore, paragraph 2 states that the supervising authority may approve that the pension claimants need not be notified regarding the merger. This also applies to issues regarding distribution of profits and reduction of share capital and reserve fund that, according to the Companies Act, are to be handled by a court.

If the responsibility for a pension commitment is transferred, the commitment has the same legal effect as if the employee had been employed by the successor from the day his employment with the predecessor began. According to the preparatory work, this provision mainly addresses fiscal issues. The act also states that once the succession of a pension commitment has taken place, the transferor is discharged from its responsibility according to the commitment.[14]

6.7 Consideration

For the successor to accept the transfer of the responsibility for pension commitments, some form of consideration from the predecessor is usually required. Most commonly, this is done through a set-off against the value of transferred assets. The consideration often corresponds to the estimated pension reserve for the commitments. The pension reserve is defined in Article 6 of the act as the debt of the business owner for obligations according to national pension plans and for the accrued part of such pensions undertaken that are not yet accounted for. However, the pension reserve does not always equal the current value of the pension commitments. Important factors to be considered when calculating the consideration are the discount interest charge used to estimate the pension reserve and the indexing set out in the commitments. The transfer of a pension fund is usually allowed with increased consideration.

Article 24 applies in cases where the transfer of pension commitments is carried out according to Article 23 of the act and the transferring company also has a pension fund. Here, the supervising authority shall decide, when considering the objective of the fund, whether and on what conditions the fund shall be transferred to the successor. The most important consideration will be the pension holders' interest in getting their pensions secured. The supervising authority decides how any potential profit will be used. Usually it agrees that the profit can remain after the transfer, unless there are particular grounds against this. The third and final paragraph of Article 24 states that if there are particular grounds, the supervising authority may provide that the pension fund, after the transfer, shall refer only those pension policy holders who had a pensions claim against the predecessor. A merger would be one situation where this might be accepted. In most cases, however, the transferred pension fund will secure the pension commitments given by the predecessor and those given by the company taking over the fund.

---

14 *Ibid*, para 3.

7. No succession of pension commitments

7.1 General remarks

If an employer decides to cease trading, it should secure the accrued part of its pension commitments by purchasing pension insurance.[15] However, this is not necessary if responsibility for the commitments has transferred according to the act or if a pension fund is securing the commitments. As long as the responsibility has not been transferred and another pension fund is not securing the commitments, the employer can purchase pension insurance to cover its commitments. If an employer ceases its business activity without transferring its pension fund, the fund must be liquidated.[16] The remaining assets within the pension fund will, after the fund has paid off its own debts, be used to purchase pension insurance to cover its commitments or, if the supervising authority approves, to pay off such claims. The employer will be forced to buy pension insurance in accordance with Article 25 of the act only if the assets in the fund are insufficient.

Article 25 applies only where an employer ceases its business operations entirely.[17] Thus, it does not apply if a subsidiary ceases to trade. There is no obligation to put pension insurance in place for commitments which exist only when a subsidiary ceases to exist or is transferred without succession of the pension commitments.

One question is how the word 'cease' should be interpreted. When does the article apply? The requirement that the employer buy insurance is important only if the employer is an individual or a legal person and the business ceases to exist, but the organisation remains. As an example, a corporation might convert from a sales company to a real estate company. However, if this means that the organisation ceases to exist, the company will go into liquidation. (In this example, a real estate company refers to a company that holds real estate as a passive capital investment and has no other kind of business.) A business operation that is temporarily put on hold while it is reorganised does not cease to exist.[18] Thus, a certain period of extension to restart the business seems to exist when a proprietor of business terminates its business operations.

7.2 Exceptions

The act contains two exceptions where the requirement to purchase pension insurance does not apply even though business operations have ceased and responsibility for the pension commitments has not been transferred. The first is when the pension commitment is credit insured and the second is when the supervising authority allows an exception. Where the commitment is insured, it is secured by the insurance. The fact that the supervising authority can grant an exception means only that the pension commitment may stay with the predecessor.

According to the second paragraph of Article 25, the supervising authority may

15 Article 25.
16 Articles 19 to 21.
17 Governmental Bill 1967:83 pp 166–167.
18 Governmental Bill 1967:83 p 156.

also allow the purchase to be spread over a maximum of three years. The provision was amended to eliminate employers' potential difficulties in paying one single premium.

The third paragraph of Article 25 states that the pension creditor may bring an action against the employer if it does not fulfil its duties according to the provision. If the creditor does not bring an action, an action may instead be brought by a trade union which may be regarded as representing the group to which the employee belongs. The employee need not be a member of the union.

8. Conclusion

In Sweden, the majority of employers are bound by collectively agreed pension schemes. This forces them to pay occupational pensions and determines the cost for the employer. Employers that are not formally bound by any agreement also commonly apply the agreed pension schemes as they are standard in the labour market. The system can therefore be labelled quasi-mandatory. As has been stated above, employers must secure their pension commitments and we have presented and discussed the three main options available in this respect. It is usually the larger companies that organise a pension fund linked to the company. The insurance solution is the easiest way for most employers to buy out their pension liabilities.

United States

Jake R Downing
Robert P Flanagan
Mary K Samsa
Seyfarth Shaw LLP

---

1. Introduction

In recent years, sponsors of traditional defined benefit pension plans in the United States have been exploring ways to reduce or eliminate annual funding obligations and volatility associated with those plans. Many plan sponsors have chosen to freeze future benefit accruals for some or all participants in favour of participant-controlled defined contribution plans. The frozen pension plans remain subject to the funding requirements set out under the US Employee Retirement Income Security Act of 1974, as amended (ERISA) and the US Internal Revenue Code of 1986, as amended. These funding requirements were made stricter through the enactment of new pension legislation in 2006. That law, the Pension Protection Act, also added increased volatility to pension asset valuation methodology. Freezing benefit accruals helps to stem the funding obligations, but it does not entirely remove the funding uncertainty associated with fluctuating asset values. As a result, many US employers continue to look for ways to hedge or eliminate the interest rate and investment risk associated with their frozen pension benefits.

This chapter describes three alternative US plans that sponsors have employed in recent years to eliminate, manage or reduce these risks. First, some US employers have attempted to completely eliminate pension liabilities through a negotiated sale of their pension plan to a third-party financial institution. The buyer assumes sponsorship of the pension plan, including all trust assets and liabilities. Second, other employers have purchased or have thought about purchasing an annuity contract from a licensed insurance company to pay future pension liabilities. In this arrangement, the annuity provider assumes the responsibility of paying benefits to retirees as they come due. Finally, some US pension trustees have revised investment strategy to manage assets in a way that causes the asset returns to track the plan's liabilities. This is referred to as liability driven investment.

2. Negotiated buy-out

In the United Kingdom, some employers have negotiated a complete buy-out of their pension assets and liabilities, essentially selling pension assets and transferring the liabilities to a third-party buyer, typically a financial institution. This approach to eliminating pension obligations has gained some traction with US employers in recent years. Under a typical negotiated buy-out, the employer forms a subsidiary corporation and transfers sponsorship of an under-funded pension plan to the subsidiary corporation.[1] The employer also transfers additional assets outside of the plan's trust to cover the plan's under-funding, but no employees or other assets are transferred to the subsidiary. A third party then purchases the subsidiary corporation and thereby assumes the assets and liabilities of the pension plan, as well as the additional assets. Generally, the third-party buyer is a large financial institution which hopes to profit on the exchange using its ability to manage the additional assets transferred to the subsidiary because these assets have not yet been contributed to the plan's trust.

While a negotiated buy-out transaction may be an appealing way for a US employer to eliminate onerous pension obligations, the Internal Revenue Service (IRS) has recently placed a hold on such transactions until further notice. The IRS issued a ruling that negotiated buy out transactions violate the US Code's 'exclusive benefit' rule.[2] Under US pension law, employee benefit plans must be established by an employer for the exclusive benefit of its employees or their beneficiaries in order to qualify.[3] According to the IRS, when an employer sells its pension plan to a third party via a negotiated buy-out, the employer–employee connection is gone and the transaction violates the exclusive benefit rule.

Notwithstanding this ruling, the IRS did offer a framework whereby lawmakers could open the door to future negotiated buy-out transactions.[4] Under this framework, the following principles would apply:

- The employer would be required to provide advance notice of the transfer to plan participants, as well as to regulators, so that the regulators had the opportunity to review and approve the proposed transaction;
- Only financially strong entities in well-regulated sectors would be permitted to acquire a pension plan in such a transaction;
- The parties would need to demonstrate that the participants' benefits and the pension insurance system would be exposed to less risk as a result of the transaction, and that the transfer would be in the best interests of the participants and beneficiaries;
- Limitations on transfers would be imposed to reduce undue concentration of risk;
- Transferees and members of their controlled groups would assume full responsibility for the liabilities of the transferred plan and would comply with post-transaction reporting and fiduciary requirements; and
- Subsequent transfer transactions would be subject to the rules applicable to the original transfer transaction.[5]

At the time of writing, the global economy is in turmoil. Given the current status of the markets and the current distrust of the financial institutions which are the major players in the negotiated buy-out universe, it seems unlikely that there will be any significant movement in favour of these transactions in the near future.

---

1 Macey, Scott J, "Enhancing Security for Frozen Pension Plan", *Journal of Compensation and Benefits*, May/June 2007.
2 Rev Rul 2008–45.
3 US Code Section 401(a).
4 US Department of the Treasury Press Release, August 6 2008.
5 *Ibid.*

3. Annuity purchase

For as long as pension plans have existed in the United States, employers have had the option to purchase an annuity contract from an insurance company to pay pension liabilities. In this kind of transaction, the employer transfers the pension plan assets to the insurance company and the insurance company agrees to pay plan benefits, typically in the form of an annuity contract. US employers have often used this approach as a way to secure the payment obligations to current and future retirees in a frozen pension plan as a step towards terminating the plan. Alternatively, the employer may wish to purchase an annuity contract for only a segment of the pension plan's population (eg, participants who have a vested benefit, but who have terminated their employment, so they are no longer accruing a benefit). The first step in pursuing an annuity purchase transaction is for the employer to identify which participants will be covered by the annuity contract. If the pension plan is frozen, the employer may look to purchase a contract to cover all existing plan liabilities as a step towards plan termination. Even if the plan is not frozen, the employer may wish to transfer some of the liabilities to an insurer to reduce the plan's overall funding exposure and volatility. In that case, the employer may limit the contract to cover only terminated vested participants. They no longer accrue a benefit and it is relatively simple to value those liabilities. Valuation becomes much more difficult for participants who are actively accruing a benefit because the total benefit for these individuals is unknown.

Purchasing an annuity contract for some participants, such as former employees, can be attractive to the plan sponsor because it reduces the plan's liabilities. This can significantly reduce a plan's funding exposure and volatility because the covered participants are removed from the plan. However, annuity purchases are relatively rare in the United States because of the cost of acquiring the contract from an insurance company. Generally, annuity providers in the United States value pension obligations for purposes of annuity bids using conservative interest rates and mortality assumptions, causing the contracts to be relatively expensive when compared to a plan's ongoing actuarial valuations. Consequently, an annuity placement is a viable approach only when a pension plan is in a strong funding position, making this a catch-22 situation. Employers with well-funded plans are often less interested in buying an expensive annuity contract because the trust investments may be performing well. A more precarious funding situation typically drives the plan trustees to explore ways to reduce liabilities. Those plans may not have sufficient assets to successfully purchase an annuity contract.

An annuity purchase transaction is carried out by the pension plan trustees, who are subject to strict fiduciary rules, including the exclusive benefit rule discussed above. Specifically, the US Department of Labour has published a regulation on how to purchase an annuity without violating the fiduciary duties owed to plan participants.[6] Under this regulation, the employer must purchase the "safest available annuity".[7] The Department of Labour provides the following list of factors which the employer should consider in selecting the safest available annuity:

---

6 DOL Regulations, Section 2509.95–1.

7 *Ibid.*

- the quality and diversification of the annuity provider's investment portfolio;
- the size of the insurer relative to the proposed contract;
- the level of the insurer's capital and surplus;
- the lines of business of the annuity provider and other indications of an insurer's exposure to liability;
- the structure of the annuity contract and guarantees supporting the annuities, such as the use of separate accounts; and
- the availability of additional protection through state guaranty associations and the extent of their guarantees.[8]

Generally, the employer would need to employ the services of an independent expert to evaluate this information and determine which annuity is the 'safest available'. The US Department of Labour has provided an exception to the safest available annuity standard where the safest available annuity is only marginally safer and disproportionately more expensive and the participants would bear a significant portion of the cost associated with the more expensive contract.[9] In most situations, this exception is meaningless because a participant in a defined benefit plan is entitled to his full accrued benefit and therefore would never bear the cost of the higher-priced contract. Generally, only in situations where the participant's accrued benefit could be increased through cost savings would the employer have the realistic ability to select an annuity other than the safest available and still satisfy the Department of Labour's standard.

As an alternative, the plan trustees could purchase an annuity contract to cover certain plan liabilities, but the plan trust could retain this annuity as a plan asset. While this type of arrangement does not reduce the plan's liabilities, holding an annuity contract in the trust could serve as an effective funding mechanism because the annuity provider would pay cash to the trust as benefits became due. In this way, the plan may be able to reduce funding volatility. Another such investment strategy is discussed in the next section.

4. Liability driven investments

As an alternative to transferring pension liabilities out of a plan through either a negotiated buy-out or a costly annuity contract, some US pension trustees have chosen to retain the pension assets and liabilities, but to change investment strategy to better manage the funding volatility. Typically, this means that the plan trustees make a fiduciary decision to move away from a traditional investment strategy with a mix of stocks and fixed-income products to a strategy using primarily long-term fixed income products that produce returns designed to match liabilities as they come due under the plan. The most common approach for a liability driven investment strategy is a structured bond portfolio.[10] This approach works best for a frozen pension plan because the plan assets do not need to earn higher rates of return

8 *Ibid.*
9 *Ibid.*
10 Renaud, Mathew J, and Mason, Galen R, "Liability Driven Investment Strategies – What ERISA Fiduciaries Need to Know", *The Investment Lawyer* Vol 14 No 9, September 2007.

to keep up with growing liabilities. In a frozen defined benefit plan that is in a strong funding position, the plan trustees can invest assets to match expected future cash outlays with fixed-income securities and a corresponding interest rate hedge to account for interest rate fluctuation.[11] This type of strategy, if properly structured and managed, can provide close to full protection against the need for additional employer cash contributions. As indicated, this approach is most effective for fully funded, frozen plans because of the limited returns associated with fixed-income assets.[12] If the plan is not frozen, the trustees may need to take on higher risk investments to earn the return necessary to offset future benefit accruals. In that situation, the hedge against market risk becomes less effective.[13]

Additionally, before making a decision to implement a liability driven investment alternative, it is important for plan fiduciaries to undertake a thorough review of the specifics of the investment strategy to confirm that all fiduciary obligations have been satisfied. While the US Department of Labour has found that a liability driven investment alternative is not, *per se*, a breach of fiduciary duty, all of the standard fiduciary obligations apply.[14]

5. Conclusion

The desire by US employers to eliminate or reduce defined benefit pension plan risks has led to a greater focus on various possible solutions. So far, however, this demand has not yielded many attractive alternatives. As discussed, the IRS has effectively blocked the negotiated buy-out alternative for the time being. Annuities remain viable, but are expensive and may be a realistic alternative only for well-funded plans. Likewise, liability driven investment strategies can reduce pension funding risk, but they are also most logical for fully funded pension plans. With recent market conditions, few such plans currently exist. US employers that wish to limit their future pension liabilities and market risk need to consult well-qualified investment advisers and legal counsel to explore alternatives based on the specific pension plan liabilities at issue. Perhaps the plan has sufficient assets to purchase annuities for terminated vested participants, or the plan may be a candidate for a more conservative investment approach, using the concepts of liability driven investments in combination with return-seeking investments. The most important point is that options do exist for managing future pension liabilities, but a 'one size fits all' option does not.

11 *Ibid.*
12 *Ibid.*
13 *Ibid.*
14 See DOL Op Ltr 2006-08A.

The end game – is buy-out really the end of the road for defined benefit schemes?

Martin Hunter
Punter Southall Transaction Services

The UK pension bulk buy-out market has roared into life over the past couple of years. Several sponsoring employers and pension scheme trustees have taken advantage of the opportunities presented by this rapidly evolving market to reduce the risk presented by their pension scheme liabilities. Does the growth of this market signal the imminent death of defined benefit pension schemes and will advisers of defined benefit pension schemes soon be searching out their local job centre?

1. Buy-out case studies

The majority of the deals done in the buy-out market recently have been driven by the sponsoring employer. Since no two pension schemes are the same, it is worth looking at the characteristics of some of the buy-out deals that have been completed to ascertain where a transaction has been able to add value to a sponsoring employer. An analysis of three of the most high-profile deals of recent times is set out below.

1.1 Cable & Wireless plc

In September 2008 details of a £1 billion deal between the trustee of the Cable & Wireless Superannuation Fund (C&W Fund) and the Prudential were announced. This was the largest single transaction in the bulk buy-out market since the new entrants joined the market in 2006. The deal was structured as a buy-in transaction and was in respect of current pensioners only, so that the pensioner liabilities will remain on the sponsoring employer's balance sheet, but the trustee of the C&W Fund will hold an annuity policy as an asset. The Prudential will make payments to the trustee, who in turn will pay the pension benefits to members.

The Cable & Wireless financial accounts for the year to March 31 2008 disclosed that the C&W Fund had a surplus of £375 million. However, due to accounting regulations no surplus was recognised on the balance sheet, as it was not considered to be possible that this surplus would lead to a refund being paid to the sponsoring employer in the future.

The premium payable to insurance companies to purchase annuities typically exceeds the value of the pension liabilities on the accounting measure, as insurers must make prudent assumptions regarding how much it will cost to pay the pension benefits in future and also have a profit motive, unlike pension schemes. Therefore, purchasing annuities with an insurance company will usually worsen the position of the sponsoring employer's balance sheet. Our analysis suggests that the amount paid to the Prudential to purchase the pensioner annuities would probably have exceeded the accounting reserve by around £100 million to £150 million. Therefore, the surplus would have reduced to somewhere in the region of £250 million and no surplus or deficit would be shown on the balance sheet. Hence, due to the significant surplus which previously existed in the C&W Fund, the transaction did not directly worsen the position of the Cable & Wireless balance sheet at the time of the deal.

The transaction will also have no direct impact on the Cable & Wireless profit and loss account, since the additional cost of the annuities above the reserve already held on the balance sheet can be absorbed by the unrecognised surplus.

In addition, the annuities were purchased using the assets held by the C&W Fund, with Cable & Wireless being required only to make a cash payment of £10 million to facilitate the deal. For a company with a market capitalisation of around £4.5 billion, this is a trivial sum.

While the transaction did not have a detrimental impact on the Cable & Wireless accounts, it did offer other benefits to the sponsoring employer. Purchasing annuities reduces the risks posed by the C&W Fund and is likely to make any future break-up and sale of Cable & Wireless slightly easier. Since speculation has been rife in the financial markets over the past couple of years regarding this possibility, this might have been a driver behind the decision to purchase annuities.

1.2 Rank plc

In February 2008 Rank plc undertook a full buy-out with Rothesay Life (a subsidiary of Goldman Sachs) for its £700 million pension scheme. (Rothesay Life later reinsured the Rank pensioners with the Prudential for £300 million, leaving it with exposure only to the deferred pensioners.)

Despite the pension scheme being in significant surplus, Rank was committed to paying cash contributions to the scheme of £30 million per annum, due to a prior agreement with the trustees. By taking advantage of the competitive prices available in the bulk buy-out market at the time of the deal, it was able to free itself from this contribution burden and also receive "at least £20 million" in surplus. Some of the surplus was also used to provide pension scheme members with increases to their pension benefits. There was no additional cash funding required from Rank to complete the buy-out and it provided significant financial gains.

In addition, the Rank share price had suffered significant falls during 2007. This led to the pension scheme being larger than Rank's market capitalisation at the time of the buy-out, which would have made it difficult for Rank to bear any volatility from the presence of the pension scheme on its balance sheet.

Overall, Rank seems to have faced a unique set of circumstances and was therefore prepared to pay the buy-out premium to benefit from being able to cease its contributions, receive a refund of surplus and remove risk from its balance sheet.

1.3 Emap plc

Towards the end of 2007 Emap plc agreed to transfer their pension liabilities to Paternoster for £170 million.

While the pension scheme was relatively small compared to the company as a whole, Emap was in the process of breaking itself up into constituent parts. This was an issue because the pension scheme would either have to be left with one of the new businesses or split across various businesses in some ratio. In either scenario the trustees of the pension scheme would want recompense for the weaker employer covenant, requiring Emap to put additional funding into the pension scheme before a restructuring could take place. In addition, any of the businesses left with all or part of the pension scheme would have their sale value depressed by the pension liabilities associated with them.

Resolving these complex issues would have taken a considerable amount of time and would have led to significant costs arising, particularly in dealing with the trustees' concerns relating to the employer covenant. The premium paid to remove these pension liabilities with an insurer was relatively small, particularly compared to the size of Emap at the time.

These case studies illustrate that the buy-out market has been able to provide solutions to a number of sponsoring employers which have helped to reduce the risk presented by their pension schemes and add value to their business. However, most of the companies and pension schemes that have done deals to date have had unique characteristics which have made buy-out attractive to them.

2. The potential size of the buy-out market

The value of private sector defined benefit pension liabilities exceeds £1 trillion in the United Kingdom. During 2007 slightly under £3 billion of bulk annuities was written and in 2008 just below £8 billion of business was done. The pie chart below illustrates the proportion of 'UK plc's' defined benefit pension liabilities which were bought out in 2007 and 2008.

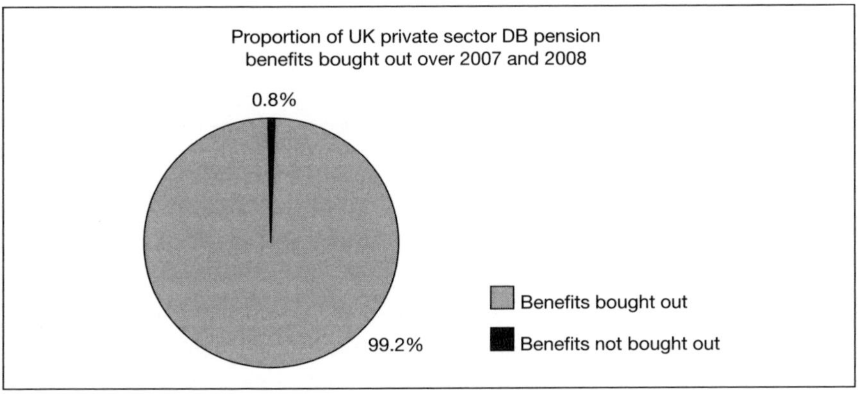

As discussed in earlier chapters, buy-out prices fell relative to their long-term level between the final quarter of 2007 and the summer of 2008. This was a result of insurance companies offering 'discounts' in their prices, in an attempt to stimulate demand for the buy-out option, build their annuity books and generate publicity for the market. (Some commentators have suggested that the lower prices were a result of the increased competition in the market. However, this theory has been disproved by the fact that lower buy-out prices started to appear in the market only from around the final quarter of 2007, despite the fact that the vast majority of the new entrants joined the buy-out market in early 2006.)

The figure above illustrates that although the UK pension bulk buy-out market has grown significantly over the last couple of years, it is still having a negligible impact on the overall size of the United Kingdom's defined benefit pension liabilities. This suggests that there are a large number of pension schemes in the United Kingdom which have no interest in buying out, despite the significant 'discounts' which have been available; the buy-out option remains prohibitively expensive for the vast majority of pension schemes.

Since the summer of 2008 buy-out prices have risen and are now close to their long-term level. Asset values have also fallen dramatically, weakening the funding positions of pension schemes. This is likely to make it even more difficult to convince those pension schemes that have not been persuaded to buy out in the last couple of years to do so in future.

3. Barriers to the growth of the buy-out market

In most cases the sponsoring employer will be the key driver behind the decision to buy out because most pension schemes target a funding level below buy-out and therefore do not have sufficient assets within their pension scheme to be able to afford to purchase annuity contracts for all members of the pension scheme. To proceed with a buy-out it will usually be necessary for the sponsoring employer to make a cash contribution to the pension scheme.

There are two key reasons why buy-out has not been viewed as a suitable use of resources by finance directors: regulation of the insurance industry and the profit motive of insurers.

Since insurance companies can and do become insolvent, their activities are highly regulated. In the United Kingdom, insurance companies are regulated by the Financial Services Authority (FSA), which requires insurance companies to hold capital reserves to back their annuity books. Insurers are required to produce a comprehensive assessment of the risks faced by their business and must typically hold enough capital to ensure that they are at least 99.5% likely to remain solvent over the next year. This corresponds to being able to demonstrate that the insurance company's capital is sufficient to allow them to withstand adverse circumstances, other than a one-in-200-year event, or worse.

Since the FSA recognises that insurance is a long-term business, regulated insurance companies are also required to demonstrate that the chance of the insurance company becoming insolvent over the long term is no more than 5%.

Typically, the FSA requires insurers to hold capital margins of around 8% of their liabilities in respect of their annuity book. This means that if an insurer takes on annuities of £100 million, they must usually hold total assets to back these annuities of around £108 million. This additional £8 million would be the capital provided by their investors.

The FSA's capital requirements also depend on the level of 'matching' between insurers' assets and their liabilities. This strongly encourages insurance companies to hold a diversified portfolio of very secure bonds, such as government bonds and high-quality corporate bonds. These assets will be of a similar duration (typically long term) to the liabilities but, due to the scarcity of very long-dated bonds, some insurers also use swaps to improve their level of matching. Inflation swaps can be used to reduce the risk of inflation increasing the value of the pension benefits, to the extent that future pension increases are linked to inflation. If an insurer does not hold a matched position, it will be required to significantly increase the amount of capital it holds to back its annuities.

These FSA requirements restrict the price which can be charged by an insurance company and lead to the value placed on pension liabilities by insurance companies exceeding the estimated cost to the pension scheme of providing the benefits directly.

In addition, insurers seek to make profit from the annuities they take on. Due to the risks involved with writing annuity business, particularly in respect of mortality and investment, investors in insurance companies might aim to make a pre-tax return on their equity of around 15% per annum. This generally means that around 15% of the premium paid to a bulk annuity provider is in respect of the insurance company's future expected profits. Finance directors are usually unwilling to transfer such a significant amount of value from their balance sheet to an insurance company.

As described above, the catalyst for the buy-out business done over most of 2007 and 2008 was the unsustainable discounts offered by some insurance companies in their pricing. However, since mid-2008 these discounts have been evaporating, so buy-out prices have now reverted to around their long-term level. This has occurred as the discounts previously offered led to expected pre-tax returns on equity as low as 6% per annum in some cases – this is extremely low given the risks involved in writing annuity business. Investors are keen to increase these expected returns towards a level of around 15% per annum, which has led to discounts disappearing.

In addition, most asset classes held by pension schemes have performed poorly during 2008, which is likely to have led to a worsened funding position. This poor asset performance, coupled with the rise in prices, is likely to have significantly increased the gap between the level of assets in the scheme and the cost of buy-out, making buy-out increasingly unaffordable. Therefore, it appears unlikely that even the limited levels of business written during 2007 and 2008 will be sustainable in future.

There are a number of pension schemes for which buy-out will never be an attractive option, as it is simply too expensive. A number of corporate sponsors are also likely to oppose the concept of buy-out, since it involves passing value to an insurer, due to the insurer's profit motive.

4. An alternative to buy-out

Given that most finance directors consider buy-out to be unaffordable, they are likely to seek an alternative method to allow them to manage the risk to their balance sheet presented by their pension scheme. Although a number of organisations have attempted to bridge the gap between the traditional buy-out option and the prices at which finance directors are willing to trade, these alternative products have, as yet, proved relatively unsuccessful. A lot of the new entrants to this area have yet to write any business and those that have, such as Citigroup and Pension Corporation, have a business model which is very unlikely to have wide applicability to the defined benefit pensions market as a whole.

Fortunately, there is an affordable alternative to buy-out which is available to all pension schemes. Over recent years a number of increasingly sophisticated tools have become available to pension schemes (of all sizes), which allow them to be de-risked to a significant extent while remaining on the sponsoring employer's balance sheet. These risks can be removed fairly easily and at a relatively cheap price.

Bonds or swaps can be used to reduce inflation risk, which arises since the pensions which will be paid in future are usually linked to inflation. There is a deep and liquid market available for inflation swaps, so this can be done at a reasonable price. (Swaps are discussed further below.)

There are also tools available which allow pension schemes to significantly reduce their investment risk, if they so choose. The most straightforward approach is to adopt a low-risk investment strategy, such as that which would be followed by an insurance company. This would involve investing in gilts or high-quality corporate bonds of a similar duration to the pension scheme's liabilities. By following such a strategy there should be a close correlation between the value of the pension scheme's assets and its liabilities.

Investing in low-risk assets such as gilts locks the pension scheme into a relatively low rate of return. While some risk-averse pension schemes might like the guaranteed nature of these returns, other pension schemes will believe that the higher expected long-term returns available from asset classes such as equities can be used to reduce the long-term cost of providing the pension scheme's benefits. However, the volatility of these returns can lead to problems, as it increases the likelihood of deficits being revealed at triennial actuarial valuations in the short term, which would lead to the sponsoring employer being required to pay deficit contributions.

Fortunately, over recent years an increasing number of investment products have been designed which allow pension schemes to reduce the volatility of their equity returns. Such a product might involve structuring various call and put options to allow the pension scheme to have collars and caps applied to its equity returns. For example, it might give up the potential for large equity returns (eg, returns above 15% per annum), which are of limited use to a pension scheme due to the difficulties associated with removing pension scheme surplus, in exchange for a guarantee that the value of the equities will not fall. The caps and collars on these investment products can be structured to suit the risk attitude of the pension scheme.

4.1 Mortality swaps

With inflation and investment risks mitigated, the last significant risk faced by a pension scheme is longevity risk – the risk that pension scheme members will live longer than expected. If it was possible for pension schemes to hedge their longevity risk at a reasonable cost, in the same way as they can currently hedge risks such as inflation, this would be the final piece in the risk management jigsaw.

A mortality swap requires a pension scheme to pay a fixed or pre-determined stream of cash flows to a counterparty (usually an insurance company or a bank) for a set period of time. This is called the 'fixed leg' of the swap. In return the counterparty pays the 'floating leg' – the cash flow required to pay benefits to members. This would be payable for the actual lifetimes of the members, which are unknown when the contract is written. By paying the fixed cash flows, the pension scheme is then able to protect itself against unexpected longevity improvements in the future, effectively locking into a fixed mortality assumption.

Although mortality swaps are bespoke products which vary between providers, they are all likely to have a fixed term of, say, 50 years. However, a pension scheme with relatively young deferred pensioners might expect to be paying pensions for the next 80 years or more. Therefore, such a swap may not provide mortality protection to the pension scheme over these last 30 years, leading to significant 'tail risk'. It is precisely this tail risk which usually causes the most concern to the scheme, since the further into the future mortality rates are projected, the more uncertain they become. To mitigate this risk, some issuers of mortality swaps include a 'final exchange', so that when the swap matures, a final payment is made to reflect the life expectancy of the remaining pensioners. The final exchange can be timed to occur at the point when the swap arrangement becomes inefficient for both parties to maintain.

There are two key risks which mortality swaps can be used to protect against:

- the risk that 'average' people actually live longer than is currently expected so that the current mortality assumption used by the scheme turns out to be 'wrong'; and/or
- the risk that a particular individual actually lives longer than expected due to random variation, even if the current mortality assumption is 'correct', which is a particular risk for smaller schemes.

Index-linked hedging can be used to protect against the former risk, where payouts to the pension scheme are based on a mortality index. Alternatively, named-lives hedging is a bespoke product which can be used to protect against the latter risk. The difference between named-lives hedging and buying an annuity with an insurer in the name of the member is that under named-lives hedging it is possible only to protect against longevity risk if desired, leaving risks such as investment with the pension scheme.

There are a number of problems associated with index-linked hedging. The experience of the scheme members could vary considerably from the index, particularly for smaller pension schemes, which could still leave the scheme exposed to significant longevity risk. For this kind of a swap to be of genuine value to a scheme, it would need to be based on the scheme's actual mortality rates, as is the case for named-lives hedging.

After a couple of years of speculation regarding whether the longevity swaps market would take off, the first deals involving pension schemes have been announced in 2009. A number of insurance companies and banks have started offering products of this type over the last few years, including the likes of Credit Suisse, Natixis, Rothesay Life (a subsidiary of Goldman Sachs) and Pension Insurance Corporation.

The reason that the longevity swaps market has taken a bit of time to get going is that there is a lack of natural counterparties which are seeking to take on longevity risk. There are very few individuals or organisations that face the opposite risk (ie, that people die earlier than expected), and are looking to remove this risk through the market. As such, the counterparties that are looking to take the opposing side of the swap are generally hedge funds, seeking an uncorrelated asset class to diversify their portfolio.

In most swaps, at the date of entering into the contract the net present values of the two cash-flow streams are expected to be identical, so that the swap has an initial value of zero. In the case of general financial swaps, such as interest rate or inflation swaps, they are usually priced using 'best estimate' assumptions. If a pension scheme is seeking to pay fixed and receive floating payments, based on the rate of inflation, it should be relatively straightforward to find a counterparty in the financial markets which would like to pay floating and receive fixed payments, to allow it to better match its own liabilities.

However, the counterparties to longevity swaps are typically hedge funds. Since they are not natural counterparties, hedge funds are likely to insist on a risk premium when pricing a longevity swap, so that the swap is not based purely on a best estimate of future expected mortality rates.

Hedge funds will also expect to be able to make profit from any swap they enter into. This profit motive, coupled with the risk premium, results in pension schemes seeking to enter into a longevity swap being required to lock into a prudent mortality assumption (which is probably more prudent than the already prudent assumption they are using to fund their liabilities). The attractiveness of longevity swaps will depend on whether the scheme is willing to lock into a more prudent mortality assumption in order to remove the uncertainty associated with the scheme's future mortality experience.

The reason that deals have started to be done in the longevity swaps market in 2009 is that prices have fallen substantially. We have been monitoring the longevity swaps market for a number of years and received a quote for one of our clients at both the start of 2007 and the start of 2009, for the same cohort of members. Over the intervening period the price had fallen significantly. This appears to be a consequence of investors being more willing to write longevity swaps business, hence requiring the mortality assumptions to be less prudent, such that the risk premium is lower.

The key determinant of the success of the longevity swaps market is the level of prudence which pension schemes are required to lock into in the mortality assumption. If pension schemes are willing to lock into these prudent assumptions to remove mortality uncertainty the market could be very successful. However, the market is still in its infancy and, at the time of writing longevity swaps are being written only for current pensioners, rather than deferred pensioners, and only for large schemes (ie, those looking to cover liabilities in excess of £100 million).

However, even without utilising the mortality swaps market it is possible for a pension scheme to protect itself against the risk of members living longer than expected. An investment strategy could be designed to provide a buffer against longevity risk, by structuring the asset portfolio to target an investment return of around London Interbank Offered Rate (LIBOR) plus 40 basis points, say. The excess return generated above LIBOR could be viewed as protection against the risk of changes in life expectancy. Although the pension scheme would still be exposed to longevity risk, hopefully any increase in the value of the pension scheme's liabilities caused by an increase in life expectancies would exceed the excess investment return generated by following this strategy.

5. The merits of the buy-out alternative

Rather than buying out the pension scheme with an insurer, the employer could therefore fund the pension scheme up to the level required to buy out (providing security to the trustees) and maintain the pension scheme on its balance sheet. The employer could then follow the steps discussed above to 'de-risk' the pension scheme.

Pension scheme trustees are required to value the liabilities of their scheme using 'prudent' assumptions. Therefore, it should be the case that in reality the actual experience of the pension scheme will be more favourable than expected. This would lead to profits (or 'surplus') appearing gradually over time, improving the funding position of the scheme.

The sponsoring employer can usually control when the pension scheme winds up and buys annuities. It could continue to run the scheme onwards until the last member has died, then wind up the scheme and collect the surplus. It could also choose to wind up at an earlier date, once a substantial proportion of the profit has been achieved and when the fixed expenses of running the scheme become a significant proportion of the cash flows. (Most schemes would expect around 50% of the net present value of the profits to be accumulated in the first 20 years.) Alternatively, the sponsoring employer could seek agreement from the pension scheme trustees to release profit from time to time under the surplus regulations, subject to this being allowed by the scheme's trust deed and rules.

A pension scheme managed in this manner should not present a burden if the sponsoring employer is sold in future. Due to the strong funding position of the scheme, a potential purchaser would have the option of buying out the liabilities with an insurer, without putting extra funds into the pension scheme, to remove the pension scheme from the balance sheet. Therefore, a price deduction to allow for the pension scheme in the transaction should not be required.

Some of the new players in the market are using this approach to manage pension schemes. Pension Corporation runs the former pension schemes of off-licence chain Threshers and communications group Telent in this way (and ran the electrical company Thorn in this manner before it bought out the benefits with its insurance arm), and Citigroup uses a similar approach with the pension scheme of Thomson Regional Newspapers. However, its business model can be applied only to an elite band of sponsoring employers and schemes – specifically, small (or shell) companies with large, well-funded pension schemes – since it involves buying the sponsoring employer in order to take control of the pension scheme. It therefore has limited applicability in the market as a whole. On the other hand, the approach itself could be followed by almost any sponsoring employer, providing a feasible and cost-efficient alternative to buy-out.

Pension Corporation and Citigroup hope that the strategy which they are adopting will allow them eventually to release significant profits from the pension schemes, while simultaneously providing security to the pension scheme members. Since they are not regulated insurance companies, they are operating under pension regulation, so there is nothing to prevent other employers from taking a similar approach to managing their own pension schemes.

6. Soft reasons for buy-out

As discussed above, on a purely financial basis buy-out is unlikely to be an attractive option for a finance director. However, there are also a number of non-financial factors which influence the buy-out decision. The key reasons that sponsoring employers tend to give for looking to offload their pension obligations can usually be distilled into the following:

- Pension schemes are too risky (particularly in terms of investment risk and longevity risk) for the employer to bear and the changing value of the pension scheme funding position leads to volatility on the employer's balance sheet.
- A pension scheme is an increasing drain on senior management time and is a distraction from running the underlying business. Pension schemes can also pose difficulties in transactional or restructuring situations.
- The sponsoring employer, unlike a life insurer, has no competitive advantage in managing pension scheme risks and therefore should not be in the business of running defined benefit pension schemes.
- Outsourcing the scheme to an insurer leads to lower administrative costs for the arrangement due to the insurer's economies of scale.

These arguments seem, on the face of things, to be relatively sound. However, we discuss each of them in turn below.

(a) Pension schemes are too risky

If a pension scheme is to be bought out, it will need to be very well funded – probably to a level above that which the trustees have been targeting in their ongoing actuarial valuations. So if the pension scheme is to buy out, a substantial cash contribution from the employer is likely to be required. If, rather than buying out the liabilities, the employer pays this contribution into the scheme, the well-funded pension scheme should pose little risk to the employer's balance sheet. Particularly if a low-risk investment strategy is in place, there should be relatively little chance of the funding level falling below 100% on the accounting basis (since the reported funding level will probably be around 135% if the pension scheme is funded to the buy-out level), which would need to happen before the scheme had an impact on the employer's balance sheet. As long as the pension scheme remains in surplus, in most cases it would have zero value on the employer's balance sheet.

Therefore, a well-funded pension scheme should not increase the volatility of the employer's balance sheet.

(b) ***A pension scheme is a drain and distraction***

With a pension scheme funded to the buy-out level, following a low-risk investment strategy, there is little need for senior management to become involved in the day-to-day management of the pension scheme. Generally, a greater amount of senior management time is required to manage pension schemes where the pension scheme deficit is a significant financial burden to the employer or the general size of the scheme is extremely large in relation to the resources of the sponsoring employer. This is because in such cases investment risk needs to be taken by the pension scheme in order to generate sufficient returns to run off the benefits from the current level of assets.

Additionally, if the scheme has sufficient assets to allow it to buy out its liabilities with an insurance company, any problems caused by the pension scheme in a transactional or restructuring situation can be solved by actually triggering the wind-up and securing the liabilities with annuity contracts.

Therefore, for a pension scheme that is fully funded on a buy-out basis, the senior management distractions and limitations on activity are minimal.

(c) ***The sponsoring employer has no competitive advantage in managing pension scheme risks***

Although most sponsoring employers do not have a competitive advantage in managing pension scheme risks, there are many other activities in which an employer engages where it does not have a competitive advantage (eg, accounting, tax and dealing with legal issues). In such cases it is normal to outsource the function to a third party who is a specialist in this area. Running a pension scheme involves a similar process, whereby services such as actuarial advice, administration and the investment of the scheme's assets are outsourced to third parties.

It is worth noting that it is not possible for insurers to manage the key risk of running an annuity book, longevity, any more effectively than pension schemes. It is possible only to be better at pricing longevity risks. While insurance companies might be best placed to price longevity risks, this will be reflected in the price of their annuities. Once an insurer has taken on a liability it cannot manage its mortality exposure, except through attempts to hedge it or offload it – options which are becoming increasingly available to both insurers and pension schemes through the nascent longevity swaps market.

Therefore, as long as the pension scheme is of sufficient size to justify outsourcing the management of the scheme to third parties, it should be possible to run it efficiently.

(d) ***Outsourcing leads to lower administrative costs***

While transferring the pension liabilities to an insurer through a buy-out will remove the expenses associated with paying the benefits, the insurer will price the expenses it will incur into the buy-out price. Large pension schemes (eg, worth at least £100 million) are actually of a sufficient size to benefit already from economies of scale. There is therefore little to be gained by combining these pension schemes in an insurance company's annuity book.

On the contrary, due to the more burdensome regulation of the insurance industry compared to the pension arena, particularly due to their reserving requirements, insurers are actually likely to require greater resources to manage their annuity book than an equivalently sized pension scheme. This means that the administrative cost of providing pension benefits is likely to be lower in the insurance environment than in the pensions environment only for the very smallest of pension schemes; typically those worth less than somewhere in the region of £1 million to £2 million.

7. Conclusion

So, is buy-out really the end of the line for defined benefit pension schemes? There will always be a few pension schemes for which the unique circumstances of their scheme and their sponsoring employer will make a buy-out attractive, despite the cost associated with this option.

However, the pension regulatory environment is currently more flexible and less onerous than the FSA-regulated insurance environment, making the provision of pension benefits through the insurance environment more costly than is the case in the pension environment. While this difference persists, and insurance companies continue to seek to make profit from the business which they write (which seems likely as long as capitalism survives!), buy-out will never be an attractive option for the majority of the United Kingdom's defined benefit pension schemes.

The future of the buy-out market

Kevin Wesbroom
Hewitt Associates LLC

---

1. Introduction

The path ahead for many UK pension plans is clear. When employers closed their plans to new entrants, they set off on a path that would inevitably, over time, lead to the eventual closure of the plan to all future accruals and to the eventual removal of the plan from the balance sheet of the sponsor – probably by means of an annuity buy-out. We are now witnessing the next phase in this process, as major household names start to close their plans to existing members. The reasons for these pension exits have been all too apparent – uncontrollable pension deficits creating mayhem on corporate balance sheets, inordinate amounts of senior management time being devoted to pensions rather than running the business, mergers and acquisitions blown off course by pension deficits and increasingly greedy trustees, egged on by the Pensions Regulator, seeking to gain control over greater swathes of corporate assets or of the company's free cash flow. Is it any wonder that finance directors and chief executives just want out?

2. Market pricing

And surprise, surprise: along come a whole host of new providers seeking to help companies do just that. The arrival of the likes of Paternoster, PIC and Lucida has transformed the ability of companies to hand over their troublesome pension obligations. But is there a catch? Of course there is: the cost. It has long been conventional wisdom that the cost of a buy-out would be prohibitively expensive – far beyond what most schemes and their sponsoring companies could expect to be able to afford. But then – bizarrely – along comes the credit crunch – bad news piled on top of bad news. In some cases it is – equity markets are back to levels of five or 10 years ago, company profitability is compromised, so surely the gap between the assets held in the fund and the cost of a buy-out, to be met from company profitability, is so huge as to be way out of reach? Perhaps it is now, but for a while this was not the case. The credit crunch that caused so much pain and stock market anguish also drove down the price of corporate bonds, which the market shunned. These are the very instruments that insurance companies purchase when they are matching their commitments under pension buy-outs. A combination of the reduced price of corporate bonds, together with a large dose of healthy competition and new players seeking to build market share and jockeying for position, drove down the prices of buy-outs in the early part of 2008. As an aside, how ironic is it that an event that has destroyed value and confidence in many long-established, respected financial institutions should lead to a price reduction and massive sales opportunity among institutions designed to cover long-term savings arrangements?

So companies suddenly found that a buy-out might be more affordable than they previously thought. With the Rank deal, where the sponsor was able to capture a £20 million surplus after the buy-out, many might have thought that we were entering a new regime of 'supermarket' buy-outs – "and would you like cashback with your purchase, Sir?". Aggressive pricing and the unproven business models of many of the new providers (or even the exits of some potential providers) might have raised questions about the security about the ultimate benefits for members, but there is no doubt that suddenly buy-outs definitely looked affordable – we may well look back on the spring of 2008 as the heyday of buy-out affordability! Since that date, insurers have been less able to pass on the full benefit of ever-widening corporate bond spreads and the collapse in equity markets means that the affordability of buy-out slipped away for many sponsors. Equally, the market turmoil will have served only to increase the desire of sponsors to rid themselves of these uncontrollable pension deficits!

3. Market innovation

Even if a full buy-out might now be unaffordable, some sponsors have looked at 'eating the elephant one bite at a time' – starting by offloading existing pensioner portfolios. One of the features of the new providers is that they have stimulated market innovation so that partial buy-outs or buy-ins have now become part of mainstream risk considerations for UK pension plans. For a scheme which has a healthy exposure to bonds to back its existing pensioner liabilities, the idea of simply swapping those bonds for an insurance policy – which at the same time removes longevity exposure – seems all too attractive. Some companies, however, may have been relying on 'sweating their assets' to meet their overall pension deficit. For them, being forced to invest in risk-reducing assets, rather than return-seeking assets, may be too painful. They may be attracted to other longevity solutions, such as the longevity swaps market, as discussed below.

4. Deferred liabilities

Getting rid of all pension liabilities still seems expensive, largely because of the high cost of dealing with deferred pensioner liabilities. In some ways this is not surprising. Consider that a deferred pension may be payable in 30 to 40 years' time, when a member finally reaches pension age. And that pension may be payable for a further 30 years after retirement. There are no investments you can buy which guarantee payments this far into the future. And what about dealing with longevity? Is it possible that within the next 50 years we will not only have found a cure for cancer, but perhaps even a cure for death itself? So we should not be surprised if the price that insurance companies want for long-term liabilities such as this is high. As an aside, we might also wonder how we ever convinced ourselves that companies should offer obligations of this nature – obligations that stretch way beyond the expected lifespan of most companies. So we need a different approach other than buy-out for dealing with deferred pensioners. Step forward the idea of enhanced transfer values (ETV) – or liability management programmes.

5. Enhanced transfer value exercises

An ETV consists of encouraging (with an extra transfer value and/or cash) deferred members to leave a defined benefit scheme and to transfer the value of their benefit into an arrangement of their choice – typically a defined contribution personal pension plan. ETV exercises suffer unduly from the M-word – 'mis-selling'. They must be unfair, people will argue, since members will never truly understand what they are giving up and will always be persuaded to accept less than fair value as an alternative, especially where cash is involved. Maybe. Certainly some of the early ETV exercises were rather dubious in this respect, pushing the boundaries of what was acceptable, partly because the employers concerned were desperate to be shot of their defined benefit liabilities.

The author believes that we are entering a new era of ETV exercises – options that will offer advantages not just to the sponsoring employer, but also to members and trustees of plans. Firstly, the level of the enhancement is likely to be higher – because employers will recognise that it is worthwhile paying higher amounts to make the offer attractive to members, as the payment is significantly less than the buy-out cost they might otherwise face. Secondly, the support offered to members under these exercises will be significantly higher than before – and will often be paid by the employer as part of the overall cost–benefit analysis. A member might not understand the intricacies of his existing pension, or how to evaluate it against an alternative defined contribution pension – but a well-informed individual financial adviser (IFA) certainly will. New breeds of IFAs are emerging to address this market opportunity. Finally, we need to recognise that a defined benefit pension in 35 years' time is not necessarily inferior to a defined contribution pension and an enhancement, perhaps in the form of cash:

- For members with significant debts or other more pressing financial obligations, the opportunity of accessing cash could be by far and away the most sensible and attractive financial option available to them.
- Can we be certain that the pension would not have been eroded by means testing? Other forms of saving may be more appropriate and efficient than pensions.
- Cash is cash – there is no need to worry about future security or protection funds (depending, of course, on which bank you put it in!).
- Do the transfer terms favour those members with less than perfect longevity prospects? Annuity specialists say that as many as 40% of annuity purchasers could qualify for enhanced terms.
- Do the transfer terms allow a single member to unlock the value of a contingent spouse's benefit that will not be used?

Companies may struggle to find the cash to pay incentives to deferred members, but the payback from these exercises could be yet another step on the path to permanently removing pension obligations and risks.

6. Pension flightpath

So between pensioner buy-ins and ETV exercises to remove deferred liabilities, we can see an eventual end of defined benefit plans in the next few decades. A route map – or flightpath or exit map – for a pension plans might take the following format:

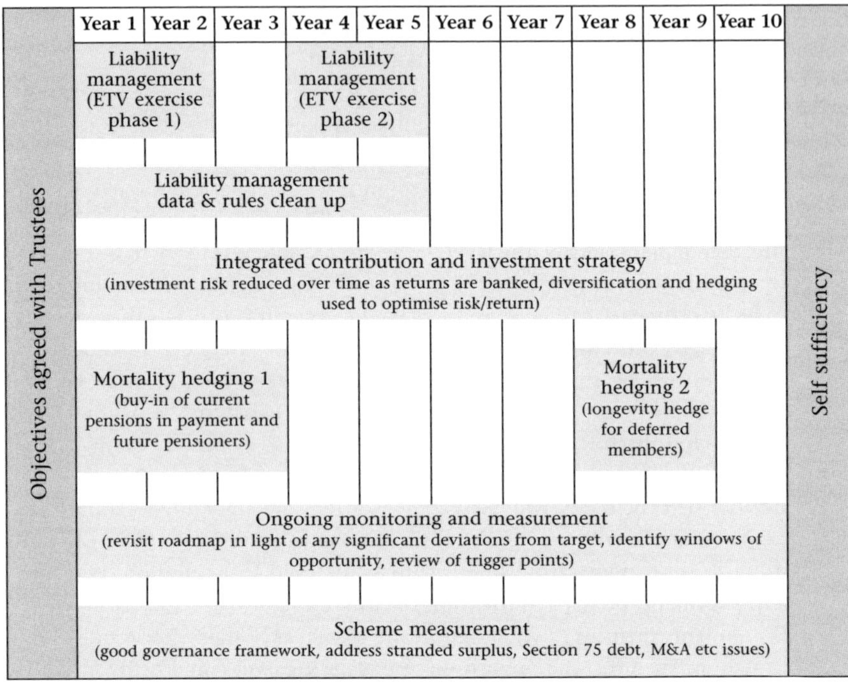

Pulling together the financing policy – the timing and level of contributions and the way they are invested – looks set to become an integral part of the managed exit programme. We expect to see more and more scheme implementing 'banking' arrangements, so that as market returns lift funding levels, the scheme makes a switch from return-seeking assets to safer bonds to ensure it locks in the gains, rather than watch them evaporate as markets turn down again. The investment process itself is becoming far more complex – there are new asset categories, new risk management techniques and a need for speedy effective decision making in times of fast-moving markets. It seems likely that many more sponsors will conclude that such an important task cannot be left to amateur trustees meeting once a quarter and they will seek to outsource the implementation of investment policy – but not the formulation of the investment strategy – to specialist external agencies, such as their investment consultants.

7. Longevity risk management techniques

Dealing with the unrewarded risk of longevity does not have to involve a buy-out policy. Buy-out involves not only removing longevity risk, but also tying up assets in a very safe – but therefore low return – investment portfolio. Some schemes will still need the extra returns that high-reward investments can generate to plug their deficit. In these cases, longevity swaps may become part of the solution. A longevity swap involves exchanging one set of cash flows – based on the actual pension payments – for another, payable for a fixed number of years for each member. Longevity risk is therefore removed, but since the contract is a swap, no assets are exchanged upfront. The full asset value can be put to work to help fund the deficit – and to meet the eventual full buy-out cost. The longevity swap can be rolled over – novated, to use the technical term – into an eventual buy-out contract so it can be a highly efficient process. Longevity swaps are being marketed not just by the same insurance companies that are active in the buy-out market, but also by capital market players. Investment banks would like to see a deep, active market in securities based on human longevity – a market opportunity for swaps which could become as big as the swap markets in interest rates and inflation. The first such trade for a UK pension fund took place in June 2009 and there is a huge backlog of pending cases. These transactions are also commonly used in the insurance space – we are on the verge of a significant breakthrough in the tools and options available to deal with one of the more difficult aspects of pension fund risk.

8. Future benefits – just defined contribution?

And in all of this – what about the workers? What are the prospects for the active members? Is their future inevitably defined contribution? Almost certainly, from the perspective that very few finance directors will ever again be persuaded to take on defined benefit obligations after the damage they have done in the past decades. But there is the possibility that defined contribution does not necessarily have to mean the individual member account basis we have accepted as the norm in the United Kingdom. We may see the emergence of new types of plan such as the collective defined contribution plans which the Department of Work and Pensions (DWP) looked at in the summer of 2008. It announced that further work would be undertaken in 2009. These plans – more helpfully referred to as target plans – are defined contribution from the finance perspective. Once the employer has paid its contribution, it can walk away, with no subsequent liability if conditions are not favourable. But the benefit is expressed in pension terms, probably as a career average style plan. We square the circle on the two conflicting designs, by having revaluation and indexation of the pension that will vary according to financial conditions. We may be back to the type of system we had in the 1970s, when schemes could not afford to pay increases after the prolonged market downturns in 1973 and 1974. So for a few years, pension increases were skipped – pensioners lost out, but schemes were able to trade through the tough times. As conditions improved, these 'lost' increases caught up and were re-instated. Target pension plans have a great opportunity to draw on the lessons of the past, to adopt cutting-edge risk mitigation strategies and to deliver what members ultimately want – a decent retirement income they can understand and plan for. They may be a way of avoiding the pension inequality between ever-more expensive final salary plans – or the lucky ones in secure buy-out contracts – and those having to live off levelled-down personal accounts. Or, being even more radical, they could solve the 'pensions apartheid' between public and private sector workers!

So future pensions, in the post-defined benefit world, might have echoes of the 1970s. In the ultimate of ironies (or is it just the circularity of events?), we could see defined benefit pensions provided predominantly by the insurance industry. The defined benefit pensions industry developed back in the very same 1970s on a self-administered basis as a response to what were perceived as unattractive terms of insured pensions contracts which had been the norm until then. The wheel may yet turn full circle.

About the authors

Juan Alonso
Senior Associate, Ashurst
juan.alonso@ashurst.com

Juan Alonso is a senior associate of the employment department in Ashurst Madrid. Mr Alonso has 10 years of experience in employment law. Prior to joining Ashurst, he was a senior associate in the employment department at Baker & McKenzie. He specialises in general employment advice, including drafting legal reports on different employment practice areas, mainly related to corporate restructuring, employment litigation before labour and administrative courts, and participation and negotiation of collective agreements and collective redundancies. He speaks Spanish, English and French.

David Archer
Director, Pitmans Trustees Limited
darcher@pitmans.com

David Archer is the managing director of Pitmans Trustees Limited and a partner in Pitmans Solicitors' pension team. He has been taking independent trustee appointments since 1992 and incorporated Pitmans Trustees Limited in 1994. Previously, Mr Archer was a solicitor with Clifford Chance in the City of London and Baker & McKenzie Australia after qualifying as a solicitor with Norton Rose in 1985.

Jonathan Bloomer
Executive chairman, Lucida plc
Partner, Cerberus European Capital Advisors
jonathan.bloomer@lucidaplc.com

Jonathan Bloomer is executive chairman of Lucida plc, a company formed to take on the assets and liabilities of corporate defined pension schemes. He is also a partner of the UK arm of Cerberus Capital, a New York-based investment manager. He was previously group chief executive of Prudential (2000-2005), and group finance director from January 1995. Prior to this he was a senior partner in Arthur Andersen's financial markets division and the managing partner of its European Insurance Practice.

Mr Bloomer was chairman of the Financial Services Practitioner Panel of the Financial Services Authority (2003-2005) and vice chairman until October 2006. He was a member of the board of the Geneva Association (2001-2005), and a member of the board of the Association of British Insurers (2000-2005). He was also a member of the Urgent Issues Task Force of the Accounting Standards Board (1995-1999).

Bas Cammelbeeck
Senior associate, Nauta Dutilh
bas.cammelbeeck@nautadutilh.com

Bas Cammelbeeck specialises in civil procedure law and pension law. Since 1998, his practice has increasingly focused on the latter.

Mr Cammelbeeck completed the postgraduate programme on pension law at the Free University

Amsterdam and is a certified pensions lawyer. He regularly advises on the pension law aspects of mergers and acquisitions. He also advises and, where necessary, litigates for companies and company pension funds on pension law issues. Since 1991 he has taught civil procedure law in the professional education programme for trainee lawyers organised by the Dutch Bar Association.

Mr Cammelbeeck graduated in law from the University of Groningen in 1977 and that same year joined Rotterdam firm Nauta Lambert Blussé, which later became part of NautaDutilh.

Jill Clucas
Of counsel, Lovells LLP
jill.clucas@lovells.com

Jill Clucas is a professional support lawyer in the pensions group at Lovells LLP. Her responsibilities include keeping clients and members of the pension team up to date on legal and regulatory changes, organising pension training events, and writing and speaking about legal developments in pensions.

Ms Clucas is currently secretary of the Association of Pension Lawyers (APL). Prior to joining the APL Main Committee, she served for five years on its Education and Seminars Sub-committee, responsible for sharing pension expertise and know-how among pension lawyers. She is a member trustee of Lovells' final salary pension scheme and is a fellow of the Pensions Management Institute.

Jake R Downing
Associate, Seyfarth Shaw LLP
jdowning@seyfarth.com

Jake R Downing is an associate in the employee benefits practice group in the Chicago office of Seyfarth Shaw LLP. He advises employers on a broad range of employee benefit matters. Mr Downing has counselled clients on qualified and non-qualified retirement and welfare plan matters regarding plan design and administration, tax qualification, fiduciary responsibility, claims procedures, disclosure requirements and general Employee Retirement Income Security Act compliance.

Marcus Fink
Senior Associate, Ashurst LLP
marcus.fink@ashurst.com

Marcus Fink is a senior associate in the pensions team at Ashurst LLP. He has a wide range of experience in all pension-related matters gained through acting for private and publicly listed UK and multinational employers and trustees. He has particular expertise in pension scheme reorganisations and mergers, deficit reduction strategies, changing scheme benefit structures, the pension aspects of corporate transactions and insolvency processes, pension scheme investment, funding negotiations and negotiations with the Pensions Regulator and the Pension Protection Fund.

Robert P Flanagan
Partner, Seyfarth Shaw LLP
rflanagan@seyfarth.com

Robert P Flanagan is a partner practising in the area of employee benefits for the Chicago office of Seyfarth Shaw LLP. Mr Flanagan serves as lead employee benefits counsel to many companies, both public and closely held. He counsels companies with regard to qualified and non-qualified retirement plans, health and welfare plans and cash and equity-based incentive compensation programmes. He advises trustees, boards of directors, investment committees and other plan fiduciaries regarding their powers and responsibilities under the Employee Retirement Income Security Act. He also assists companies on employee benefits issues in the context of mergers and acquisitions.

Peter Hammerich
Partner, Bugge, Arentz-Hansen & Rasmussen
ph@bahr.no

Peter Hammerich is a partner in Bugge, Arentz-Hansen & Rasmussen in Oslo, Norway. He is head of the firm's asset management group and works with all aspects of asset management legislation and asset management, including insurance and pension issues.

He is recommended in *Chambers* (Band I, Regulatory), *Who's Who Lawyer, Legal 500 (Pensions)* and *PLC Which Lawyer?*

Mr Hammerich is the author of several publications within his fields of expertise.

Steven Hull
Partner, Ashurst LLP
Steven.Hull@ashurst.com

Steven Hull is a partner at international law firm Ashurst LLP. He has over 20 years' legal experience of a wide range of pension-related maters in acting for employers and trustees. He has particular expertise in pension scheme reorganisations and mergers, deficit recovery and funding issues, changing benefit structures, the pension aspects of corporate transactions, and dealing with the legislative regime introduced by the Pensions Acts 1995 and 2004 and Finance Acts 2004 and 2009.

Prior to joining Ashurst LLP in 2005, Mr Hull established and led the pensions team for over five years in the London office of a large US law firm. Prior to that, he spent over 12 years training, qualifying and becoming a partner in the pensions team at a well-known London law firm. His time there included a two-year secondment to the employee benefits department of a large New York law firm.

Martin Hunter
Consultant, Punter Southall Transaction Services
Martin.Hunter@pstransactions.co.uk

Martin Hunter joined Punter Southall in 2004 and initially advised pension scheme trustees. In 2006 he transferred to Punter Southall Transaction Services, the specialist transactions consulting division within Punter Southall, where he advises private equity houses and corporate entities on the acquisition and disposal of defined benefit pension schemes. He also advises companies on the ongoing management of their pension liabilities, including offering advice on valuation negotiations, liability reduction exercises and other de-risking strategies.

Mr Hunter is co-author of an extensive research report into the pension bulk buy-out market, entitled *The End Game? – An analysis of the bulk buy-out market & other de-risking solutions*. He is also a member of the Punter Southall buy-out team.

Mr Hunter graduated from Keble College, Oxford, with a BA in mathematics in 2003 and became a fellow of the Institute of Actuaries in 2008.

Paz de la Iglesia
Associate, Ashurst
paz.delaiglesia@ashurst.com

Paz de la Iglesia is an associate in the employment department of Ashurst Madrid. Ms de la Iglesia has eight years' experience in employment law. Prior to joining Ashurst, she worked at Uría & Menéndez, one of Spain's top law firms. Ms de la Iglesia specialises in employment and social security law. She advises on employment contracts, social security matters, the suspension and termination of employment contracts, substantial modification of work conditions, functional and geographic mobility, compensation systems and policies, administrative and contentious proceedings, and outsourcing and legal audits. She also helps companies to apply and obtain work and residence permits. Ms de la Iglesia is fluent in Spanish and English and speaks intermediate French.

Jenny Jilmstad
Legal counsel, Ashurst Advokatbyrå AB
jenny.jilmstad@ashurst.com

Jenny Jilmstad is legal counsel and head of the employment group at Ashurst Stockholm. Ms Jilmstad handles current employment law matters for Swedish and international clients, as well as the employment aspects of different mergers and acquisitions.

Prior to joining Ashurst in 2008, Ms Jilmstad worked in employment law at Baker & McKenzie, between 1999 and 2007. In 2002 she worked at Baker & McKenzie's London office. Ms Jilmstad has also worked as an employment law expert at Sveriges Byggindustrier.

Rosamund Lee
Senior manager, Pitmans Trustees Limited
rlee@pitmans.com

Rosamund Lee is a solicitor in the pensions department at Pitmans. She has wide experience of all aspects of occupational and personal pension schemes, particularly drafting and advisory work. She worked in private practice in London for 11 years and then went in-house and worked for Friends Provident for four years before joining Pitmans in 2005.

Francisco de León
Senior associate, Ashurst
francisco.deleon@ashurst.com

Francisco de León is a senior associate in the corporate department of Ashurst Madrid. Ashurst is a leading international law firm with 13 offices in 12 countries. Mr de León has 12 years' experience in insurance law and worked at Clifford Chance prior to joining Ashurst. He specialises in general corporate law, M&A and joint ventures, and has particular experience in the insurance and financial services sector. He is fluent in Spanish and English and speaks intermediate German.

Tobias Neufeld
Partner, Taylor Wessing
t.neufeld@taylorwessing.com

Tobias Neufeld is a German qualified lawyer and a partner in the employment department at Taylor Wessing, an international full-service law firm with over 280 partners and more than 1,200 employees. Mr Neufeld's work is focused on employment and pensions law advice for transactions and restructurings, as well as advisory work including pension scheme closures, buy-outs, benefit adjustments and related litigation. He has a master's degree in insurance law and worked in the London, Frankfurt and Munich offices of two international law firms before joining Taylor Wessing in June 2009. Mr Neufeld is a certified employment law specialist in Germany and is also qualified as a solicitor in England and Wales.

Penny A Pilzer
Of counsel, Lovells LLP
penny.pilzer@lovells.com

Penny Pilzer is a lawyer in the pensions group at Lovells LLP. She advises employers, trustees and financial institutions on a wide variety of pension issues, including closures to accruals, structuring buy-outs and buy-ins, negotiations relating to corporate reorganisations and transactions, defined contribution plan design and day-to-day compliance with tax and pensions laws. Clients include Prudential Assurance, Royal Mail and the trustees of the McKinsey and Interpublic pension schemes.

Ms Pilzer is a member of the Investment sub-committee of the Association of Pension Lawyers and the Money Purchase Committee of the Society of Pension Consultants. In 2007, she was asked by the Department of Work and Pensions to assist its independent Deregulatory review, and was seconded to work on the Review's policy team. She is a graduate of the University of Michigan and Harvard Law School, and is qualified in the United States and the United Kingdom.

Matthew Preston
Senior associate, Herbert Smith LLP
matthew.preston@herbertsmith.com

Matthew Preston is a senior associate in Herbert Smith LLP's pensions team. His nine years' post-qualification experience is wide ranging and includes advising companies and trustees in relation to corporate transactions and complaints to the Pensions Ombudsman, as well as the day-to-day running of pension schemes. In particular, he has recent experience in advising on major acquisitions and applications to the Pensions Regulator for clearance.

Mr Preston is a full member of the Association of Pension Lawyers and speaks regularly at the firm's client seminars.

Mary K Samsa
Partner, Seyfarth Shaw LLP
msamsa@seyfarth.com

Mary K Samsa is a partner in the employee benefits practice group in the Chicago office of Seyfarth Shaw LLP. She has been ranked by *Chambers* for 2009 and 2008 as "Up and Coming" in the employee benefits area. She is lead partner for her clients in the area of qualified retirement plans (eg, 401(k) and pension plans) with respect to compliance and fiduciary counselling. She also focuses on the area of executive compensation (both domestically and internationally, and with respect to for-profit as well as not-for-profit entities). Ms Samsa is considered one of the lead partners for her firm on international employee benefits issues specifically relating to mobile employee issues and international M&A transactions. She is a certified public accountant with a master's in taxation.

Hunter Thyne
Director, Hunter Employee Benefits Law (Pty) Ltd
Hunter.Thyne@HunterLaw.co.za

Hunter Thyne obtained a bachelor of commerce (1992) and a bachelor of laws (1995) from the University of Natal. He also completed master's in tax law at the University of Witwatersrand (2001).

Mr Thyne has spent time working for an international bank, various South African insurers and asset managers, which he advised on the administration of retirement funds and assisted in designing products specific to retirement funds.

He was an associate at Edward Nathan (now Edward Nathan Sonnenburgs Inc) in the Johannesburg pension funds department. In 2005 Mr Thyne and his fellow colleagues in the department left to start Hunter Employee Benefits Law (Pty) Ltd, the first legal practice specialising solely in retirement fund law in South Africa. Mr Thyne is currently a director of Hunterlaw.

Mr Thyne has 11 years' experience in retirement fund law and is a committee member on the South African Pension Lawyers Association.

Edmund Truell
Founder, Pension Corporation
Truell@pensioncorporation.com

Edmund Truell is the founder of Pension Corporation, which was set up in 2006 to provide pension insurance or the selling of bulk annuities to UK defined benefit pension schemes. It has also pioneered the direct acquisition of corporate assets with large pension schemes. Pension Corporation now has schemes totalling nearly £5 billion of assets under its stewardship.

Edmund has 22 years' experience in private equity and debt market. He led the 1998 buy-out and formation of Duke Street Capital (DSC), having been Chief Executive since 1994. He created Duke Street Capital Debt Management in 2000 and built it into one of Europe's largest and most successful CDO managers. It was sold to Babson Capital in 2004

Edmund was Chairman of the British Venture Capital Association from 2001–2002. He is a Trustee of the Galapagos Conservation Trust.

Kevin Wesbroom
Principal consultant, Hewitt Associates LLC
Kevin.wesbroom@hewitt.com

Kevin Westbroom is an experienced pension consultant who has been advising high-profile clients for over 30 years. He is a qualified actuary who has been involved with many different aspects of pension, investment and broader employee benefits, including the establishment of Hewitt's UK defined contribution team. He is currently the UK lead for global risk services, a fusion of actuarial and investment skills designed to help clients make sense of rapidly changing investment markets and new developments such as buy-out and risk-driven solutions.

He continues to act as pension adviser on a number of client assignments and one-off references. He is practising what he has been preaching about phased retirement by working four days a week. If his views about the shape of future pensions are right, then his final phasing into full time retirement, and the end of private sector defined benefit pension provision, could come together in 10 years' time!

Klaus Henrik Wiese-Hansen
Senior lawyer, Bugge, Arentz-Hansen & Rasmussen
kwh@bahr.no

Klaus Henrik Wiese-Hansen is a senior lawyer in the asset management group at Bugge, Arentz-Hansen & Rasmussen in Oslo, Norway. Mr Wiese-Hansen's role involves working with securities legislation, capital markets and regulatory legislation and asset management in general, including investment fund management, insurance and pension issues. Mr Wiese-Hansen is recommended in *Legal 500* (Pensions) and has written several publications within the fields of expertise.

Mark Wood
Chief executive, Paternoster UK Limited
mark.wood@paternoster.uk.com

Mark Wood began his career with Price Waterhouse where he qualified as a chartered accountant specialising in financial services, particularly life insurance. He has held a number of senior positions in the financial services industry at Commercial Union, Barclays, Axa UK plc (chief executive, 1996–2001) and Prudential – UK and Europe (chief executive, 2001–2005).

Initially backed by Numis, and then with £500 million of equity financing from a number of institutions including Deutsche Bank, Mr Wood founded Paternoster in December 2005. Paternoster is a regulated insurance company that takes on the risks associated with companies' final salary/defined benefit pension schemes.